T0284665

BIRDING
Texas

HELP US KEEP THIS GUIDE UP TO DATE

Every effort has been made by the author and editors to make this guide as accurate and useful as possible. However, many things can change after a guide is published—regulations change, facilities come under new management, and so forth.

We would love to hear from you concerning your experiences with this guide and how you feel it could be improved and kept up to date. While we may not be able to respond to all comments and suggestions, we'll take them to heart, and we'll also make certain to share them with the author. Please send your comments and suggestions to falconeditorial @rowman.com.

Thanks for your input!

BIRDING
Texas

Where, How, and When to Spot Birds across the State

RANDI MINETOR
Photography by NIC MINETOR

ESSEX, CONNECTICUT

An imprint of Globe Pequot, the trade division of
The Rowman & Littlefield Publishing Group, Inc.
4501 Forbes Blvd., Ste. 200
Lanham, MD 20706
www.rowman.com

Falcon and FalconGuides are registered trademarks and Make Adventure Your Story is a trademark of
The Rowman & Littlefield Publishing Group, Inc.

Distributed by NATIONAL BOOK NETWORK

Copyright © 2024 The Rowman & Littlefield Publishing Group, Inc.

All interior photographs by Nic Minetor unless otherwise noted
"Parts of a Bird" drawing on p. 16 by Todd Telander
Maps by The Rowman & Littlefield Publishing Group, Inc.

All rights reserved. No part of this book may be reproduced in any form or by any electronic or mechanical
means, including information storage and retrieval systems, without written permission from the publisher,
except by a reviewer who may quote passages in a review.

British Library Cataloguing in Publication Information available

Library of Congress Cataloging-in-Publication Data

Names: Minetor, Randi, author. | Minetor, Nic, photographer.
Title: Birding Texas : where, how, and when to spot birds across the state / Randi Minetor ; photography by
    Nic Minetor.
Description: Essex, Connecticut : Falcon Guides, [2024] | Includes bibliographical references and index.
Identifiers: LCCN 2024002083 (print) | LCCN 2024002084 (ebook) | ISBN 9781493072422 (paper ; alk. paper) |
    ISBN 9781493072439 (electronic)
Subjects: LCSH: Bird watching—Texas. | Birding sites—Texas. | Birds—Texas.
Classification: LCC QL684.T4 M56 2024 (print) | LCC QL684.T4 (ebook) | DDC 598.072/34764—dc23/
    eng/20240312
LC record available at https://lccn.loc.gov/2024002083
LC ebook record available at https://lccn.loc.gov/2024002084

♾️™ The paper used in this publication meets the minimum requirements of American National Standard for
Information Sciences—Permanence of Paper for Printed Library Materials, ANSI/NISO Z39.48-1992.

The author and The Rowman & Littlefield Publishing Group, Inc., assume no liability for accidents
happening to, or injuries sustained by, readers who engage in the activities described in this
book.

CONTENTS

CONTENTS

ACKNOWLEDGMENTS

No matter where we go, the generosity and enthusiasm of local birders has never failed us, pointing us in the right direction to find our target species or helping us with field identifications, or just getting us "on the bird." We don't know the names of most of the people who helped us sort out sparrows and wrens in the desert at Big Bend, spy thrashers at bird blinds on the Lower Rio Grande Valley, or find missing shorebirds on Bolivar Flats, but we are grateful to every single one of them.

In particular, we must thank the staff members at Texas's many national wildlife refuges, Audubon bird sanctuaries, World Birding Centers, and state, county, and city parks who pointed us in the right direction for groove-billed ani, common black hawk, scaled quail, and dozens of other specialty species. A stranger named Lucas Pittman happened to be standing with us on the Shin Oak Observation Deck at Balcones Canyonlands National Wildlife Refuge when the long-sought black-capped vireo finally put in an appearance. He courteously called our attention to it, which led to the photo of the elusive vireo in this book—for which we are very grateful. A woman we met in Big Bend whose name we never learned told us of several places in west Texas to find birds we had sought for weeks; a kind woman at Mustang Island gave us detailed and exacting directions to the nesting platform occupied by two aplomado falcons. These incidents and many others confirmed for us once again that birders are the best people in the world.

We are very grateful to birders closer to our Upstate New York home whose rare bird alerts and personal guidance led us to birds that did not put in an appearance for us in Texas: Dominic Sherony, Jill Church Heimrich, Robert Buckert, Jules Wagner, Nick Kachala, Willie D'Anna, Josh Ketry, Andy Garland, Kyle Gage, Bill Howe, Dick Horsey, Greg Lawrence, Pat Martin, Mike Tetlow, Tom and Jeanne Verhulst, Michael Gullo, and Andrew Guthrie. Dominic Sherony provided many of his own excellent photos to help us finish this book, and Gil Eckrich and Jason Vassallo each contributed a photo of a rarity we did not manage to capture on our own. Dominic and Mike Tetlow also provided much-needed assistance in reviewing our photos to be sure of all identifications, helping us improve our skills, and ensuring this book's quality and accuracy.

As always, the team at Falcon Guides has produced a great book. We thank editorial director David Legere, both for his supervision and for giving us the opportunity once again to spend months birding one of the most exciting regions of the country. Everyone at Falcon contributes so much time, effort, and artistry to books in this series, and we can't thank them enough. Our brilliant agent, Regina Ryan, continues to keep our publishing careers

ACKNOWLEDGMENTS

on track as she has for more than fifteen years, taking extraordinary care of us so we can pursue our passions throughout the region and beyond.

Finally, to the friends and family who support us in all our efforts, we so appreciate your generosity of spirit when it comes to our literary endeavors. Ken Horowitz, Rose-Anne Moore, Martin Winer, Bruce Barton, Lisa Jaccoma, Kevin Hyde, Martha and Peter Schermerhorn, Ruth Watson, John King, Cindy Blair, Paula and Rich Landis, and all the others scattered across the country: You make every chapter fun, and there are no words strong enough to express our gratitude.

INTRODUCTION TO
BIRDING TEXAS

Texas! The name instantly conjures visions of all kinds of things that are bigger there, from vast horizons to the state fair to massive cuts of steak. Texas birding is no exception to this rule—the state has earned a reputation for attracting hundreds of bird species to its many disparate habitats, making it one of the hottest birding destinations in the United States.

In this book you'll find identification and location information for more than 250 of the most likely bird species you will encounter on a trip here, as well as references to nearly 300 wildlife refuges, marshes, beaches, parks, lakes, rivers, riparian areas, deserts, plains, grasslands, woodlands, and other areas where birds congregate.

With its position at the midpoint between the nation's east and west coasts, the largest of the contiguous forty-eight states becomes the dividing line for the continent's distinct eastern and western bird populations. Here meadowlarks from both halves of the continent meet within a narrow territory in the middle of the state, as do eastern and western kingbirds, bluebirds, screech-owls, and other bifurcated pairs of species that differ in finely defined ways. Along the banks of rivers and streams, kingfishers of the west—green and ringed kingfisher—meet up on the same shores with belted kingfisher, the only species of its kind in the eastern United States. Here you can find forest and grassland birds in the state's eastern half and prairie and desert birds in the west, so a birding trip to Texas invariably produces a long list of sightings no other state can supply.

At the same time, Texas's expansive size and southerly position in the contiguous United States places it on the border between northern and southern birding as well, further increasing the diversity of species here. While northern cities, including Dallas, Fort Worth, Austin, and Waco, host birds associated with higher eastern latitudes, birding changes significantly in San Antonio, Houston, Corpus Christi, and Brownsville, bringing birds whose ranges reach into Central America to habitats and feeders in south Texas. The result is a birder's paradise, where visitors and residents looking to add to their life lists can tally impressive numbers of species.

Whether you've recently turned to birding as a new hobby or you've been watching and seeking out birds for decades, you'll find abundance in Texas, an unending variety of dependable and unexpected species to keep you busy for a morning, a vacation, a season, or a lifetime.

Geography and Habitats

In its 268,597 square miles of landmass, Texas holds an unmatched variety of habitats for resident and migrating birds. Its coastline along the Gulf of Mexico, saltwater and freshwater marshes, northern successional forests, open farmland and plains, Lower Rio Grande Valley, vast desert expanses, brushlands, and western mountains all offer opportunities for dependable sightings of much-sought-after birds.

The Gulf Coast

Some 367 miles of Gulf coastline offer birders a remarkable opportunity to find nearly every species that frequents the nation's eastern seaboard, as well as a number of more westerly birds. While beaches can be crowded with tourists and residents throughout much of the year, a number of areas protected specifically for birds and marine life offer spectacular birding without the crush of people seeking sun, sand, and surf.

Bolivar Flats Shorebird Sanctuary in Galveston offers one of the easiest and most productive places in the country to view shorebirds, allowing birders to drive right out onto the beach and observe tens of thousands of migrants in spring and fall. Long-billed curlew; piping, snowy, Wilson's and black-bellied plovers; American golden plover; western, white-rumped, Baird's, least, stilt, pectoral, and semipalmated sandpipers; whimbrel; black-necked stilt; American avocet; American oystercatcher; black skimmer; marbled godwit; ruddy turnstone; red knot; and a variety of gulls and terns all make Bolivar Flats a critically important stopover on their way north from Central and South America. Birds migrating through here make their way to destinations in the east and west, many species flying all the way to their breeding grounds in Canada's Arctic tundra and even to Alaska, so the mix of species can be spectacular here.

Farther down the coast, the treasure trove that is Aransas National Wildlife Refuge brings you to one of the only places in the southern United States where the endangered whooping crane spends the winter. Any time of year, Aransas yields sightings of great blue, tricolored, and little blue herons; great, snowy, and cattle egrets; reddish egret; black-crowned and yellow-crowned night-herons; white and white-faced ibis; wood stork; and roseate spoonbill, while clapper and king rails and sora also wander out from between tall reeds to give birders occasional but satisfying glimpses.

The Lower Rio Grande Valley

Topping many birding organizations' lists as the most desirable and productive birding destination in America, the southern tip of Texas is not only loaded with birds that can be seen nowhere else in the United States but also makes them remarkably easy to see. Geographically, this southernmost area of Texas dips far down along the border with Mexico, making it only logical that birds usually seen south of the border would find their way into this area. Wildlife centers all along the Texas-Mexico border make the most of this phenomenon by luring birds with feeders, placing them in areas that are easy to access by birding tourists, and keeping them filled all year.

Here's where you'll find green jay; great kiskadee; plain chachalaca; curve-billed thrasher; buff-bellied hummingbird; black-crested titmouse; clay-colored thrush; Inca dove; white-tipped dove; olive sparrow; groove-billed ani; golden-fronted and ladder-backed woodpecker; hooded, Altamira, Scott's, and occasional Audubon's orioles; green and ringed kingfisher; common pauraque; and southern birds with wider ranges: common ground dove, painted bunting, verdin, yellow-breasted chat, blue grosbeak, and many others. Our personal favorite stop is Hugh Ramsey Park in Harlingen, but you won't want to miss any of the hot spots that also offer ponds with least grebe, black-bellied whistling duck, white and white-faced ibis, and more. Be sure to visit Bentsen–Rio Grande Valley State Park/ World Birding Center in Mission, Estero Llano Grande State Park World Birding Center in Llano Grande, Resaca de la Palma State Park/World Birding Center in Brownsville, Sabal Palm Sanctuary in Brownsville, Santa Ana National Wildlife Refuge in San Juan, and the National Butterfly Center in Mission.

The combination of semitropical habitat, the Rio Grande, and its verdant riparian corridor creates a birding paradise—albeit an often overheated one. Most of the birds you can see here are present year-round, so consider visiting in the shoulder seasons of April and September/October rather than in the heat of summer to preserve your electrolytes and protect your skin from intense sunlight. Winter can also provide exceptional birding opportunities here, though the most popular nature centers can become crowded as snowbirds arrive from up north, making parking and access to viewing somewhat more challenging.

The Chihuahuan Desert and the Davis/Guadalupe Mountains

The landscape changes dramatically the farther west you travel in Texas, and soon palm trees are replaced with yucca, ocotillo, agave, prickly pear, strawberry cactus, and Turk's head cactus. In this harsher environment, the birds change significantly as well, providing birders with a completely different but equally bountiful experience in one of the only remaining Chihuahuan deserts on the continent.

Big Bend National Park draws hundreds of thousands of visitors annually—and you will find on any visit that most of these visitors are birders. They turn up in the park's Rio Grande Village to find the common black hawks that nest there in a remarkably public spot, right in the middle of a mowed area (marked with signs, so you can't miss it) on the way to the picnic grounds. Verdin, blue grosbeak, Eurasian collared-dove, white-winged dove, Inca dove, black-chinned hummingbird, acorn and golden-fronted woodpeckers, black and Say's phoebes, western kingbird, western wood-pewee, vermilion and ash-throated flycatchers, and greater roadrunner are common here, while common poorwill and lesser nighthawk put in veiled appearances at night.

Birds abound all over the park, especially close to the river, but two spots are must-stops in Big Bend. Dugout Wells provides one of the few water features, limited though it is, anywhere in the park beyond the Rio Grande: a working well with a windmill generating power for it. This tiny bit of moisture attracts many birds to this fairly concentrated area, including scaled quail, black-throated sparrow, black-tailed gnatcatcher, cactus wren, crissal thrasher, dickcissel, pyrrhuloxia, verdin, Scott's oriole, and two highly sought-after nocturnal residents: western screech-owl and elf owl.

The second and far more challenging quest is for the Colima warbler, a drab little brown bird that has only one dependable location in the United States: the Chisos Mountains in the heart of Big Bend. This elusive little warbler shows itself only in late April and early May, when daily heat can rise to 114 degrees Fahrenheit in Big Bend, and it usually sings along one of several trails that ascend into the mountains. Any hike to see this bird begins before dawn at about 5,400 feet in elevation and climbs to as high as 6,800 feet (though the bird usually reveals itself through song between a third and halfway to that altitude). If you simply must see every bird in Texas, you'll need to take on this challenge; but depending on your overall health and tolerance for heat, you may decide you don't need to see every bird in Texas after all. Whatever your decision, stop at the Chisos Basin Visitor Center to find out exactly where the bird has been seen in the past few days, and take twice the amount of water you think you will need.

Central Texas

The forested hills and canyons in the Waco and Austin areas of eastern Texas serve as the breeding grounds for two much-sought-after birds: black-capped vireo and golden-cheeked warbler. These two little Texas specialties bring thousands of visitors to places like Balcones Canyonlands National Wildlife Refuge—especially its Doeskin Ranch and Shin Oak Observation Deck areas—as well as Lost Maples State Natural Area, another favorite nesting place for the vireo and warbler.

To locate these birds before they get down to incubating their eggs and thus become secretive and very difficult to find, visit between the end of March and the first week of May, while the males continue to sing on territory. Be sure you know each bird's song well before you go looking for them, as using playback (recordings of their songs) is considered harassment of these protected birds. This is where Cornell Lab of Ornithology's miraculous Merlin Bird ID app can be a big help: It listens to the birds you are hearing around you and tells you what they are. (This game-changing app is free, and it has saved us all kinds of time as we search for specific birds.)

Many other more common birds share habitat with these two Texas specialties, including painted bunting, dickcissel, eastern and western kingbirds, lesser goldfinch, white-eyed vireo, blue grosbeak, yellow-billed cuckoo, the ever-elusive northern bobwhite, Bewick's wren, scissor-tailed flycatcher, yellow-breasted chat, black-crested titmouse, Carolina chickadee, white-winged dove, red-bellied woodpecker, indigo bunting, and cedar waxwing, so there will be plenty to keep you interested and occupied while you wait for the desired warbler or vireo to make a brief appearance.

Exotics

You may be well aware of the abundance of exotic bird species—birds whose normal range would not include North America—that roam some Texas cities. Whether these colonies of chattery, gregarious, and charismatic birds grew from a few escaped pets, a failed pet store owner's mass release, private collections in botanical gardens, or some other mysterious source has been cause for considerable speculation among birders for generations. While Texas does not provide habitat for as many exotic species as does Florida or California, it has impressive flocks of red-crowned parrot, monk parakeet, red-vented bulbul, and a number of others.

We have included some of these birds in this book, based on the recommendations of the American Birding Association (ABA) and their accepted records of breeding populations. The hot spots we have provided for these birds may lead to sightings of additional species, as many parrots and parakeets enjoy the same kinds of habitat and may vie for their own territory in fairly limited surroundings. Spotting many of these birds is virtually inevitable in some parts of Texas—try Oliviera Park in Brownsville at sunset or most city parks in Houston—so if you see something unexpected, take note. It may turn out to be a life bird you can "count" according to ABA guidelines.

Optics and How to Choose Them

If you are new to birding and have not yet acquired your own binoculars or decided on the need for a spotting scope, we offer some basic guidance.

1. Yes, you need binoculars. Birds rarely land close enough to give you a good, satisfying look, especially if you're examining an unfamiliar wing pattern, an alternate seasonal plumage, or details you've never seen in person before. Binoculars are key to your enjoyment of the birds, but which binoculars are right for you? Here are the most important things to understand when purchasing a pair for your birding enjoyment:

- **Look for the magnification and diameter formula,** usually stamped on the focus knob. For example, it may say 7 x 35, 8 x 42, or 10 x 40. The first number indicates the number of times the binoculars magnify the image of the bird—so if the first number is "8," it means you will see the bird at eight times its normal size. You may believe, then, that a magnification of 10 or more would be the best for your purposes, but before you leap to buy such a pair, try it out in person. You may find that 10x binoculars are too heavy to hold still, making the additional magnification an expensive waste. Many birders are most comfortable with a factor of 8.

- **The diameter number** (35, 40, 42, or 50) tells you how much light comes through the large end of the binoculars. The number is the diameter of the lens itself; the larger it is, the brighter and clearer the image will be when it reaches your eye. Binoculars with a larger diameter are especially good in low-light situations, like when you're trying to see the mating dance of the American woodcock at dusk or you're attempting to spot a barn owl calling in a dim forest.

- **The secret is the multicoating.** Why are your grandfather's 10 x 50 binoculars, purchased in the 1960s, not nearly as good for birding as a modern pair at 7 x 35? Optics technology has come a long way over the past fifty years, eliminating distortions like the blue and yellow fringe around objects you may see through your granddad's pair. "Fully multicoated" means every piece of glass inside and out—as many as eighteen surfaces—is layered with coatings that reduce glare, distortion, fringing, and other issues that can keep you from seeing a bird clearly.

- **Get past the sticker shock.** Cheap binoculars are not going to cut it in the field, so if you're a committed birder and want the best experience possible, you're going to have to spend a little money. There's good news on this front, however: Several top manufacturers have developed excellent binoculars at a price point of about $250, so you don't need to stretch for a top-of-the-line pair in the $1,200 range to have perfectly serviceable optics.

2. Do you need a spotting scope? It's a valid question, especially if you're new to birding, and one you need to answer in your own time. To get an idea of the possibilities a scope opens up for you, participate in a field trip with your local birding association and look through several of the scopes other birders use. Remember how you felt the first time you saw a bird through a good pair of binoculars? The leap from binoculars to a scope is equally dramatic. If you do decide to purchase your own scope, keep in mind that the tripod is every bit as important as the magnification and diameter—on a windy day or when you're standing on a busy boardwalk, you'll be glad you chose a slightly heavier, more stable tripod that keeps your scope from vibrating.

Bird Classifications

The American Ornithological Society and the American Birding Association have teams of experts who have spent years determining the exact biological category each bird belongs in, what family of birds it belongs to within that category, and what its taxonomic (Latin) name should be. This is critically important work for our scientific understanding of birds, their evolution, and the discovery of new species through DNA analysis and other methods.

Bird taxonomy informed this book, but we also relied on our own field experience, gathered through more than thirty-five years of birding, and our use of a wide range of field guides. In this book we have endeavored to group birds within their taxonomic families, but also in a manner that will make it easy to compare one bird to another for purposes of identification. So you'll find all the wading birds grouped together, as well as all the swimming birds, the birds of prey, and so on. This enhances the usability of this guide, allowing you to focus on studying the bird's field marks in relation to others in the same general habitat.

Seasonal Plumage and Other Mysteries

As if the process of identifying each bird was not confounding enough, most birds lose their bright breeding plumage once the mating season is over. All birds molt at least once a year, dropping their old feathers and replacing them with new ones, but not all of them change the look of their plumage from one season to the next. When they do, it can result in considerable frustration for birders struggling to identify individuals in a mixed flock of what the 1980 Peterson *Field Guide to the Birds* famously dubbed "confusing fall warblers."

To help you sort out the field marks (or lack of them) when the birds make it the hardest to do so, we have provided detailed descriptions of nonbreeding plumage for each of the birds that make this transition. Many fall warblers look nearly identical in their nonbreeding plumage, with perhaps a single feature that differs, so you can make careful comparisons of the descriptions to determine which species you may be seeing. Remember that the bird's habitat, food choices, song, and behavior are still the guiding factors to its identification, especially when the plumage provides few clues.

Many waterfowl go through two periods of molt each year, based on their nesting and breeding schedule. Male ducks lose their bright feathers soon after nesting, changing over to a drab appearance called "eclipse" plumage as early as the last week of June. This is particularly evident in wood ducks, which go from a coat of many colors to a brown mantle with a white patch at the throat. In early winter, when other species of birds are still cloaked for fall, male wood ducks and other waterfowl regain their stunning plumage in preparation for attracting their mate.

Birding by Ear

One of the most important skills you need to bird in any area of the world is an ability to identify birds by song. It's not as difficult as you may think—the more you listen in the field and practice with recordings, the clearer it will become that each bird has a distinctly different way of expressing itself. Even if you have embraced the Merlin Bird ID app, which identifies every song and chip note it can hear in seconds, it's worth making the effort to learn at least the most common songs on your own. You may be amazed at how satisfying it is to identify several common birds without relying on an app—and your non-birding friends will think you're a genius.

We have provided phonetic transcriptions of each bird's song or call in this book, with popular phrases and mnemonics to help you learn some of the most common and familiar calls. That being said, there is no substitute for a good smartphone app that puts every bird's song in your pocket. Some apps serve as an adjunct to field guides (or are part of a field guide app, such as iBirdPro, National Geographic Birds, Sibley eGuide, Audubon Birds Pro, and Peterson Birds), so you can choose a bird and listen to all the variations of its song. Others actually teach you how to tell one bird's song from another and how to remember each song. Highly recommended teaching apps include Larkwire, Chirp!, and IKnowBirdSongs; each is available for a one-time fee. Many of these apps use songs from the Macaulay Library at the Cornell Laboratory of Ornithology, one of the most respected and extensive resources for bird information in North America.

If you are daunted by the idea of learning bird songs, let us say this: You will be amazed at how much time it saves you in the field. Start by learning the ten most common birds in your own backyard—for example, house sparrow, northern cardinal, common grackle, blue jay, northern mockingbird, American robin, Carolina chickadee, red-winged blackbird, mourning dove, Carolina wren. Each of these birds has a distinctive song, making this sampler an excellent starting point in learning what makes one song different from another. With these ten (or ten others you choose) firmly in your mind, you'll be able to identify these birds in the field whether you actually see them or not, allowing you to apply more of your time and effort to finding more-unusual birds on each field trip.

Rare, Endangered, and Extirpated Species

Setting expectations in advance will help you come home from any birding excursion with the satisfaction that you saw what you came to see. That's why we need to be up front about the birds that are very difficult to see in Texas, as well as the birds that were once part of the landscape and are not any longer.

The US Fish and Wildlife Service lists five species that once lived in Texas and are now extinct: Bachman's warbler (the last known individual in the world was seen in 1988), ivory-billed woodpecker (2004), passenger pigeon (1914), Carolina parakeet (1910), and Eskimo curlew (1987).

In addition to the extinct birds, the US government classifies these three Texas birds as federally endangered: northern aplomado falcon, interior least tern, and black-capped vireo. Piping plover is considered federally threatened, meaning it is likely to become endangered in the foreseeable future.

The Texas Parks and Wildlife Department has its own current list of species that are endangered or of special concern at the state level. Sightings of these are possible, and this book provides the most likely places to find some of them, but they may be difficult to locate even in their accustomed hot spots.

- **State threatened species:** reddish egret, white-faced ibis, swallow-tailed kite, bald eagle, peregrine falcon, white-tailed hawk, piping plover, sooty tern, tropical parula
- **State endangered species:** wood stork, brown pelican, red knot, northern aplomado falcon, interior least tern, southwestern willow flycatcher, black-capped vireo

Why are these birds—some of which are fairly common in other parts of the country—becoming scarce in Texas? Audubon Texas presents us with a frightening picture: Bird populations are under siege as the climate changes and habitats become compromised or unlivable, or disappear altogether. A total of twenty-eight species in Texas are considered highly vulnerable to habitat loss and changing conditions, including much-sought-after species like Montezuma quail, broad-tailed hummingbird, hook-billed kite, aplomado falcon, black-capped vireo, golden-cheeked warbler, Botteri's sparrow, and many others. Another forty-eight species are in a moderately vulnerable position as heat levels rise, water sources disappear, and barrier islands are submerged by rising sea levels.

The loss of bird species would be devastating to birders, but it has far-reaching implications for all residents of Texas. Hummingbirds, orioles, and other nectar-eating birds carry pollen from one plant to another, making them critically important in sustaining many kinds of native plant species. Many birds eat insects—a swallow of any variety, for example, eats thousands of insects daily—reducing populations that would otherwise devour crops, become a widespread nuisance, and spread diseases like West Nile virus, chikungunya, dengue fever, and Zika virus. Seed- and fruit-eating birds play an important role in dispersing seeds through their droppings, replanting forests and meadows with native plants. Vultures and other carrion eaters clean up roadkill and devour animals that die in the wild. In short, the decline of diversity in the avian world will have a profound and widespread impact on human lives and activities.

There's another side of climate change for birders, however. Major storms, changes in habitat, and shifts in food availability bring rare sightings of birds from other parts of the United States and beyond to Texas's shores and forests. Pairs of limpkins, for example, found their way out of central Florida in 2021 and into many southeastern and south-central states including Texas, following the ongoing, widespread dispersion of an invasive giant apple snail from South America. Trindade petrel, a species of the South Atlantic waters off the Brazilian coast, made the official Texas bird list in 2022. Small-billed elaenia, a South

American species and long-distance migrant south of the equator, showed up in Corpus Christi in May 2021. Many less-exotic vagrants appear after hurricanes roil the Gulf of Mexico, delighting birders from all over the Southeast who make their way to the Texas coast.

If you live in Texas or you're planning a trip here in the near future, check the rare bird alert lists for each state compiled by the American Birding Association at birding.aba .org. Here you'll find quick links to all the discussions on the birding mailing lists across the country. Birders love to share information, so you are likely to find detailed directions to specific sightings.

Birding Ethics in the Age of Social Media

While your life list is your own and you have the option of counting whatever bird sightings you choose, some aspects of birding ethically are not optional. The American Birding Association provides this Code of Birding Ethics, and you will find that the vast majority of birders you meet follow this to the letter.

American Birding Association Code of Birding Ethics

Reproduced with permission. For more information about the American Birding Association, visit aba.org.

1. Promote the welfare of birds and their environment.

1(a) Support the protection of important bird habitat.

1(b) Avoid stressing birds or exposing them to danger, exercise restraint and caution during observation, photography, sound recording, or filming.

- Limit the use of recordings and other methods of attracting birds, and never use such methods in heavily birded areas or for attracting any species that is Threatened, Endangered, of Special Concern, or is rare in your local area.
- Keep well back from nests and nesting colonies, roosts, display areas, and important feeding sites. In such sensitive areas, if there is a need for extended observation, photography, filming, or recording, try to use a blind or hide, and take advantage of natural cover.
- Use artificial light sparingly for filming or photography, especially for close-ups.

1(c) Before advertising the presence of a rare bird, evaluate the potential for disturbance to the bird, its surroundings, and other people in the area, and proceed only if access can be controlled, disturbance minimized, and permission has been obtained from private landowners. The nesting sites of rare birds should be divulged only to the proper conservation authorities.

1(d) Stay on roads, trails, and paths where they exist; otherwise, keep habitat disturbance to a minimum.

2. Respect the law, and the rights of others.

2(a) Do not enter private property without the owner's explicit permission.

2(b) Follow all laws, rules, and regulations governing use of roads and public areas, both at home and abroad.

2(c) Practice common courtesy in contacts with other people. Your exemplary behavior will generate goodwill with birders and non-birders alike.

3. Ensure that feeders, nest structures, and other artificial bird environments are safe.

3(a) Keep dispensers, water, and food clean and free of decay or disease. It is important to feed birds continually during harsh weather.

3(b) Maintain and clean nest structures regularly.

3(c) If you are attracting birds to an area, ensure the birds are not exposed to predation from cats and other domestic animals or dangers posed by artificial hazards.

4. Group birding, whether organized or impromptu, requires special care.

Each individual in the group, in addition to the obligations spelled out in Items 1 and 2, has responsibilities as a Group Member:

4(a) Respect the interests, rights, and skills of fellow birders, as well as people participating in other legitimate outdoor activities. Freely share your knowledge and experience, except where code 1(c) applies. Be especially helpful to beginning birders.

4(b) If you witness unethical birding behavior, assess the situation and intervene if you think it prudent. When interceding, inform the person(s) of the inappropriate action and attempt, within reason, to have it stopped. If the behavior continues, document it and notify appropriate individuals or organizations.

Group Leader Responsibilities [amateur and professional trips and tours]:

4(c) Be an exemplary ethical role model for the group. Teach through word and example.

4(d) Keep groups to a size that limits impact on the environment and does not interfere with others using the same area.

4(e) Ensure everyone in the group knows of and practices this code.

4(f) Learn about and inform the group of any special circumstances applicable to the areas being visited (e.g., no audio playback allowed).

4(g) Acknowledge that professional tour companies bear a special responsibility to place the welfare of birds and the benefits of public knowledge ahead of the company's commercial interests. Ideally, leaders should keep track of tour sightings, document unusual occurrences, and submit records to appropriate organizations.

Why follow this code? Naturally, it's good for the birds, even if it means you don't have the opportunity to get a good look at a rarity or add a bird to your life list. There's another facet we must take into consideration in the age of social media, however: Infractions can be photographed or recorded, and your peccadillo in the field can become a matter of indelible public record.

A vivid example of this took place in September 2017, when a crowd of birders in Norwich, England, on a "twitch"—a hunt for a rare bird sighted and staked out by other birders—actually trespassed on private land and damaged a fence in an attempt to frighten and flush a rare grasshopper sparrow into the open. This process of "organized flushing" is frowned upon and regarded as unethical in birding circles all over the world, but some birders consider this an acceptable practice. The rare sparrow, most likely already exhausted from somehow finding itself in unfamiliar territory thousands of miles from its accustomed home, may suffer even more from this disruption as it tries to rest and feed. Impatient birders, however, neglect to take the bird's welfare into consideration in their zeal to catch a glimpse of it and add it to their life lists.

This particular group of birders clashed with wardens on the property, however, and one individual began recording video of the exchange. The resulting 8-minute tantrum, as remarkably patient wardens attempted to reason with the agitated birders, now lives on X (formerly Twitter), YouTube, and author James Common's blog (commonbynature.com/2017/09/21/birders-behaving-badly/) for folks like us to see from half a world away. Whether these birders ever actually saw the sparrow is not noted, but their faces, voices, and words will linger on the internet for many years; and they no doubt took some grief from others in their own community for placing their chance at a rare bird sighting over someone's private property, basic civility, and—most important for our purposes—the health and safety of the bird.

The moral is simple: Behave yourself in the field, and put the bird's survival before your zeal to check off a sighting or get a great photo. It's the right thing to do for the birds, and it will keep you from getting a bad reputation that lives forever online.

HOW TO USE THIS GUIDE

On each page, you'll find photographs and details that will help you identify the birds you see, and determine the best places to find them.

Field marks: In addition to the photos, we have listed the features that differentiate this bird from others. These descriptions begin with a breeding male and are followed by breeding female and any changes for nonbreeding plumage.

Size: The bird's approximate length (L) or height (H) (for tall wading birds like great blue heron) and wingspan (WS) can be important to its identification.

Similar species: Misidentifications are easy to make, as every birder knows. We've simplified the process of elimination by providing the key field marks that may indicate that the bird in your sights is not what you think it is.

Season: The time of year you are most likely to see this bird.

Habitat: Birds wander, but they tend to stay close to their nesting sites and to the areas in which they can find food. We provide the most likely habitat for each.

Food source: This will help you determine whether the bird you seek can find its food in the place you're looking. If you don't see trees loaded with berries, for example, you're not likely to find waxwings.

Nest: Many of the birds in this book do not nest and breed in Texas. For the ones that do, we've provided the probable nest location—in a tree above 50 feet, for example, or on the ground among reeds and tall grasses.

Call: Nothing beats a recording of an actual birdcall, but the phonetic transcriptions you find here may help you match the kind of call you're hearing so that you can narrow down the possibilities for identification. If male and female have different calls, both are provided.

Hot spots: Here you'll find three to six places in Texas where the bird has been seen season after season or year after year. To determine these hot spots, we toured Texas and visited hundreds of birding locations while completing the photography for this book, using our personal experience to determine which places yielded the most sightings and provided a high-quality experience in general. We rejected some sites because they were on private or restricted property, they did not provide a safe place to leave a vehicle, or there was no clear path to the birding location.

I also applied science to the task. I used the sightings reported by tens of thousands of birders in eBird, the crowdsourced database developed and managed by the Cornell

Laboratory of Ornithology at Cornell University. Rather than delving back through decades of sightings to find where a bird may have been seen historically, I used data collected over the past five years—providing you with the most up-to-date information about where each bird has been seen most recently and consistently. I looked not only for a long list of sightings of a specific species—these, after all, could all be a single bird seen by a large group on one day—but also for year-after-year sightings of that species, a sign that this hot spot drew the desired species consistently.

You will see that many of the hot spots are cited repeatedly—for example, Estero Llano Grande State Park World Birding Center, Hugh Ramsey Park, Big Bend National Park, Village Creek Drying Beds in Arlington, Salineño Wildlife Preserve, Resaca de la Palma State Park, Mitchell Lake Audubon Center, and many others. We hope this emphasis speaks to the obvious point: These are the best places to bird to find the greatest number of species in one place. Make note of these as you plan your exploration of Texas.

Each of these hot spots includes the nearest town or city, the state, and GPS coordinates for the entrance or location. (Please note: GPS coordinates *do not* mean "Stand here and you'll see this bird." They are simply provided to make certain you reach the right wildlife refuge, forest, beach, lake, or parking area.)

Range map: This map shows the season and areas of Texas in which the bird is usually seen.

Map Key

Winter
Migration (spring or fall)
Summer (breeding)
Year-round

Birders know well that no sighting is guaranteed. Birds have minds of their own, and they can decide to move hours or seconds before you arrive; they also may choose a new place to rest, feed, and raise their young from one year to the next. We have provided information about the type of habitat each bird prefers so that you can search in suitable places if the birds reject a particular beach, a salt marsh disappears as the sea level rises, or a section of forest does not produce a hardy berry crop in a given year.

PARTS OF A BIRD

We have used plain English terms throughout the descriptions in this book, but this illustration will help you determine which area we mean.

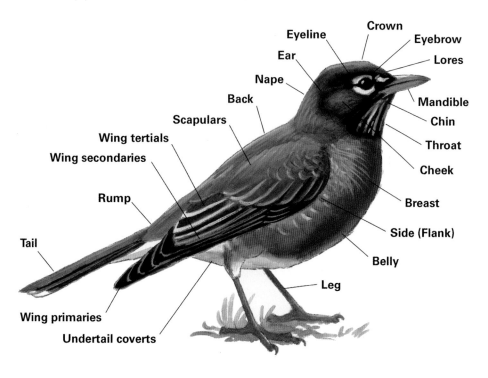

LOON

COMMON LOON
Gavia immer

This loon seeks the Texas coast's open water in winter and passes over most of the state during migration.

Field marks: Black head, black bill, red eye; pinstriped collar ending in a black band; striking checkerboard pattern on back, white breast. Nonbreeding plumage is slate gray with a white eye ring and collar-like white notch around neck.

Size: L: 26"–32", WS: 41"–52"

Similar species: Red-throated loon is smaller and grayer, with thin bill and more white on face (and is not usually seen in Texas). Double-crested cormorant is all black with a yellow bill.

Season: Winter and early spring

Habitat: Coastal waters, lakes and other open water

Food source: Fish

Nest: In secluded spots along lakeshores with easy access to water (not in Texas)

Call: Plaintive trill that has become synonymous with wilderness: a tremolo of ten or twelve beats in quick succession; also a yodeling call: *woooWAHwha, woooWAHwah*

Hot spots: Port Aransas Jetty, Port Aransas, 27.8348271 / -97.046015; Matagorda Island State Park, Port O'Connor, 28.3352839 / -96.4529228; Moody Gardens, Galveston, 29.2744864 / -94.8543092; Lookout Point, Palacios, 28.6956886 / -96.2338185; Lake o' the Pines, Alley Creek Park, Rock Springs, 32.7984553 / -94.5892366.

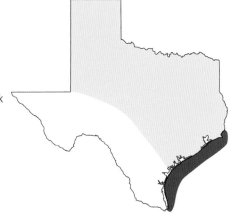

GREBES

PIED-BILLED GREBE
Podilymbus podiceps

The region's second-smallest grebe prefers brackish waters in winter, with scattered individuals on freshwater lakes and ponds in summer.

Field marks: Tan overall with a darker grayish back; distinctive thick bill turns white with a black band in breeding season.

Size: L: 13", WS: 16"

Similar species: Eared grebe is larger, more strikingly marked, and has red eyes. Least grebe is smaller and darker, with a black bill and yellow eyes.

Season: Year-round

Habitat: Ponds, lakes, marshes in secluded areas

Food source: Crayfish and other small crustaceans, small fish

Nest: Well hidden among marshland reeds, usually where water is a foot deep or more

Call: Rising bark with evenly spaced syllables: *wa-wa-wa-wa- Whu, Whu, Whu, Whu,* slowing down until it trails off

Hot spots: Any pond, marsh or small lake at a low elevation may host this common grebe, and they often appear among mixed flocks of overwintering waterfowl in ocean and gulf waters just offshore. The calm water between beaches and barrier islands often contains these grebes, as do large open marshes.

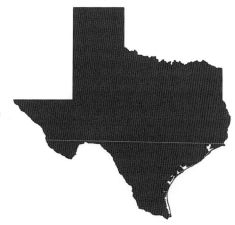

EARED GREBE
Podiceps nigricollis

The world's most common grebe's breeding plumage is easy to spot with its golden-washed cheek feathers, its thin bill and brilliantly red eye, and its slim neck. In Texas, most eared grebes are seen in their muted winter plumage.

Field marks: Breeding: Dark brown overall with rusty sides; bright gold feathers behind the eye; crested head, very thin black bill, and red eye. Nonbreeding: Dark gray with white sides; white from front of neck to chin; black cap, red eye.

Size: L: 14", WS: 21"

Similar species: Pied-billed grebe is smaller and more compact, and is brown overall with a thicker, whitish bill. Least grebe has a yellow eye and is even smaller.

Season: Winter

Habitat: Shallow marshes, lakes and ponds, usually on or near salt water in winter

Food source: Brine shrimp, brine flies, small fish

Nest: Among rushes and cattails in wetlands (not in Texas)

Call: Rising, elongated single note, ending in a short croak; female call is similar but shorter.

Hot spots: Oyster Lake, Collegeport, 28.6135254 / -96.2118928; Benbrook Lake/North Holiday Park, Benbrook, 32.6510088 / -97.4747562; Mitchell Lake Audubon Center, San Antonio, 29.3105956 / -98.4996938; Quintana Beach and Jetty, Freeport, 28.9343 / -95.2987; Packery Channel Park, Corpus Christi, 27.6264996 / -97.2204369.

LEAST GREBE
Tachybaptus dominicus

Tiny, slate gray, and striking with its sharply contrasting yellow eye, the least grebe lives primarily in Mexico and farther south, but a healthy population lives in the southernmost part of Texas.

Field marks: Small and uniformly dark gray, with a whiter tuft at the rump; its yellow eye and all-gray bill make this grebe easy to distinguish from pied-billed grebes. Nonbreeding plumage is browner.

Size: L: 10", WS: 11"

Similar species: Pied-billed grebe is slightly larger, lighter brown, and has a heavy white bill with a black stripe in breeding season. Nonbreeding eared grebe is larger, with a longer neck and a bright red eye.

Season: Year-round

Habitat: Wetlands of fresh or brackish water, small lakes, and ponds, especially with low vegetation

Food source: Mostly insects and larvae, tiny vertebrates, tadpoles

Nest: In vegetation on the edge of a wetland or pond

Call: A high squeak, accompanied by a low-pitched trill; pairs in courtship chatter rapidly in a trill duet.

Hot spots: Laguna Atascosa National Wildlife Refuge, Brownsville, 26.2295776 / -97.3466982; San Benito Wetlands, Harlingen, 26.1739485 / -97.6235167; King Ranch, Kingsville, 27.5183197 / -97.9093409; Estero Llano Grande State Park, Weslaco, 26.1268335 / -97.9578167; Salineño Wildlife Preserve, Salineño, 26.514616 / -99.1155021.

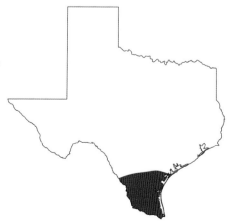

WATERFOWL

CANADA GOOSE
Branta canadensis

This northern bird's winter range now extends into northern and eastern Texas.

Field marks: Brown body, lighter brown breast; black neck, black head with white band around throat and cheeks; gray bill; white vent.

Size: L: 25"–43" (considerable variation), WS: 75"

Similar species: Greater white-fronted goose has pink bill and legs, white patch on face at edge of bill, and is lighter colored overall. Cackling goose is smaller with a shorter neck.

Season: Winter

Habitat: Any body of water near grasses or farm fields

Food source: Grass, human crops (rice, corn)

Nest: A pile of sticks and grasses in a field or lawn near water (generally not in Texas)

Call: *Honk-a-honk, honk-a-honk* when taking flight or communicating in a flock

Hot spots: Inks Lake State Park, Buchanan Dam, 30.7329965 / -98.3682132; Rough Creek Park, Granbury, 32.4186558 / -97.7858895; Dallas Southside Wastewater Treatment Plant, Dallas, 32.6456988 / -96.6391754; Chisholm Park, Fort Worth, 32.8578425 / -97.1722648; Country Club Lake/ Williamson Park, Bryan, 30.6424167 / -96.3609123.

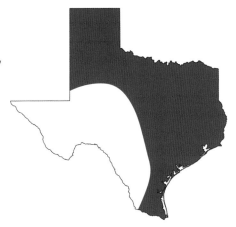

CACKLING GOOSE
Branta hutchinsii

Smaller than a Canada goose, with a shorter neck and more sloping forehead, this goose often hangs out in flocks of its larger cousin.

Field marks: Brown body and breast; black neck, black head with white band around throat and cheeks; small, triangular black bill; short, stocky neck; white rear underside.

Size: L: 24"–26", WS: 43"

Similar species: Canada goose is very similarly marked, but is larger with a lighter breast, a longer neck, and nearly twice the wingspan.

Season: Winter

Habitat: Any body of water near grasses or farm fields

Food source: Grass, human crops (rice, corn)

Nest: In the Arctic, not in Texas; a pile of sticks and grasses in a field or lawn near water

Call: Single barked *honk*, similar to a Canada goose, but higher in pitch

Hot spots: Leroy Elmore Park, Lubbock, 33.5337785 / -101.9051548; Lobo Lake Park, Levelland, 33.5804728 / -102.3766029; McDonald Lake, Amarillo, 35.1589333 / -101.91717; Lake Wellington, Wichita Falls, 33.8738362 / -98.5757303; North Fork Buffalo Creek Reservoir, Iowa Park, 33.9843637 / -98.7533569. Also scattered individuals in ponds near Galveston from December to February.

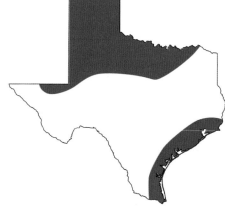

SNOW GOOSE
Anser caerulescens

Two phases display very different plumage: white in adulthood and the dark juvenile "blue goose."

Field marks: White face and body; pink bill and legs; black wing primaries.

Size: L: 25"–31", WS: 53"

Similar species: Ross's goose is smaller with a diminutive bill. Mute swan is larger with a longer, curved neck and orange and black bill.

Season: Winter in the western panhandle and east Texas; migration through much of the state

Habitat: Open fields and wetlands

Food source: Aquatic plants, young crop seedlings, wild rice and millet, some berries

Nest: On the ground in the Arctic tundra

Call: A loud *honk*, higher-pitched than a Canada goose

Hot spots: McGee Lake, Amarillo, 35.2810102 / -101.6586828; Leroy Elmore Park, Lubbock, 33.5337785 / -101.9051548, and other parks with ponds in the area; Hagerman National Wildlife Refuge (especially Middle Branch Inlet of Lake Texoma), Sherman, 33.7388657 / -96.7589092; San Bernard National Wildlife Refuge, Cedar Lake, 28.884594 / -95.562815; ponds at Soil Conservation Service Site 6 Dam on CR 2102, Kenedy, 28.7959909 / -97.9677587.

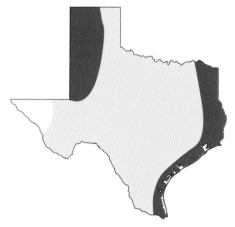

GREATER WHITE-FRONTED GOOSE
Anser albifrons

The white band around the bill and the bright orange legs make this overwintering bird easy to spot in a mixed flock.

Field marks: Grayish tones overall with darker banding across the belly; dark head with white band on face at the base of the bill, pink bill; white tail coverts, white band on end of tail; bright orange legs.

Size: L: 26"–34", WS: 42"–60"

Similar species: Canada goose and cackling goose have a white patch on the head and a black neck.

Season: Winter in southeastern areas; widespread spring and fall migrant throughout the state

Habitat: Open fields and marshes

Food source: Plants

Nest: On the Russian and Siberian tundra

Call: Laughing three-note call: *but-a-WAH, but-a-WAH*

Hot spots: Darst/Ricefield Roads area, Kendleton, 29.4249608 / -95.9442913; ponds at Soil Conservation Service Site 6 Dam on CR 2102, Kenedy, 28.7959909 / -97.9677587; San Bernard National Wildlife Refuge, Cedar Lake, 28.8938016 / -95.5819988; Dallas Southside Wastewater Treatment Plant, Dallas, 32.6456988 / -96.6391754; Brazoria National Wildlife Refuge Auto Loop Tour, Clute, 29.0599843 / -95.267568.

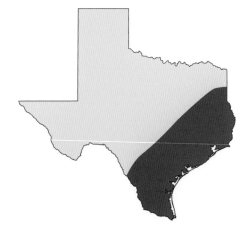

BLACK-BELLIED WHISTLING DUCK
Dendrocygna autumnalis

These distinctive ducks travel in flocks and often roost together in trees.

Field marks: Gray head with noticeable peak, white eye ring, bright red bill; gray neck, tawny breast and back; black wings with prominent white stripe, black underside; pink legs and feet.

Size: L: 20"–22", WS: 30"

Similar species: Fulvous whistling duck has a buff head and breast and no white wing stripe.

Season: Year-round

Habitat: Marshes with large bodies of water, open fields

Food source: Aquatic plants, grasses, farm grains, some insects and snails

Nest: In a tree or thicket, sometimes on the ground

Call: A high, squeaky chatter or a distinctive whistle: *dih-doo-WHEE-di-WEE-duh*

Hot spots: Village Creek Drying Beds, Arlington, 32.7842795 / -97.1266181; Mason Creek Park, Katy, 29.8073589 / -95.7906103; Kuykendahl Detention Pond, The Woodlands, 30.188372 / -95.535857; Kaufer-Hubert Memorial Park, Loyola Beach, 27.3196959 / -97.6841211; Estero Llano Grande State Park/World Birding Center, Weslaco, 26.1268335 / -97.9578167; and on just about any pond in any park from Houston south to McAllen.

WOOD DUCK
Aix sponsa

One of America's most colorful ducks; the male's facial markings and green cap are particularly distinctive.

Field marks: Male has green cap with crest at back of head, dark face with white outlines; ruddy breast, yellow flanks, green back; long tail with rusty undertail coverts. Female has white oval around eye; gray head and back, brown to buff flanks with contrasting spots. Eclipse plumage: Male turns gray-brown with green cap, red eye, gray face with white streaks; whitish throat, green wash on back and wings, gray breast and flanks.

Size: L: 17"–20", WS: 30"

Similar species: Mallard male has a bright green head, pale back, and a shorter tail.

Season: Year-round in east Texas and in the Amarillo area, winter in southern Texas

Habitat: Ponds and lakes sheltered by trees; wetlands with high grasses

Food source: Plants, insects, small aquatic animals, amphibians

Nest: In a tree cavity or nest box

Call: Female has a *whir-up, whir-up* repeated call; male has a high-pitched whistle.

Hot spots: This very common duck can be found in pairs or small flocks on virtually every pond in the state east of Abilene, and in the mid-southern part of the state in winter. A permanent population also lives on ponds throughout the Lubbock and Amarillo metropolitan areas.

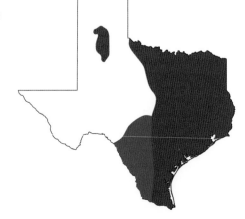

MALLARD
Anas platyrhynchos

The most common dabbling duck in the United States, the mallard is found in virtually every lake, pond, or large puddle in any metropolitan area.

Field marks: Male has green head, yellow bill; white collar, rusty breast, pale brown body, black and white tail. Female is uniformly brown with a paler head and black crown and line through the eye, orange bill with a dark center spot; blue speculum on wings with a white outline; orange legs.

Size: L: 20"–26", WS: 35"

Similar species: American black duck is darker overall with a lighter head and no wing speculum. Northern shoveler has much longer gray bill, a white breast, and rusty flanks. Ring-necked duck has navy blue head, gray bill with a white outline, and black back.

Season: Year-round in metro areas; a winter resident south of Midland and Waco

Habitat: Open water from small ponds and wetlands to large lakes, usually close to shore. Mallards also feed in farm fields and other open land areas.

Food source: Insects, freshwater invertebrates, worms, seeds, crop leavings, aquatic plants

Nest: On the ground in grassland, marshes, and near lakes and ponds

Call: The stereotypical *quek, quek, quek*

Hot spots: Mallards can be found in or near any body of water in wild places or in coexistence with humans. Ponds in mall parking areas, housing developments, and schoolyards all host mallards, as do harbors, piers, and parks where people feed them (not a recommended practice).

GADWALL

Mareca strepera

One of the many ducks that breed far north and overwinter in Texas, the gadwall male's black rump and gray bill set it apart from other dabblers.

Field marks: Male is a drab brown duck with a gray head and sloping forehead, reddish scapulars on wings, black rump and undertail coverts, yellow legs, and gray bill in breeding plumage. In nonbreeding season, the male becomes uniformly mottled brown with a gray head. Female is a mottled brown with white secondaries and a yellow bill.

Size: L: 19"–23", WS: 31"–36"

Similar species: Mallard female has blue speculum. American black duck has purple speculum.

Season: Winter

Habitat: Large ponds and small lakes with tall reeds and aquatic plants

Food source: Pond vegetation, tiny water animals

Nest: In prairies near water; midwestern United States and farther north

Call: Female quack is higher pitched than a mallard; male emits a narrow *mepp*.

Hot spots: Any park with a sizable pond or lake may host a pair or small flock of gadwalls in winter. These are particularly dependable: Lake Willow/Waco Wastewater Treatment Plant, Waco, 31.5161422 / -97.0753241; Aransas National Wildlife Refuge Wildlife Drive, 28.2403924 / -96.818819; Bentsen–Rio Grande Valley State Park/World Birding Center, Mission, 26.1849709 / -98.3793885; Abilene State Park/Lake Abilene, Buffalo Gap, 32.2316256 / -99.8920619; Jenna Welch Nature Center I-20 Pond, Midland, 31.9630947 / -102.1210903.

NORTHERN PINTAIL
Anas acuta

The long tail and dapper brown and white neck make this large duck distinctive.

Field marks: Brown head, white breast with a white stripe up each side to the head, gray body, black undertail coverts; long, black "pin" tail. Female is light brown with mottling through the wings and body and a dark gray bill.

Size: L: 20"–25", WS: 30"–35"

Similar species: No other duck species in Texas resembles a male northern pintail. Females may be confused with cinnamon teal females, but female northern pintail has a smaller bill and a plainer head.

Season: Winter

Habitat: Ponds, marshes, and waterways in marshes

Food source: Seeds and grains, insects, small crustaceans

Nest: In northern United States and Canada, on the ground near freshwater or brackish marshes and lakes

Call: Male call a high whistled *eeowee*; female call a chattered *quack*

Hot spots: In addition to these spots, wastewater treatment plants can be exceptional places to find overwintering ducks. Check your local plant before traveling far to see them. San Bernard National Wildlife Refuge, Moccasin Pond Loop, Cedar Lake, 28.884594 / -95.562815; Roy G. Guerrero Colorado River Metro Park, Austin, 30.246172 / -97.7049763; Aransas National Wildlife Refuge Wildlife Drive and Dagger Point, 28.2403924 / -96.818819; Choke Canyon State Park—Calliham Unit, 28.4717282 / -98.3394384; Kaufer-Hubert Memorial Park, Loyola Beach, 27.3196959 / -97.6841211.

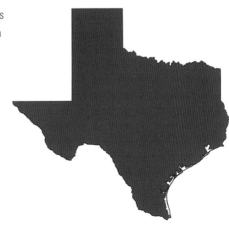

AMERICAN WIGEON
Mareca americana

Find this striking dabbler on ponds with abundant food at the surface.

Field marks: Male's head has a bright green stripe from lores to nape and a white or cream-colored cap; rufous flanks and underside, pinkish back, black wing tips; white undertail coverts and black rump and tail. Female is mottled rufous from back to underside, with a mottled gray head. Both have light blue bill with black tip, white wing patch with a green speculum. Nonbreeding adult male resembles female.

Size: L: 19"–23", WS: 30"–33"

Similar species: Green-winged teal is smaller and has a deep russet face and head, with no white cap.

Season: Winter

Habitat: Ponds, lakes, marshes

Food source: Leaves of many kinds of aquatic plants

Nest: Wigeons breed in the northern Midwest, Great Lakes, and Canada

Call: Male call a high-pitched *whew-woo-wee*; female call a barking quack

Hot spots: Aransas National Wildlife Refuge Visitor Center area, 28.2403924 / -96.818819; San Bernard National Wildlife Refuge, Cedar Lake, 28.884594 / -95.562815; Sunset Lake Park and Indian Point, Portland, 27.8525492 / -97.3559312; Trading House Creek Reservoir, Hallsburg, 31.5510378 / -96.9629288; Hargesheimer Wastewater Treatment Plant, Potosi, 32.2966233 / -99.7645843.

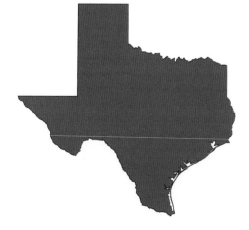

NORTHERN SHOVELER
Spatula clypeata

This duck's outsized bill makes it easy to identify in any season.

Field marks: Breeding male has green head, long gray bill; white breast and undertail coverts, rufous flanks, black tail. Nonbreeding male has gray head, yellow bill; gray breast and rufous flanks. Female is mottled brown with large yellow bill.

Size: L: 17"–20", WS: 27"–30"

Similar species: Mallard has much smaller yellow bill.

Season: Winter

Habitat: Marshes, both freshwater and saltwater; also lakes and ponds in flat areas

Food source: Aquatic insects and tiny animals; pond vegetation

Nest: In high vegetation; northern-midwestern United States and Canada

Call: Male call a low *chuk-chuk*; female a nasal *chik-chik*

Hot spots: Any city, state, or county park with a pond may have a flock of shovelers overwinter there, especially in the eastern half of the state and in the panhandle. Some prime spots for large flocks include Anahuac National Wildlife Refuge, Bolivar Peninsula, 29.609066 / -94.535253; Aransas National Wildlife Refuge Visitor Center area, 28.2403924 / -96.818819; Leonabelle Turnbull Birding Center, Port Aransas, 27.8275297 / -97.0789558; Union Grove Wildlife Management Area, Stillhouse Hollow Lake, Harker Heights, 31.0109757 / -97.5938272; McDonald Lake, Amarillo, 35.1589333 / -101.91717.

BLUE-WINGED TEAL
Spatula discors

One of the nation's smallest ducks overwinters in large flocks on Texas's lakes and ponds.

Field marks: Male has blue head with white crescent before the gray bill, spotted brown body, white patch at hip, blue wing patch with white border, green speculum (both usually only visible in flight). Female is grayish brown with a distinct lighter pattern, dark line through the eye, white at base of bill and at throat.

Size: L: 15"–16", WS: 23"–30"

Similar species: Green-winged teal has bold green and rufous head, solid gray flanks.

Season: Year-round in eastern Texas, winter in the west; some summer breeding flocks in the panhandle

Habitat: Shallow ponds and wetlands

Food source: Plants, seeds

Nest: On the ground in tall grass, near water

Call: Male call a high-pitched *chee, chee*; female a midrange *quack*

Hot spots: Any open body of water in the state is likely to have a population of blue-winged teal in the right season. Some of the most dependable spots include Leonabelle Turnbull Birding Center, Port Aransas, 27.8275297 / -97.0789558; San Bernard NWR Moccasin Pond Loop, Cedar Lake, 28.884594 / -95.562815; San Angelo State Park, San Angelo, 31.4677918 / -100.5033213; Cullinan Park, Sugar Land, 29.6355459 / -95.6603193; John Bunker Sands Wetland Center, Combine, 32.6137185 / -96.5008752.

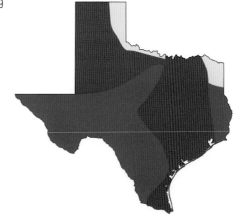

CINNAMON TEAL
Spatula cyanoptera

This striking western duck is most easily found in south Texas, mingling with large flocks of winter teal.

Field marks: Adult male is a bright rust color overall with a dark gray bill, black back, black tail; wings are dark with a pale blue shoulder and white underwing. Females are buff overall with a longer dark bill, dull blue wing patch, and white underwing. Nonbreeding male resembles female, but with a somewhat more rusty color.

Size: L: 15"–17", WS: 22"

Similar species: Eurasian wigeon has a rust-colored head but with a cream cap and gray back; it is rarely seen in Texas.

Season: Year-round in westernmost Texas, winter along the Lower Rio Grande; a migrant elsewhere

Habitat: Shallow ponds, wetlands, marshes

Food source: Aquatic plants, insects, small invertebrates, seeds

Nest: In marsh grasses less than 2 feet tall (only in west Texas)

Call: Male has a rattling call like wooden beads clacking against one another; female's call is a low, harsh quack.

Hot spots: Estero Llano Grande State Park World Birding Center, Llano Grande, 26.1268335 / -97.9578167; B.J. Bishop Wetlands, Presidio, 29.541114 / -104.317778; Twin Buttes Reservoir, San Angelo, 31.3774555 / -100.5366611; Lake Casa Blanca International State Park, Laredo, 27.5338322 / -99.4412898; Leonabelle Turnbull Birding Center, Port Aransas, 27.8275297 / -97.0789558.

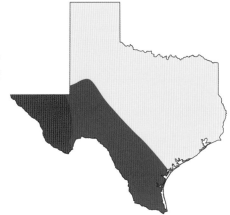

GREEN-WINGED TEAL

Anas crecca

America's smallest duck sports a bold facial pattern in breeding plumage.

Field marks: Breeding male has a rufous head with a green band from the eye to the back of the head; gray wings and flanks with a white bar on forward flank. Nonbreeding male is brown overall with visible green speculum. Female is mottled brown overall with a buff streak at the tail; green speculum is visible at rest.

Size: L: 12"–15", WS: 21"–25"

Similar species: Blue-winged teal has a blue head with a white crescent at the base of the bill, blue wing patch.

Season: Winter

Habitat: Lakes, ponds, and wetlands

Food source: Seeds, grasses, aquatic insects, small crustaceans

Nest: In a depression on the ground, some distance from water; Canada and the northern United States west of New England

Call: Brief, staccato whistles from male; laughing *haw-haw* quack from female

Hot spots: While these birds can be on any body of water in Texas during the winter, they are most numerous downstate and in ponds nearest the Gulf coast and Lower Rio Grande. Leonabelle Turnbull Birding Center, Port Aransas, 27.8275297 / -97.0789558; South Padre Island Birding and Nature Center, South Padre Island, 26.1374628 / -97.1739367; Estero Llano Grande State Park World Birding Center, Llano Grande, 26.1268335 / -97.9578167; Lake Casa Blanca International State Park, Laredo, 27.5338322 / -99.4412898; Mitchell Lake Audubon Center, San Antonio, 29.3105956 / -98.4996938.

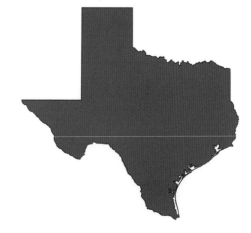

MOTTLED DUCK
Anas fulvigula

A year-round resident, this dabbling duck's yellow bill helps differentiate it from a female mallard.

Field marks: Male is a warm brown overall with buff streaks and a lighter head, a yellow bill with a black spot at the lower base, and orange legs and feet. Female is lighter overall but very similar.

Size: L: 21"–23", WS: 30"

Similar species: Female mallard has an orange bill with a dark center spot and a blue speculum with bold white border. American black duck is darker overall with a drab greenish bill.

Season: Year-round

Habitat: Ponds, marshes, freshwater pools, stormwater collection areas

Food source: Plants, rice, small crustaceans, insects, small fish

Nest: On the ground or in short vegetation, usually near water

Call: A raspy, repeated *cra-a-b*; female call a low quack

Hot spots: Galveston Island State Park, Galveston, 29.1956654 / -94.9559069; Leonabelle Turnbull Birding Center, Port Aransas, 27.8275297 / -97.0789558; Kaufer-Hubert Memorial Park, Loyola Beach, 27.3196959 / -97.6841211; Hazel Bazemore Park Hawkwatch Platform, Corpus Christi, 27.8660551 / -97.6427346; South Padre Island Birding and Nature Center, South Padre Island, 26.1374628 / -97.1739367.

CANVASBACK
Aythya valisineria

Identify this large diving duck by its red head, white back, and the slant of its forehead.

Field marks: Red head sloping forward to the dark bill; black breast, white back and flanks, black rear. Female has tan head with sloping forehead, white line through the eye, light body, tan rear.

Size: L: 19"–24", WS: 30"–36"

Similar species: Redhead is smaller and has darker back, rounded head, light blue bill with black tip.

Season: Winter

Habitat: Lakes, bays, and marshes

Food source: Seeds, tubers, and roots of aquatic plants, especially the sago pondweed; some snails and insect larvae

Nest: In areas of marsh vegetation, anchored to tall reeds and grasses; areas of the American Midwest and West and western Canada

Call: Male call a short *coo*, which can sound like a cackle when flocks call at once; female call a harsher *kiih*

Hot spots: Canvasbacks may appear on any reservoir, wastewater treatment plant pool, or large pond from November through March. These spots get larger and more dependable flocks: Salineño Wildlife Preserve, Roma, 26.5148584 / -99.1162062; Laguna Atascosa National Wildlife Refuge, Brownsville, 26.2338009 / -97.3643036; Fort Worth Nature Center and Refuge, Fort Worth, 32.8398612 / -97.4810886; Hagerman National Wildlife Refuge, Sherman/Denison, 33.7385706 / -96.7527511; Trading House Creek Reservoir, Hallsburg, 31.5510378 / -96.9629288.

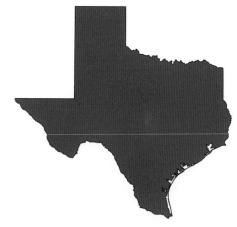

REDHEAD
Aythya americana

The smaller of the redheaded ducks, often found wintering in large flocks on lakes and ponds.

Field marks: Rounded red head; black breast and rear, gray body; bluish bill with a black tip. Female is brown, often with a whitish area around the bill; bill is dark gray, tipped in black.

Size: L: 18"–22", WS: 30"–34"

Similar species: Canvasback has dark bill, sloping forehead, and white back and is larger.

Season: Winter

Habitat: Saltwater bays, freshwater lakes

Food source: Seeds and roots of aquatic plants, small fish, mollusks, insects

Nest: Near water in tall reeds and grasses; prairies in the American and Canadian west

Call: Male call a *wuh-whooa*, arcing upward before descending; female a harder *queh*, like a quack

Hot spots: Packery Channel Park, Corpus Christi, 27.6264996 / -97.2204369; San Luis Pass, Galveston, 29.0892519 / -95.1187706; Village Creek Drying Beds, Arlington, 32.7842795 / -97.1266181; Benbrook Lake in Mustang Park, Fort Worth, 32.6098812 / -97.4725914; Horizon City RO ponds, Agua Dulce, 31.680525 / -106.15563; Amistad National Recreation Area Spur 406 area, Del Rio, 29.5522277 / -101.0230652.

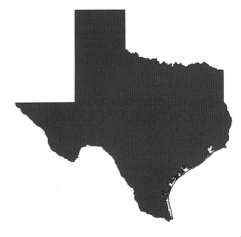

RING-NECKED DUCK
Aythya collaris

You'll have to look closely to find the reddish-brown "ring" around this duck's neck.

Field marks: Note the peaked back of the head. Dark purple head, yellow eye, gray bill with white ring and black tip; black back, light gray flanks with a white bar extending upward, black rear. Female is brown overall, with a white line through the eye, a white area just before the bill, and a gray bill with a black tip.

Size: L: 14"–18", WS: 24"–30"

Similar species: Greater scaup has a dark head with a greenish hue. Lesser scaup has a peaked head, no white on the bill, whiter sides, and a lighter back.

Season: Winter

Habitat: Freshwater ponds, marshes, bogs with considerable vegetation

Food source: Pondweed seeds and tubers, other aquatic plants, mollusks, waterborne insects and invertebrates

Nest: Among marsh plants, directly over water

Call: Brief whistled note from male; sharp, repeated quack from female

Hot spots: Santa Ana National Wildlife Refuge, San Juan, 26.0787993 / -98.1330503; Choke Canyon State Park—Calliham Unit, 28.4717282 / -98.3394384; Charles A. Guy Park, Lubbock, 33.5119625 / -101.8964211; Lewisville Lake Environmental Learning Area, Lewisville, 33.0662579 / -96.9750008; Goodnight Ranch Community Ponds, Austin, 30.1573524 / -97.7579449.

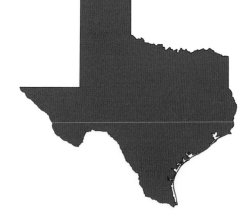

LESSER SCAUP
Aythya affinis

Look for large flocks of this diving duck over the winter.

Field marks: Dark head appears glossy navy blue in the right light; the pointed peak at the top rear is the best indication of a lesser (rather than greater) scaup. Yellow eye, gray bill; black breast and rear, gray back, white flanks.

Size: L: 16"–18", WS: 24"–30"

Similar species: Greater scaup is slightly larger, with a rounded head (no peak) that may appear greenish in sunlight.

Season: Winter

Habitat: Ocean bays, lakes, estuaries

Food source: Aquatic invertebrates

Nest: On the ground in areas of high grasses and sedges, on dry land or near lakes; western United States prairies and marshes (not in Texas)

Call: Male call a bubbly series of high-pitched *piffs*; female a hoarse, repeated *quick*

Hot spots: Laguna Point Recreation Area, Port Mansfield, 26.5527582 / -97.4171998; Oso Bay Wetlands Preserve, Corpus Christi, 27.7143059 / -97.3327732; Oak Thicket Park, Lake Fayette, 29.9479812 / -96.727066; Lake Willow, Waco Wastewater Treatment Plant, 31.5161422 / -97.0753241; White Rock Lake, Dallas, 32.8337313 / -96.7121315.

BUFFLEHEAD
Bucephala albeola

North America's smallest diving duck overwinters in ponds, lakes, and bays throughout Texas.

Field marks: Male has large white area on back of the black head, small bill, black back, white flanks and underside, gray tail. Nonbreeding male loses much of the white area on the head, retaining a patch on each side. Female is all brown with a darker back and head, white oval patch on each side of the head.

Size: L: 13"–14", WS: 21"–24"

Similar species: Hooded merganser is much larger and has a thin black bill, as well as rusty flanks and distinctive white striping.

Season: Winter

Habitat: Ponds, lakes, inlets, Gulf of Mexico

Food source: Insects, mollusks, crustaceans, some seeds found underwater

Nest: In cavities, often those left behind by northern flickers (not in Texas)

Call: A single syllable: *quah*; a continuous *qua-qua-qua* during breeding season

Hot spots: South Padre Island Birding and Nature Center, 26.1374628 / -97.1739367; Wildlife Drive, Aransas National Wildlife Refuge, 28.2403924 / -96.818819; Lafitte's Cove, Galveston, 29.2169006 / -94.9349016; Sibley Nature Center, Midland, 32.0349286 / -102.0706594; Sunset Bay, White Rock Lake, Dallas, 32.8337313 / -96.7121315.

HOODED MERGANSER
Lophodytes cucullatus

The showiest of the mergansers is also the smallest.

Field marks: Male has black head with large white crest it raises during breeding season, thin bill, black back and chest with unique white striping, rusty flanks. Female is all brown with a reddish-brown crest, yellow bill, and long tail held upward. Nonbreeding adult (July–September, not usually seen in Texas) is brown overall with no crest.

Size: L: 17"–19", WS: 24"–26"

Similar species: Bufflehead is much smaller and black overall, with a thicker, gray bill.

Season: Winter, with some passing through during migration in west Texas

Habitat: Ponds and streams in wooded areas; also swamps and marshes

Food source: Crayfish and other crustaceans, insects, small fish, snails, small amphibians, underwater plants and seeds

Nest: Ten to 20 feet above ground in a hollow tree, often near water (not in Texas)

Call: A deep, rolling, descending croak, like a frog; females utter a grunting *quack.*

Hot spots: Look for pairs of these ducks rather than large flocks. South Texas Botanical Gardens, Corpus Christi, 27.6525275 / -97.4068666; Rollover Pass, Bolivar Peninsula, Galveston, 29.5100602 / -94.5008326; Canyon Lake Gorge, Canyon Lake, 29.9118677 / -98.2391453; Kirby Lake, Abilene, 32.3724227 / -99.7345734; TX 90 Pond and Mockingbird Lane, Navasota, 30.4354941 / -96.0374447.

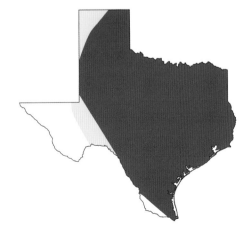

RUDDY DUCK
Oxyura jamaicensis

The bright blue bill, black cap, and rufous body make the male stand out from rafts of wintering ducks.

Field marks: Male in breeding plumage has a white face, large black cap covering the top third of the head, bright blue bill, rufous body with tail often pointed upward, white belly visible in flight. Female is brown overall with a darker cap and a dark line across the white cheek. Nonbreeding male is grayish-brown overall but retains the white cheeks and black cap; bill is gray.

Size: L: 15", WS: 19"–23"

Similar species: Nothing compares in breeding plumage. Nonbreeding black scoter (rarely seen in Texas) is larger and drabber overall, with less white on the face.

Season: Winter

Habitat: Freshwater ponds, lakes, and marshes

Food source: Aquatic vegetation, algae, water insects, crustaceans, mollusks

Nest: Floating among reeds in ponds or marshes; western United States and Canada (not in Texas)

Call: A low, guttural call like a wet belch

Hot spots: Lakes, ponds, and wastewater treatment plants throughout the state may host ruddy ducks through the winter. Here are some known bodies of water where they have congregated for the past five or so years: Bryan Beach, Freeport, 28.9020747 / -95.3488313; Leonabelle Turnbull Birding Center, Port Aransas, 27.8275297 / -97.0789558; Choke Canyon State Park—Calliham Unit, 28.4717282 / -98.3394384; Lake Veridian, Arlington, 32.794057 / -97.0886707; Eldorado Wastewater Treatment Plant, Eldorado, 30.8636077 / -100.5874192.

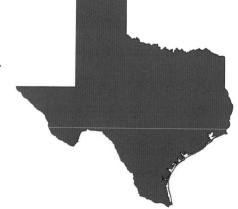

DUCK-LIKE BIRDS

COMMON GALLINULE
Gallinula galeata

The candy-corn bill and laughing cackle make this sleekly patterned bird (formerly known as common moorhen) distinctive and unmistakable in local marshes.

Field marks: Brown above and bluish-gray below with a large white area on the tail, white flank stripe between the gray sides, and brown wings. The bill is bright red with a yellow tip, with considerable variation among birds of different ages.

Size: L: 13"–15", WS: 21"–23"

Similar species: American coot is all black with a white bill.

Season: Year-round near the Gulf coast, summer further inland; predominantly in east Texas with scattered individuals further west

Habitat: Freshwater ponds, streams, and marshes with tall reeds

Food source: Water plants and seeds, small invertebrates

Nest: On stems or branches of plants along the edge of water

Call: Falsetto *huh-huh, huh, huh-huh* in nonrhythmic pattern, like a cartoon laugh

Hot spots: Choke Canyon State Park—Calliham Unit, 28.4717282 / -98.3394384; Leonabelle Turnbull Birding Center, Port Aransas, 27.8275297 / -97.0789558; Aransas National Wildlife Refuge Wildlife Drive, 28.2403924 / -96.818819; Sheldon Lake State Park, Sheldon, 29.8820575 / -95.1858783; Sabal Palm Sanctuary, Brownsville, 25.85233 / -97.4176839.

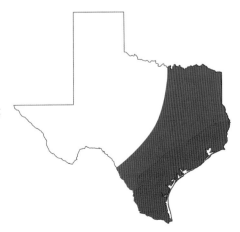

AMERICAN COOT
Fulica americana

Large flocks of these all-black birds gather in marshes and ponds throughout the winter.

Field marks: All black with small white stripes on the tail, white bill, greenish-yellow legs, red eye. Adults have a red spot at the top of the bill.

Size: L: 15", WS: 24"–26"

Similar species: Common gallinule has a red and yellow bill.

Season: Year-round

Habitat: Saltwater inlets, bays, and marshes; freshwater ponds and wetlands

Food source: Water plants, many small aquatic animals, occasionally bird eggs

Nest: On a pallet of plant materials anchored to reeds in a marsh or wetland

Call: A midrange clucking: *pukka, pukka, pukka*; more abbreviated as an alarm call

Hot spots: Any body of water throughout the state may have its resident flock of coots. Here are some with large, dependable flocks year-round: Lake Travis, Bob Wentz Windy Point Park, Austin, 30.4128174 / -97.9008651; Choke Canyon State Park—Calliham Unit, 28.4717282 / -98.3394384; Leonabelle Turnbull Birding Center, Port Aransas, 27.8275297 / -97.0789558; O. H. Ivie Reservoir, Concho Park, Leaday, 31.554908 / -99.71049; Leroy Elmore Park, Lubbock, 33.5337785 / -101.9051548.

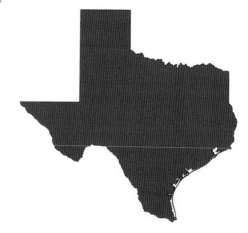

PURPLE GALLINULE
Porphyrio martinica

Strikingly iridescent, this colorful, ground-foraging marsh bird more than lives up to its name.

Field marks: Adult has bright blue-to-purple head, neck, breast, and underside; light blue forehead shield, bright orange-red bill with yellow tip, greenish back and wings, white undertail coverts, black tail; bright yellow legs with large, yellow, three-toed feet. Juvenile has light brown head and neck, brown bill, white breast and underside, light brown flanks, greenish back and wings, yellow legs, white undertail, greenish tail.

Size: L: 13"–14", WS: 22"

Similar species: Common gallinule has a similar bill, but is gray and dark brown overall with a white flank stripe below the wings.

Season: Spring and summer

Habitat: Freshwater marshes with tall grasses for cover and floating plants (water lilies and such) for nesting

Food source: Water lilies, leaves and tubers of other aquatic plants, some insects, snails, small fish, frogs

Nest: In vegetation above water or on the water's surface

Call: Low, descending *kuck-kuck-kuck-kuck-kuck*; a higher-pitched *kick-kick-kick* in flight

Hot spots: South Padre Island Birding and Nature Center, 26.1374628 / -97.1739367; Leonabelle Turnbull Birding Center, Port Aransas, 27.8275297 / -97.0789558; San Bernard NWR Moccasin Pond Loop, Cedar Lake, 28.884594 / -95.562815; Brazoria National Wildlife Refuge Auto Loop Tour, Clute, 29.0599843 / -95.267568; Brazos Bend State Park, Thompsons, 29.3735739 / -95.6230259.

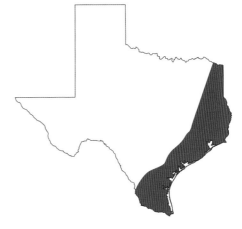

PELICANS, CORMORANTS, AND ANHINGA

AMERICAN WHITE PELICAN
Pelecanus erythrorhynchos

A large white bird with a big pouch under its bill, this pelican is found on islands in freshwater lakes.

Field marks: White overall; long orange bill, orange legs and feet, black primary wing feathers.

Size: L: 62"–72", WS: 108"

Similar species: Northern gannet (unusual in Texas) has black primaries, a tan cap, and a gray bill.

Season: Winter in east Texas and along the Gulf coast; spring and fall migration throughout the state

Habitat: Islands in freshwater lakes and ponds

Food source: Fish

Nest: On islands, building low mounds of mud and debris

Call: A throaty croak

Hot spots: These birds may congregate in any area with a large body of water. Here are some of the most dependable places: King Ranch, Santa Gertrudis Unit, Kingsville, 27.5183197 / -97.9093409; Leonabelle Turnbull Birding Center, Port Aransas, 27.8275297 / -97.0789558; Aransas National Wildlife Refuge Wildlife Drive, 28.2403924 / -96.818819; Quintana Neotropical Bird Sanctuary, Quintana, 28.9336226 / -95.3087246; Fort Parker State Park, Forest Glade, 31.5943304 / -96.5309058.

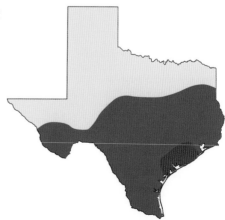

BROWN PELICAN
Pelecanus occidentalis

The unmistakable denizen of Texas Gulf shores gathers in flocks at every port, bridge, and pier.

Field marks: Adult has yellow head in breeding season with dark brown nape and neck (white in nonbreeding), and huge gray-to-brown bill with underhanging pocket for catching and transporting fish. Gray-brown back and wings, dark brown breast and underside, brown legs and feet. Juvenile has brown head and neck and whitish underside. Plunging dive while catching fish helps identify these birds over water.

Size: L: 50"–53", WS: 79"–80"

Similar species: American white pelican is all white with black trailing edge of wings. Double-crested cormorant is smaller and all black with a bright yellow-orange bill.

Season: Year-round

Habitat: Open ocean and ocean shores

Food source: Fish

Nest: On the ground among thick vegetation or in a shrubby area; sometimes in an exposed treetop

Call: Mostly silent; young emits a low growl/groan in the nest.

Hot spots: Any trip to the Gulf of Mexico will yield brown pelicans. Watch bridge and causeway railings, posts at piers and wharves, and beaches for groups of pelicans. A scan of the Gulf from any beach will reveal pelicans skimming just above the water as they watch for fish, and then executing their complex, twisting dive maneuver to catch them.

DOUBLE-CRESTED CORMORANT
Nannopterum auritum

Very common seabird on Gulf shores and large freshwater lakes.

Field marks: Black overall; orange lores, gray bill; white tufts on crown during breeding. Juveniles have pale or tan throat and underside.

Size: L: 32"–33", WS: 50"–54"

Similar species: Neotropic cormorant is smaller, and breeding birds have a white V at the base of the bill.

Season: Winter through much of the state; summer in the panhandle

Habitat: Open water, especially along the Gulf shore; also inland at large lakes and flowing rivers

Food source: Fish, crustaceans

Nest: In rocky or sandy areas along lake or river shoreline

Call: Mostly silent, with some grunting during nesting

Hot spots: Virtually every beach wall, rocky outcropping, offshore island, and sandbar has its own complement of double-crested cormorants; many large inland lakes and reservoirs provide homes to these large, dark birds as well. You do not need a special hot spot to find one—just go to any beach or shoreline overlook and scan the horizon. Cormorants sit low in the water, making them look similar to loons, so check carefully for the bright orange-yellow bill to make the identification.

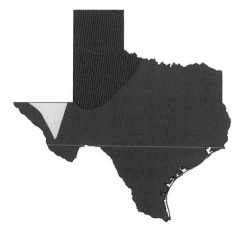

NEOTROPIC CORMORANT
Nannopterum brasilianum

Look closely at this bird's smaller, slimmer size and the white outline between its bill and throat to tell it apart from its double-crested relatives.

Field marks: Black overall, with orange skin outlined in white at the base of the bill; in breeding plumage, white feathers appear behind the ear.

Size: L: 22"–24", WS: 40"–42"

Similar species: Double-crested cormorant is larger and bulkier; lacks the white V at the base of the bill.

Season: Year-round

Habitat: Bays, inlets, and estuaries along the Gulf coast; also found inland at large lakes that have plenty of fish

Food source: Fish, crustaceans

Nest: In a small tree or dead snag not far from water

Call: A deep, low-pitched grunt, very like a wild hog

Hot spots: Every inlet and beach along the Gulf coast has its own population of neotropic cormorants, usually intermixed with double-crested cormorants. Beaches on the barrier islands all along the Gulf coast (Bolivar, Galveston, Quintana, South Padre, and others) are perfect places to seek sightings of neotropics.

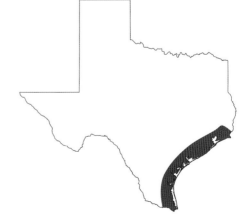

ANHINGA
Anhinga anhinga

The lacy white mantle over black wings, long neck, and very long tail make anhingas fairly easy to identify.

Field marks: Adults are black overall with a long, bright yellow bill, longer tail than a cormorant, and a white wash over black wings. Juveniles have a cream to light brown head, neck, throat, and upper breast.

Size: L: 34"–36", WS: 45"

Similar species: Double-crested and neotropic cormorants are smaller and have shorter necks and tails and a shorter bill.

Season: Year-round near the Gulf coast; spring through fall inland

Habitat: Slow-moving fresh water, including shallow rivers, streams, and drainage canals; also bays and inlets along the Gulf coast

Food source: Mostly small fish

Nest: In the crotch of a tree near water

Call: Usually silent except during nesting, when they may croak to one another with a dry, rattling sound.

Hot spots: Hazel Bazemore Park Hawkwatch Platform, Corpus Christi, 27.8660551 / -97.6427346; Lake Findley, Alice, 27.7888887 / -98.0641977; Estero Llano Grande State Park World Birding Center, Llano Grande, 26.1268335 / -97.9578167; Fisheries Field Station, Brownsville, 25.9850902 / -97.5309134; Brazos Bend State Park, Thompsons, 29.3735739 / -95.6230259.

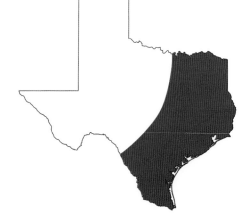

GULLS AND TERNS

LAUGHING GULL
Leucophaeus atricilla

Named for its cackling call, this black-headed gull is one of the most widespread gull species on Texas's Gulf coast.

Field marks: Breeding adult has black head extending to the neck, partial white eye ring, heavy red bill that droops slightly at the end; white body, dark wings, white tail with black band at the end, black legs. Nonbreeding adult has white head streaked in gray at the back, black bill.

Size: L: 16"–17", WS: 40"–42"

Similar species: Little gull (very rare) is smaller, has a slim bill, and has a dark underwing. Bonaparte's gull is smaller and has a thin black bill and light gray wings.

Season: Year-round

Habitat: Gulf beaches, salt marshes, large and small lakes

Food source: Insects and invertebrates, shellfish, berries, human trash

Nest: On the ground in a salt marsh, hidden among grasses

Call: Repeated *kyah, kyah*, increasing in speed until it sounds like a human laugh

Hot spots: Laughing gulls are prevalent from the Bolivar Peninsula to Brownsville, with populations spreading inland through Houston and as far west as Zapata along the border. Their year-round presence, especially on beaches, makes them easy to find for vacationers as well as residents.

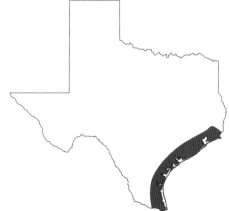

RING-BILLED GULL
Larus delawarensis

The most common gull in America, this scavenger turns up in flocks in parking lots, in mowed grassy areas, and at your outdoor restaurant table.

Field marks: Breeding adult has white head and body; yellow bill with black ring near the tip, gray wings, black wing tips, yellow legs. Juveniles have varying degrees of brown streaking over the head, body, and wings; pink bill with black tip, pink legs.

Size: L: 17.5"–19", WS: 47"–48"

Similar species: Herring gull is larger and has a yellow bill with a red spot. Laughing gull has a black hood in breeding season, and has darker wings year-round.

Season: Winter

Habitat: Ocean beaches, lagoons, inlets, marshes, parks, parking lots, landfills

Food source: Human discards, fish, rodents, eggs and chicks from other birds' nests

Nest: In a depression on the ground; in colonies on an island or other protected area

Call: Piercing *keey-oh, keey-oh*, or a harsh, high-pitched barking call

Hot spots: You will see these ubiquitous birds every time you visit the beach, go to a supermarket or park, or venture into any wilderness area that contains a lake or large pond. Ring-billed gulls often stand in large flocks in parking areas waiting for food scraps to drop from unsuspecting humans' vehicles. Outdoor dining can be a challenge where they congregate— near the Gulf coast or in areas with lakes or reservoirs.

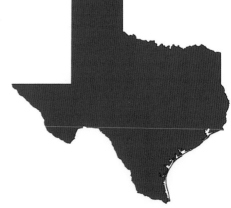

HERRING GULL
Larus argentatus

More numerous on the Atlantic Ocean side of the state, this common gull confuses birders with its many plumage variations.

Field marks: Breeding adult has white head and breast, yellow eye, heavy yellow bill with red spot on lower mandible; gray wings with black tips, white tail, pink legs. Nonbreeding adult is similar but with brown streaking on the head and neck. Juveniles in first and second winter have extensive brown mottling over the head, breast, underside, tail, and wings, with black wing tips and a dark brown band at the end of the tail. Extent of streaking will vary from one bird to the next.

Size: L: 24"–26", WS: 55"–58"

Similar species: Great black-backed gull is larger with black wings. Lesser black-backed gull is slightly smaller and has darker gray wings and yellow legs. Ring-billed gull is smaller and has a yellow bill with a black ring.

Season: Primarily winter

Habitat: Gulf beaches, barrier islands, wetlands, and large lakes

Food source: Fish, aquatic invertebrates, shellfish, carrion, other birds, human discards

Nest: On the ground on the beach or an island not far from shore

Call: A squeal followed by a high *hyah-hyah-hyah-hyah*, not unlike a human laugh. Other calls include a long whistle ending in a high-pitched squeal.

Hot spots: Quintana Beach and Jetty, Freeport, 28.9343 / -95.2987; San Luis Pass, Galveston, 29.0892519 / -95.1187706; Matagorda Bay Nature Park, Matagorda, 28.5976351 / -95.9782791; Brownsville Landfill, Brownsville, 25.9380025 / -97.3939785; Lake Ray Hubbard, Rowlett, 32.9026503 / -96.5447617.

CASPIAN TERN
Hydroprogne caspia

The oversized, boldly red bill on this largest tern is the key to its identification.

Field marks: White head with black cap past its eye, large red bill with dark gray tip, pale gray wings with dark primaries, black legs. Nonbreeding adult has streaky gray cap.

Size: L: 20"–23", WS: 50"–53"

Similar species: Royal tern is smaller and has thinner orange-red bill. Common tern is much smaller and has thinner black cap; its orange bill had a black tip.

Season: Winter along the coast; scattered sightings of migrating birds in spring and fall during stopovers at lakes and reservoirs

Habitat: Gulf shore, lakes and rivers near the Gulf with gravel shores

Food source: Fish, occasional crustaceans

Nest: In the sand on seashores and lake beaches; northeastern Atlantic Ocean, central Canada, western United States, and Pacific coast (not in Texas)

Call: A single raspy croak

Hot spots: South Padre Island Birding and Nature Center, 26.1374628 / -97.1739367; Laguna Atascosa National Wildlife Refuge, Brownsville, 26.2338009 / -97.3643036; Port Aransas Jetty, Port Aransas, 27.8348271 / -97.046015; Apffel Park/East Beach, Galveston, 29.33169 / -94.73242; TX 48 Shrimp Basin Bridge/Zapata Memorial Boat Ramp, Brownsville, 26.0023329 / -97.2999001.

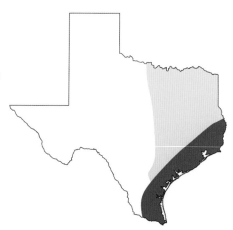

ROYAL TERN
Thalasseus maximus

Smaller and sleeker than the Caspian tern, this tern has a slimmer red bill and a more pronounced crest.

Field marks: Breeding adult has white head with black cap and pointed crest on back of head, red-orange bill, pale gray wings with black tips, white tail, black legs. Nonbreeding adult's white forehead tapers to black shading; black line from eye to crest. Juvenile's bill is more yellow, with white forehead, black shading on back of head, mottled wings, yellow legs.

Size: L: 18"–20", WS: 40"–42"

Similar species: Caspian tern is larger and has heavier bill. Common tern has a red bill with a black tip, and red legs in breeding plumage.

Season: Year-round, with much higher concentrations in winter

Habitat: Gulf beaches, saltwater bays and inlets

Food source: Fish, water invertebrates

Nest: On coastal islands, in a hollow dug in the sand

Call: Single note *cur-rick*; also very high, short trill

Hot spots: Just about any beach will have its share of royal terns. Here are some places where they gather in flocks: Apffel Park/East Beach, Galveston, 29.33169 / -94.73242; San Luis Pass, Galveston, 29.0892519 / -95.1187706; Padre Island National Seashore, visitor center area, 27.4244237 / -97.2973251; Port Aransas Jetty, Port Aransas, 27.8348271 / -97.046015; 8 Mile Beach/Sunny Beach, Galveston, 29.2349195 / -94.8829937.

FORSTER'S TERN
Sterna forsteri

Telling Forster's and common terns apart can be tricky. Generally, Forster's is slightly larger, and breeding birds have no gray or black on the primaries. Common terns usually migrate along the Texas coast, but do not linger long.

Field marks: Breeding adult has black cap extending to the nape, orange bill with black tip, white body, pale gray wings with white primaries, deeply forked white tail, orange legs. Nonbreeding bird has white head with large black spot just behind the eye, darker wing primaries.

Size: L: 13"–15", WS: 30"–31"

Similar species: Common tern is smaller, retains most of its black cap in nonbreeding plumage, and has a redder bill.

Season: Year-round along the Gulf coast, winter in east Texas; passing over west Texas and the panhandle during migration

Habitat: Ocean shoreline, salt marshes

Food source: Fish, tadpoles, mollusks, crustaceans

Nest: Built on a foundation of dead plants in salt marshes

Call: High-pitched *keek, keek, keek* and lower, rapid clicking or chucking sound

Hot spots: Any Gulf beach may yield Forster's sightings, but these regularly receive larger flocks. South Padre Island Birding and Nature Center, 26.1374628 / -97.1739367; Packery Channel Park, Corpus Christi, 27.6264996 / -97.2204369; Port Aransas Jetty, Port Aransas, 27.8348271 / -97.046015; Quintana Beach and Jetty, Freeport, 28.9343 / -95.2987; Rollover Pass, Bolivar Peninsula, Galveston, 29.5100602 / -94.5008326.

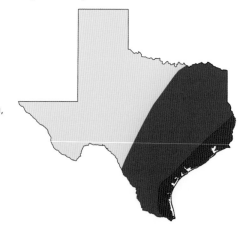

BLACK SKIMMER
Rynchops niger

With its elongated shape, oversized lower mandible, and spellbinding water-skimming behavior, black skimmer is a favorite among coastal birders.

Field marks: Black mantle from top of head to wing tips, white underside, white forehead, orange and black bill with longer lower mandible, orange legs.

Size: L: 18"–19", WS: 42"–45"

Similar species: American oystercatcher has similar coloring but lacks the pronounced bill configuration.

Season: Year-round, with higher concentrations in winter

Habitat: Sandbars, beaches, salt marshes, estuaries, bays

Food source: Fish, shrimp

Nest: In a depression on the ground, hidden by vegetation

Call: Single note *duh, duh, duh*; faster in flight or as an alarm

Hot spots: Bolivar Flats Shorebird Sanctuary, Galveston, 29.3711371 / -94.7287083; San Luis Pass, Galveston, 29.0892519 / -95.1187706; Matagorda Bay Nature Park, Matagorda, 28.5976351 / -95.9782791; Aransas National Wildlife Refuge Wildlife Drive, 28.2403924 / -96.818819; Port Aransas Jetty, Port Aransas, 27.8348271 / -97.046015.

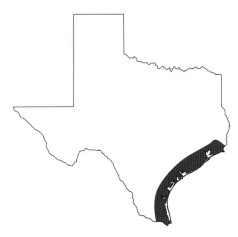

HERONS AND EGRETS

GREAT BLUE HERON
Ardea herodias

The tallest of the long-legged waders, this majestic bird stands quietly and waits for prey, then grabs or stabs its target in a split-second attack.

Field marks: Gray-blue with grayish legs, large bill, yellow lower mandible, black crown, long plumes from neck. In flight, legs extend far beyond tail, neck curls in, and darker flight feathers become visible.

Size: H: 46", WS: 72"

Similar species: Tricolored heron has white underbelly. Little blue heron is darker blue and half as tall.

Season: Year-round wherever there is open water

Habitat: Fresh- and saltwater marshes, grasslands, any pond with ample fish

Food source: Fish, small mammals, frogs, birds, insects

Nest: High in trees in colonies (rookeries), often some distance from feeding grounds

Call: Hoarse croaking *bwaaaaah*; alarm is a series of chuffing sounds like *bwaak, bwaak, bwaak.*

Hot spots: The most common tall wading bird in North America, the great blue heron can be seen easily at virtually any small lake, inland pond, tidal marsh, and wetland wildlife refuge throughout Texas.

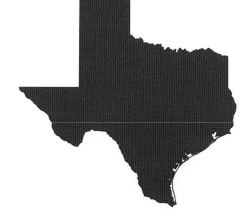

GREAT EGRET
Ardea alba

Texas's tallest egret is a sight to behold. Pure white with a long, curving neck, it's easy to see as it stands motionless and waits for prey to swim by.

Field marks: All white, long yellow-orange bill, black legs and feet.

Size: H: 39", WS: 51"

Similar species: Snowy egret has a black bill with yellow lores, black legs, and yellow feet.

Season: Year-round on the Gulf coast, summer in east Texas; migration through west Texas

Habitat: Salt- and freshwater marshes, mudflats, other wetlands along the Gulf coast; also inland lakes, wetlands, and farm fields

Food source: Fish, frogs, other small wetland creatures

Nest: In colonies, high in trees

Call: Low, squawking *caaaah*, dropping still lower at the end

Hot spots: Numerous and easy to distinguish from other long-legged birds, great egrets can be found anywhere there is open water. Before making a special trip to the coast to find an egret, check any retention pond or drainage canal in a suburb, at a mall, or in an open area.

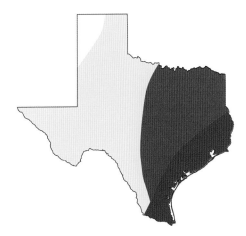

SNOWY EGRET
Egretta thula

This elegant member of the heron family sports long plumes during the breeding season; its bright yellow feet make it unique among egrets.

Field marks: All white; long white plumes from head and chest during breeding season, slender black bill, yellow lores, black legs with yellow feet.

Size: H: 24", WS: 41"

Similar species: Great egret is significantly larger and has a yellow bill and black feet. Cattle egret is smaller and has a shorter bill and black feet (red during breeding).

Season: Year-round along the Gulf coast, summer in populated areas of east Texas, the western end of the Rio Grande Valley, and around lakes in the panhandle; migration elsewhere in eastern and central Texas

Habitat: Marshes (salt, brackish, and freshwater), ponds, wetlands

Food source: Fish, small crustaceans, worms, frogs, insects

Nest: In colonies, toward the tops of trees or tall shrubs

Call: Croaking *maaaw, morr*; higher pitched than great egret or great blue heron

Hot spots: Snowy egrets congregate in areas with water, even when it's limited: the Gulf coast, the Lower Rio Grande Valley, ponds, lakes, canals, slow streams, or wetlands. In addition to the wetlands along the Gulf coast, try these city parks: White Rock Lake, Dallas, 32.8337313 / -96.7121315; Benbrook Lake in Mustang Park, Fort Worth, 32.6098812 / -97.4725914; Maxey Park, Lubbock, 33.5702868 / -101.9019926; Keystone Heritage Park, El Paso, 31.8209406 / -106.5630008; Brackenridge Park, San Antonio, 29.4629383 / -98.4698155.

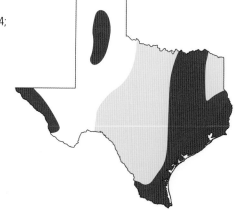

TRICOLORED HERON
Egretta tricolor

Smaller than the great blue heron and strikingly marked, this heron is a year-round, dependable sighting on the Gulf coast. Find it in the quiet waters of freshwater and saltwater marshes.

Field marks: Steel-blue back, wings, neck, and head; streak of white outlined with rusty red down the front of the long neck, white underparts, pink legs (yellow in juveniles), blue-gray bill tipped with black.

Size: H: 26", WS: 36"

Similar species: Great blue heron has blue-gray underparts, heavier yellow bill.

Season: Year-round

Habitat: Coastal marshes, inland freshwater wetlands

Food source: Fish, small crustaceans, insects, frogs

Nest: In colonies with other herons and egrets, high in trees

Call: Nasal, rasping two-syllable *wiwur, wiwur*; alarm call is a continuous grunting.

Hot spots: Tricolored herons are as easy to find as great and snowy egrets and great blue herons—virtually any body of water or perpetually wet area will have them. Cove Harbor Bird Sanctuary, Rockport, 27.9969687 / -97.0727921; East End Lagoon Nature Preserve, Galveston, 29.333603 / -94.7454326; San Bernard National Wildlife Refuge, Cedar Lake, 28.884594 / -95.562815; Port Aransas Wetland Park, Port Aransas, 27.825 / -97.071; South Padre Island Birding and Nature Center, 26.1374628 / -97.1739367.

LITTLE BLUE HERON
Egretta caerulea

Often standing still enough to blend with its surroundings, this dark blue and purple bird stays in the shadows while patrolling for prey.

Field marks: Uniformly dark blue with gray legs, light bluish bill. Head and neck may be dark purple in mature adults. Juvenile is pure white with gray bill and greenish legs.

Size: H: 24", WS: 40"

Similar species: Great blue heron is much larger, lighter colored, and has a yellow bill. Tricolored heron is somewhat taller and has white underparts and a white streak down the front of its neck. Cattle egret is smaller, with a shorter neck and darker bill than a juvenile little blue heron.

Season: Year-round on the Gulf coast, summer in east Texas

Habitat: Fresh- and saltwater wetlands and marshes, wet fields, estuaries, quiet streambeds, drainage canals along roadsides

Food source: Fish, small crustaceans, dragonflies, frogs

Nest: Short trees, shrubs, usually concealed by vegetation

Call: Series of harsh *mow, mow, mow* croaks in flight; short staccato croaks while stationary. These may vary in length and frequency.

Hot spots: Like the great blue and tricolored herons, the little blue heron is widespread and abundant in its range. Try these dependable stops for all Texas long-legged waders: Cove Harbor Bird Sanctuary, Rockport, 27.9969687 / -97.0727921; East End Lagoon Nature Preserve, Galveston, 29.333603 / -94.7454326; San Bernard National Wildlife Refuge, Cedar Lake, 28.884594 / -95.562815; Port Aransas Wetland Park, Port Aransas, 27.825 / -97.071; South Padre Island Birding and Nature Center, 26.1374628 / -97.1739367.

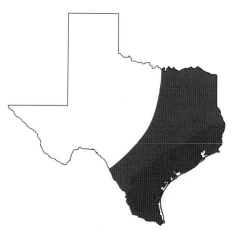

REDDISH EGRET
Egretta rufescens

A wader of southern climates, this egret stays close to the coast in shallow saltwater marshes. Its population appears to be declining throughout the region.

Field marks: Rufous head and neck, blue skin around eye, pink bill with black tip, grayish-blue body and wings, gray legs. Juvenile may have pinkish-gray head and neck instead of reddish; some juveniles are pure white with gray legs, but retain the pink and black bill.

Size: L: 29"–31", WS: 46"

Similar species: Little blue heron is smaller and is dark blue overall with a gray-blue bill. Juvenile tricolored heron is more brilliantly rufous, with the reddish color carrying into the wings.

Season: Year-round

Habitat: Saltwater marshes, bays, estuaries

Food source: Fish

Nest: In mangrove swamps, in a tree just above the water

Call: A series of single, low, grunting notes, accompanied by bill clattering during courtship

Hot spots: Apffel Park/East Beach, Galveston, 29.33169 / -94.73242; Galveston Island State Park, Galveston, 29.1956654 / -94.9559069; Matagorda Bay Nature Park, Matagorda, 28.5976351 / -95.9782791; Charlie's Pasture South Boardwalk, Port Aransas, 27.81398 / -97.080079; Indian Point, Corpus Christi, 27.8525492 / -97.3559312.

CATTLE EGRET
Bubulcus ibis

This egret gets its name from its relationship with livestock, foraging for insects that large animals kick up as they move around a pasture. The bird even stands on animals' backs to catch fleas, flies, and ticks.

Field marks: Short, stocky, short-billed, all-white egret with a yellow bill and black legs and feet. When breeding, this egret develops light orange areas on its head, back, and neck/chest, and its legs turn red.

Size: H: 20", WS: 36"

Similar species: Snowy and great egrets are larger and have bills more than twice the length. Great egret has a long neck. Snowy egret has yellow feet.

Season: Year-round

Habitat: Open fields, often sharing a pasture with cattle, horses, or other large animals

Food source: Primarily insects, foraged on the ground (or off the backs of cattle)

Nest: In the tops of trees in a swamp or marsh

Call: Flight call is a measured *ruh, ruh*; conversation among groups of birds is a clucking not unlike chickens.

Hot spots: Drive along any highway in Texas and watch the open fields for these abundant birds dotting the landscape, especially in spring and summer. They are often seen actually standing on a cow's back, just as their name would suggest. When there are no cattle, the birds can be seen with their heads down, foraging for insects on mowed lawns or in farm fields. In west Texas they congregate in large numbers at reservoirs and wastewater treatment plants.

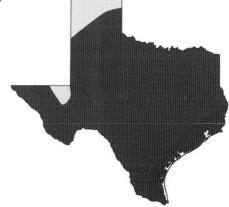

GREEN HERON
Butorides virescens

A quiet, secretive hunter, the green heron moves slowly among tall grasses at the edges of estuaries or ponds and waits for prey to reveal itself.

Field marks: Dark green back, chestnut neck and head, dark crest, long dark bill, yellow legs. Often seen hunkered down on the edge of a creek or riverbank, then standing with neck extended to full length. Young birds have white streaks on chestnut neck.

Size: H: 18", WS: 26"

Similar species: Night-herons are white, gray, and black, with no chestnut or green areas. American bittern is a lighter brown overall, though neck is similarly streaked. Least bittern is a bright yellow-brown.

Season: Most often seen in spring and fall

Habitat: Banks of creeks, ponds, and rivers; usually seen low and close to the water

Food source: Primarily fish

Nest: Hidden in a tree from ground level to 30 feet up, usually (but not always) near a water source

Call: A low, throaty *ga-wuh*; a surprisingly high *kyur* alarm call; a chattering *kuh-kuh-kuh* when something gets too close to the nest

Hot spots: Like the other long-legged waders in Texas, green heron may appear at the edge of any pond, lake, estuary, drainage canal, retention pond, or other still body of water, especially in protected wetlands. With patience, just about any visit to a wetland, pond, or wastewater treatment plant will yield a green heron sighting.

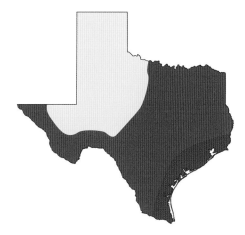

BLACK-CROWNED NIGHT-HERON
Nycticorax nycticorax

Secretive and nocturnal, this heron reveals itself by flying at dusk to its wetland feeding grounds. By day it roosts in trees, often on branches overhanging an open wetland.

Field marks: Stocky bird with black back and crown; gray wings, chest, and neck; white forehead above black bill, red eye, yellow legs. Juveniles have streaky brown chest and underparts, mottled gray and brown back, yellowish bill.

Size: H: 25", WS: 44"

Similar species: Yellow-crowned night-heron has a white crown and cheeks; a longer, thinner neck. Bitterns are browner or more brightly colored (least).

Season: Year-round

Habitat: Salt- and freshwater marshes, ponds, shallow wetlands

Food source: Fish and aquatic animals, shellfish, reptiles, amphibians, insects

Nest: On an island or deep in a swamp, usually in a tree or hidden in cattails

Call: Cackling series of *kwak kwok* syllables when flushed or in flight

Hot spots: Candelaria Wetlands, Candelaria, 30.085828 / -104.683994; McAlister Park, Lubbock, 33.5422531 / -101.9487476; Estero Llano Grande State Park World Birding Center, Llano Grande, 26.1268335 / -97.9578167; Charlie's Pasture South Boardwalk, Port Aransas, 27.81398 / -97.080079; 8 Mile Beach/Sunny Beach, Galveston, 29.2349195 / -94.8829937.

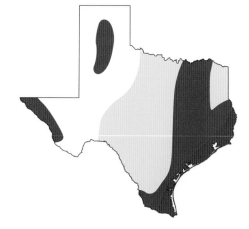

YELLOW-CROWNED NIGHT-HERON
Nyctanassa violacea

The striking facial pattern of this heron, with its bright yellow crown, makes it easy to distinguish from its black-crowned cousin. Despite its name, the yellow-crowned night-heron can be seen easily in the middle of the day.

Field marks: Gray body, wings, and neck with darker gray flight feathers. Adults have a black and white facial pattern with a white cheek and bands of black, a yellow crown, and a plume in breeding season. Juveniles have streakier chest and neck, wings covered in white dots. Yellow legs and red eye are present in both juveniles and adults. Thick, dark bill is shorter than black-crowned night-heron.

Size: H: 24", WS: 42"

Similar species: Black-crowned night-heron is stockier, has a shorter neck, and lacks the yellow crown. Bitterns are brown.

Season: Summer

Habitat: Coastal ponds, salt marshes

Food source: Crabs and other small crustaceans, insects, small fish

Nest: High in oak and pine trees near water or low in thick shrubs, often in colonies with other heron species

Call: A single barked syllable: *rowf*

Hot spots: Apffel Park/East Beach, Galveston, 29.33169 / -94.73242; Galveston Island State Park, Galveston, 29.1956654 / -94.9559069; Leonabelle Turnbull Birding Center, Port Aransas, 27.8275297 / -97.0789558; Hugh Ramsey Park, Harlingen, 26.1857402 / -97.6641657; Barton Creek Wilderness Park, Austin, 30.269106 / -97.8241937; Hermann Park (McGovern Lake), Houston, 29.7168676 / -95.3921521.

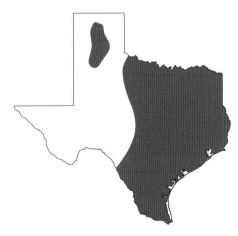

IBISES AND SPOONBILL

WHITE IBIS
Eudocimus albus

A long-legged wader with a bright red, decurved bill, this bird is easy to identify among large groups of tall waders.

Field marks: White overall with black wing tips, long bill curving downward, red legs. Juvenile has a brown-black body with a white leading edge of the wing, gray neck and head, yellow-green bill and legs.

Size: H: 22"–26", WS: 42"

Similar species: All egrets have straight yellow or black bills. Juvenile little blue heron has a yellow-green bill and legs. White-faced ibis is dark colored overall.

Season: Year-round on the Gulf coast; spring and fall migration in easternmost Texas

Habitat: Grassy marshes, open ponds and pools

Food source: Insects, crustaceans

Nest: In a tree, above water

Call: Grunting *unk-unk-unk* (male); squealing from female

Hot spots: White ibis turns up on the Gulf coast, in ponds and marshes, and along drainage canals and retention pools. Here are some very dependable spots: Bolivar Flats Shorebird Sanctuary, Galveston, 29.3711371 / -94.7287083; Brazoria National Wildlife Refuge Auto Loop Tour, Clute, 29.0599843 / -95.267568; Aransas National Wildlife Refuge Wildlife Drive, 28.2403924 / -96.818819; Padre island National Seashore Bird Island Basin, 27.4721051 / -97.312088; Delores Fenwick Nature Center, Houston, 29.5426223 / -95.3106022.

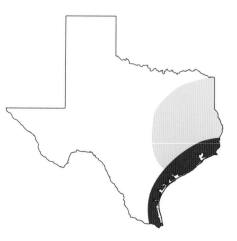

WHITE-FACED IBIS
Plegadis chihi

A permanent resident along the Gulf coast and a conspicuous migrant throughout the state, this bird is easy to distinguish from its all-white relatives.

Field marks: In breeding plumage, rusty iridescent head, neck, and breast; bright white line around pink-to-red facial skin, red eye, long gray bill curved downward, iridescent green wings and tail, reddish underside, bright red legs. Nonbreeding and juvenile have dark gray head, neck, breast, and underside; white on face disappears, but red eye and facial skin remain.

Size: L: 23"–24", WS: 36"

Similar species: Glossy ibis (infrequent in Texas) has very similar plumage, but the skin on its face is dark and the white lines on its face in breeding plumage are finer than the ones on the white-faced ibis.

Season: Year-round on the Gulf coast; spring and fall migration throughout the state

Habitat: Wetlands and secluded ponds

Food source: Insects, worms, small crustaceans

Nest: In the thick of marsh cattails and other tall aquatic plants

Call: A repeated honk as it flies out of a wetland; a low, single *whunk* grunt while feeding

Hot spots: High Island Smith Oaks Sanctuary, Bolivar Peninsula, 29.573681 / -94.3898535; Brazoria National Wildlife Refuge Auto Loop Tour, Clute, 29.0599843 / -95.267568; San Bernard National Wildlife Refuge, Cedar Lake, 28.884594 / -95.562815; Leonabelle Turnbull Birding Center, Port Aransas, 27.8275297 / -97.0789558; Laguna Atascosa National Wildlife Refuge, Brownsville, 26.2338009 / -97.3643036; Richland Creek Wildlife Management Area, Cayuga, 31.9832577 / -96.0818564.

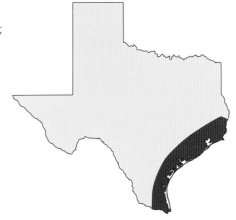

ROSEATE SPOONBILL
Platalea ajaja

The bright pink plumage, long silvery bill, and unusual feeding behavior make this tall wading bird a favorite among birding tourists and Texas residents.

Field marks: White head and neck with black vertical band between the head and neck; long light gray bill with a spoon-shaped tip; bright pink wings, back, and underside; darker pink legs with gray knees and feet. Juvenile birds are whiter with a pale pink wash.

Size: L: 32"–34", WS: 50"

Similar species: No other tall waders in Texas are pink or have the long bill with the spoon-shaped end.

Season: Year-round on the Gulf coast

Habitat: Coastal wetlands, shallow ponds

Food source: Small fish, aquatic invertebrates; the bird searches for prey in the mud with its feet and sweeps them up with its spoonbill.

Nest: In colonies on islands in shallow waters, in trees about 15 feet above the water

Call: A low, throaty grunt, often punctuated by clacking its bill

Hot spots: Bolivar Flats Shorebird Sanctuary, Galveston, 29.3711371 / -94.7287083; Aransas National Wildlife Refuge Wildlife Drive, 28.2403924 / -96.818819; Galveston Island State Park, Galveston, 29.1956654 / -94.9559069; Leonabelle Turnbull Birding Center, Port Aransas, 27.8275297 / -97.0789558; Cove Harbor Bird Sanctuary, Rockport, 27.9969687 / -97.0727921.

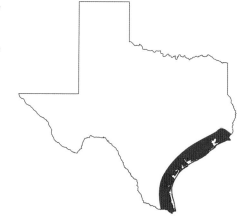

CRANES

SANDHILL CRANE
Antigone canadensis

Sandhill cranes use the Texas panhandle as a critical migratory stopover, gathering there by the thousands in spring and fall. In winter they can be found in open fields with streams across the state.

Field marks: Tall gray bird with a whitish face and red crown, gray bill, some red on the wings; long, black legs.

Size: H: 38"–41", WS: 73"–80"

Similar species: Whooping crane is white with black primary wing feathers. Great blue heron is bluer, has a distinctive head pattern, and is larger. White-faced ibis is darker colored overall, with iridescence, and has a long, curving bill.

Season: Winter throughout the state; spring and fall migration in northeast Texas and the panhandle

Habitat: Ponds in flat areas, marshes, farm fields

Food source: Seeds, grains, plants, small mammals, reptiles, amphibians, insects

Nest: On the ground, usually near water

Call: Repetitive, rattling *ooh-ah, ooh-ah, ooh-ah*

Hot spots: Oso Bay Wetlands Preserve, Corpus Christi, 27.7143059 / -97.332773; Brazos Bend State Park, Thompsons, 29.3735739 / -95.6230259; Palo Duro Canyon State Park, Lake Tanglewood, 34.9651086 / -101.671257; Lake Ransom Canyon, Lubbock, 33.5304843 / -101.6825438; CR 202 at Nueces River, Uvalde, 29.1818405 / -99.8945618.

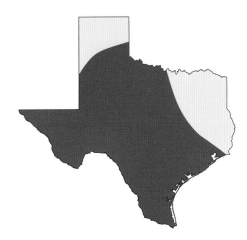

WHOOPING CRANE
Grus americana

These endangered white cranes—the tallest birds in North America—migrate every year to Aransas National Wildlife Refuge to spend the winter.

Field marks: Very tall, all-white bird with a red crown and malar stripe, yellow and gray bill, black primary wing feathers, and dark legs. Juveniles have faded brown feathers on head, neck, and body.

Size: L: 52"–54", WS: 87"

Similar species: Sandhill crane is gray overall. Great egret is not as tall, has an all-white head and body and a bright yellow bill. Snowy egret is smaller and has a black bill and yellow feet.

Season: Winter

Habitat: Marshes, tidal flats, and open farmland

Food source: Small aquatic invertebrates, frogs, mice, voles, snakes, grains

Nest: In potholes in marshes among aquatic plants, in northern Canada

Call: An elongated, high-pitched *whoop*

Hot spots: The only absolutely dependable place in Texas to see whooping cranes in winter is on the Gulf coast at Aransas National Wildlife Refuge, 28.2403924 / -96.818819. The Wildlife Tower on the refuge usually offers the best viewing. Small flocks or individuals may drop into farm fields or other open areas in late fall or early winter on the way to the refuge, but these are usually isolated incidents.

RAILS

KING RAIL
Rallus elegans

Larger and brighter colored than clapper rail, king rail makes both brackish and freshwater marshes its home.

Field marks: Rufous head and neck with gray area behind eye, black cap, yellow bill, neatly patterned back, rufous breast and underside to rear flanks, black rear with pronounced white bars. Female is drabber overall.

Size: L: 15", WS: 51"

Similar species: Clapper rail is grayer and lacks the bright rufous coloring.

Season: Year-round

Habitat: Brackish and freshwater marshes

Food source: Water insects, small crustaceans, frogs, plant seeds, small shellfish

Nest: Hidden among marsh grasses and reeds

Call: Descending series of *chk-chk-chk-chks*

Hot spots: Tyrrell Park, Beaumont, 30.0140991 / -94.1460037; Guadalupe Delta Wildlife Management Area, Long Mott, 28.5027523 / -96.8324876; Suter Wildlife Refuge, Corpus Christi, 27.7085274 / -97.3379721; Laguna Atascosa National Wildlife Refuge, Brownsville, 26.2338009 / -97.3643036; Tiocano Lake, Harlingen, 26.2116649 / -97.8146911.

CLAPPER RAIL
Rallus crepitans

Poking its way along the edges of reedy coastal saltwater marshes, the clapper rail is the easiest to see of the rail species.

Field marks: Gray overall with a lighter gray/buff breast, gray face with a black stripe through the red eye, and a black cap. In flight, the rail displays a reddish-brown upper wing and pinkish legs.

Size: L: 14"–15", WS: 19"–20"

Similar species: King rail is more boldly patterned, especially in its black and white–barred underside and bright orange breast and throat. Virginia rail is much smaller.

Season: Year-round

Habitat: Saltwater marshes along the Gulf coast

Food source: Small crustaceans and fish, frogs, invertebrates, insects

Nest: Hidden in the salt marsh reeds and grasses

Call: A rhythmic clicking, like striking two rocks together; female call is more vocal: *kuk-kuk-kuk-kuk* with a descending trill at the end.

Hot spots: Goose Island State Park, Rockport, 28.13255 / -96.985052; San Bernard National Wildlife Refuge, Cedar Lake, 28.884594 / -95.562815; Apffel Park/East Beach, Galveston, 29.33169 / -94.73242; Rollover Pass, Bolivar Peninsula, Galveston, 29.5100602 / -94.5008326; South Padre Island Birding and Nature Center, 26.1374628 / -97.1739367.

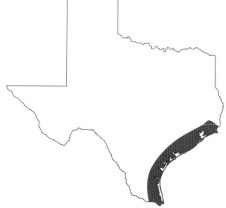

PLOVERS

BLACK-BELLIED PLOVER
Pluvialis squatarola

This large plover is easy to spot, with its black face, neck, breast, and underside in breeding plumage; black underwings in any season.

Field marks: Breeding adult has white head with grayish cap; black face, breast, and underside; short black bill, white undertail coverts, mottled gray and white mantle, black legs; black "armpits" visible in flight. Nonbreeding bird has gray head and breast, light gray to white underside, mottled gray mantle.

Size: L: 11.5"–13", WS: 25"–29"

Similar species: American golden plover has black undertail coverts, warm tan tone on back and wings.

Season: Spring and fall migration; also winter, with larger flocks in winter

Habitat: Beaches, wetland mudflats, open fields and pastures with standing water and muddy areas

Food source: Small invertebrates

Nest: On open tundra; the Arctic region

Call: High-pitched whistled *peeu, peeu-ee*

Hot spots: Any sandy beach on the Gulf coast is likely to have several black-bellied plovers among the mixed shorebirds over the winter, but these spots are particularly dependable: Bolivar Flats Shorebird Sanctuary, Galveston, 29.3711371 / -94.7287083; Apffel Park/East Beach, Galveston, 29.33169 / -94.73242; Leonabelle Turnbull Birding Center, Port Aransas, 27.8275297 / -97.0789558; Aransas National Wildlife Refuge Wildlife Drive, 28.2403924 / -96.818819; Matagorda Bay Nature Park, Matagorda, 28.5976351 / -95.9782791.

SNOWY PLOVER
Charadrius nivosus

This pale little plover favors the Gulf coast beaches in winter, but it breeds in the west Texas plains.

Field marks: Breeding bird has buffy brown head and back with black forehead, black eye with black ear patch, black line on side of short neck, black bill. White face, throat, breast, and underside; brown legs. Nonbreeding adult is grayer above with no forehead stripe or ear patch, dark line at neck; white throat, breast, and underside.

Size: L: 6"–6.5", WS: 17"–18"

Similar species: Wilson's plover is darker overall with a black breast band in breeding plumage and a longer, heavier bill. Semipalmated plover is darker with white forehead, orange bill with black tip, and orange legs. Piping plover is lighter overall with a narrow, unbroken dark breastband, an orange bill with black tip, and orange legs.

Season: Winter on the Gulf coast, summer in west Texas

Habitat: Gulf coast beaches, coastal plains, and barrier islands

Food source: Various invertebrates

Nest: A scrape in open ground lined with pebbles and grasses, usually in a protected area away from foot traffic

Call: A trilled *prrrrt*; sometimes a high-pitched *tur WEET*

Hot spots: Bolivar Flats Shorebird Sanctuary, Galveston, 29.3711371 / -94.7287083; San Luis Pass, Galveston, 29.0892519 / -95.1187706; Matagorda Island State Park, Port O'Connor, 28.3352839 / -96.4529228; Blue Barns Road and Johnson Draw, Midland, 31.8943881 / -101.8181723; San Angelo State Park, San Angelo, 31.4677918 / -100.5033213.

KILLDEER
Charadrius vociferus

Nesting on golf courses, in parking lots, and in other human-populated areas, the killdeer feigns a broken wing to lure potential predators away from its nest.

Field marks: Brown or rufous cap, white face with bold markings, two wide black rings across the throat and breast, rufous-brown back and wings, white underside, bright rufous rump; wide, white stripe the length of the wings visible in flight.

Size: L: 9"–10.5", WS: 20"–24"

Similar species: Semipalmated plover is smaller, has a yellow bill, and has only one ring around its neck.

Season: Year-round

Habitat: Large mowed lawns, golf courses, open prairie, farm fields

Food source: Insects and small invertebrates, especially worms and grasshoppers

Nest: In an area with gravel—a field, parking lot, golf course, or roof

Call: A piercing, repeated *kill-DEER, kill-DEER*

Hot spots: Flocks of killdeer are likely to mix with migrating and resident shorebirds on beaches, as well as ground feeders on landscaped properties and in mowed parks all over Texas. These birds are so plentiful and easy to spot that you should have no trouble ticking them off your list.

OYSTERCATCHER

AMERICAN OYSTERCATCHER
Haematopus palliatus

With its clownish features and propensity for chatter, the East Coast's oystercatcher makes itself unmistakable on local beaches.

Field marks: Black head and neck, orange eye and long orange bill, white chest and underside, brown back and wings, white stripe on wings visible in flight, white rump, pale yellow legs.

Size: L: 17"–21", WS: 32"

Similar species: Black skimmer has a more tapered body, a black back and wings, and a two-toned orange and black bill with a longer lower mandible.

Season: Year-round

Habitat: Gulf coast beaches

Food source: A variety of shellfish, including oysters

Nest: In a scrape in the sand on ocean beaches

Call: A variety of hurried *peeps*, sung in quick succession; also short, single *peeps*, longer *pee-uy* calls in flight

Hot spots: Bolivar Flats Shorebird Sanctuary, Galveston, 29.3711371 / -94.7287083; Port Aransas Jetty, Port Aransas, 27.8348271 / -97.046015; Oyster Lake, Collegeport, 28.6135254 / -96.2118928; Indian Point, Corpus Christi, 27.8525492 / -97.3559312; South Padre Island Birding and Nature Center, 26.1374628 / -97.1739367.

STILT AND AVOCET

BLACK-NECKED STILT
Himantopus mexicanus

The stylishly marked stilt breeds in marshes along the Gulf coast, as well as in the El Paso area.

Field marks: Male is black above from forehead to tail, black and white face; long, slim black bill; white below from face to undertail coverts, black wings, long red legs. Female has a brown-black back.

Size: L: 14"–15", WS: 25"–29"

Similar species: American avocet male has a light brown head and an upcurving bill; nonbreeding female has a grayish-white head.

Season: Year-round along the Gulf coast, summer along the western Rio Grande Valley; a migrant throughout the rest of the state

Habitat: Salt- and freshwater marshes

Food source: Small aquatic animals, tadpoles, insects, some seeds

Nest: In marshy areas

Call: Repeated *kik-kik-kik*, harsher when alarmed

Hot spots: Bolivar Flats Shorebird Sanctuary, Galveston, 29.3711371 / -94.7287083; Moody Gardens, Galveston, 29.2744864 / -94.8543092; Brazoria National Wildlife Refuge Auto Loop Tour, Clute, 29.0599843 / -95.267568; Port Aransas Wetland Park, Port Aransas, 27.825 / -97.071; Ewald Kipp Way, El Paso, 31.785065 / -106.527189.

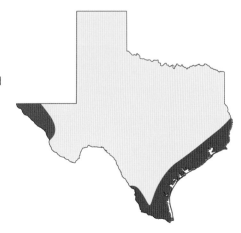

AMERICAN AVOCET
Recurvirostra americana

This striking marsh-loving bird uses Texas waters for overwintering, migration, and breeding.

Field marks: Light brown head, neck, and breast; long, upcurved bill; white body and tail, wide black stripes on back visible in flight, black wings with wide white stripe, gray legs. Nonbreeding female has a grayish-white head.

Size: L: 18"–20", WS: 31"–37"

Similar species: Black-necked stilt has black and white head, red legs.

Season: Winter on the Gulf coast, summer in the panhandle and around El Paso; avocets migrate across much of Texas as well.

Habitat: Salt- and freshwater marshes; also the edges of ponds and lakes

Food source: Aquatic insects, crustaceans, plants

Nest: On a beach or mudflat near a water source

Call: Continuous, high-pitched *mee-tee-meet-meet-meet*

Hot spots: Maxey Park, Lubbock, 33.5702868 / -101.9019926; Playa at 103rd Street and Slide Road, Lubbock, 33.5009345 / -101.9249268; Fred Hervey Wastewater Treatment Plant, El Paso, 31.9493008 / -106.3423004; Bryan Beach, Freeport, 28.9020747 / -95.3488313; Charlie's Pasture South Boardwalk, Port Aransas, 27.81398 / -97.080079.

SANDPIPERS AND SNIPE

LONG-BILLED CURLEW
Numenius americanus

The largest shorebird in North America spends the winter on the Gulf coast of Texas.

Field marks: Rusty overall with a brown and rufous mottled back, wings, and tail; bright rufous patches on wings. Long, pink and black bill curves notably downward. Dull pinkish-brown legs.

Size: L: 20"–25", WS: 28"–35"

Similar species: Whimbrel is smaller, has a shorter curving bill, and is grayer overall. Hudsonian godwit also has a rufous chest and underside, but it is smaller and its bill curves upward.

Season: Winter, though scattered individuals may show up on mudflats or near ponds throughout the state in other seasons.

Habitat: Tidal mudflats, open farmland, prairies

Food source: Insects, aquatic crustaceans and invertebrates

Nest: A scrape on the ground amid short vegetation, in plains west of Texas

Call: A trill followed by elongated, high-pitched *peeer, peeeer, peeeer*; also a high, reedy, two-syllable *wee-eet, wee-eet* to signal a mate

Hot spots: Bolivar Flats Shorebird Sanctuary, Galveston, 29.3711371 / -94.7287083; Laguna Atascosa National Wildlife Refuge, Brownsville, 26.2338009 / -97.3643036; Packery Channel Park, Corpus Christi, 27.6264996 / -97.2204369; Padre Island National Seashore Bird Island Basin, 27.4721051 / -97.312088; South Texas Ecotourism Center, Laguna Vista, 26.09276 / -97.29624.

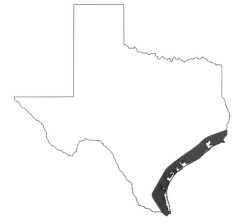

SANDERLING
Calidris alba

Easy to identify as they run back and forth on beaches just above the waves, these birds often move in large flocks.

Field marks: Breeding adult has reddish head and neck, short black bill, white underside, scaled black and brown wings, black legs; white wing stripe visible in flight. Nonbreeding bird is pale gray above, white below, with black bill and legs.

Size: L: 8", WS: 15"–17"

Similar species: Least and semipalmated sandpipers are smaller and lack the reddish breeding plumage. Least sandpiper has greenish legs in all seasons.

Season: Winter

Habitat: Gulf beaches, tidal mudflats

Food source: Invertebrates, occasional insects

Nest: On tundra in the Arctic region, in a depression in the ground

Call: Whistling chatter or high-pitched *wip-wip-wip-wip*

Hot spots: No beach is complete without its flock of sanderlings, whether they form a single family unit or number in the hundreds. If you visit any of the Gulf of Mexico beaches from late September through early April, you will see these birds running up the beach as they avoid the incoming surf, and then dashing down it in remarkable unison to partake of whatever the tide brought in. Their distinctive plumage and regimented behavior helps differentiate them from the least and semipalmated sandpipers.

LEAST SANDPIPER
Calidris minutilla

The smallest sandpiper provides a simple way to tell it apart from others in its class: its yellowish legs.

Field marks: Breeding adult has brown head, chest, back and wings, with black scales over the brown on wings; small bill that droops down at the end, white underside, yellow-green legs. Nonbreeding bird is gray instead of brown, but with a brownish head.

Size: L: 6", WS: 12"–13"

Similar species: Semipalmated sandpiper is slightly larger, has a straight bill and black legs. Western sandpiper is more rufous on head and back and has a longer bill and black legs.

Season: Late fall to early spring in south Texas; migratory with long stopovers through the rest of the state, especially around wastewater treatment plants

Habitat: Gulf and lake beaches, tidal mudflats, moist open fields, stormwater treatment areas

Food source: Small invertebrates, insects, some plant seeds

Nest: In northern Canada, in a hollow on the ground

Call: A high trill, interspersed with a *cheep* or *chirreep*

Hot spots: Least sandpipers are widespread and numerous, traveling in small flocks during spring and fall migration and remaining in larger flocks to canvas beaches and other fertile ground for food. You will encounter them on any beach or mudflat from October through early May, often in mixed flocks of sanderlings, semipalmated sandpipers, and other small shorebirds.

LONG-BILLED DOWITCHER
Limnodromus scolopaceus

It's nearly impossible to tell this bird apart from its short-billed cousin except in breeding season, when the long-billed has heavily barred flanks.

Field marks: Breeding adult has dark orange head with white eyebrow stripe, long bill; rufous neck, breast, and belly; scaly brown, black, and white pattern on wings and back; flanks barred with black streaks; yellow legs. Nonbreeding bird is gray overall with white eyebrow, white underside.

Size: L: 11"–12", WS: 18"–20"

Similar species: Short-billed dowitcher has spotted breast and flanks and an imperceptibly shorter bill. Red knot is smaller and has a short bill.

Season: Winter along the coast; spring and fall migration farther north

Habitat: Marshes, mudflats, wetlands

Food source: Worms, small crustaceans, snails, insect larvae, moss, seeds

Nest: On open tundra; northernmost Alaska

Call: A rattling call followed by a musical *peeta-peeta-wee-too*

Hot spots: Bolivar Flats Shorebird Sanctuary, Galveston, 29.3711371 / -94.7287083; San Bernard NWR Moccasin Pond Loop, Cedar Lake, 28.884594 / -95.562815; Suter Wildlife Refuge, Corpus Christi, 27.7085274 / -97.3379721; Dallas Southside Wastewater Treatment Plant, Dallas, 32.6456988 / -96.6391754; Kirby Lake, Abilene, 32.3724227 / -99.7345734.

WILSON'S SNIPE
Gallinago delicata

The snipe's distinctive patterning and rounded body make it a standout among mixed shorebird flocks.

Field marks: Black and buff–striped head, long gray bill, brown and buff–striped back, spotted brown breast, heavily barred flanks, white belly, orange tail, yellow legs.

Size: L: 10"–11", WS: 18"–20"

Similar species: American woodcock is larger and has a buff breast, flanks, and underside, with no barring.

Season: Winter

Habitat: Open, flooded fields; marshes, swamps, and other wetlands

Food source: Insect larvae, small crustaceans, tiny mollusks

Nest: In a hollow on the ground in a grassy field

Call: Repeated *kut-kut-kut* or rhythmic *tuck-a-tuck-a-tuck-a-tuck-a*

Hot spots: Brazos Bend State Park, Thompsons, 29.3735739 / -95.6230259; Southeast Greenway, Mueller, 30.2904776 / -97.6929778; John Bunker Sands Wetland Center, Combine, 32.6137185 / -96.5008752; 8 Mile Road/Sportsman's Road, Galveston, 29.2539795 / -94.8935137; Aransas National Wildlife Refuge Wildlife Drive and other areas, 28.2403924 / -96.818819.

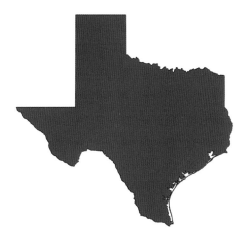

SPOTTED SANDPIPER
Actitis macularius

The spotted sandpiper's continuous dipping and nodding earns it the nickname "teeter-tail."

Field marks: Brown face with darker brown cap, white line above eye, black line through eye, orange bill; white breast heavily spotted in brown, white underside with lighter spotting, brown back and wings' short white wing stripe visible in flight. Nonbreeding plumage lacks the spots, and the bill is dull beige.

Size: L: 7.5", WS: 13"–15"

Similar species: Solitary sandpiper is larger and darker, has white spots on its back and wings, and has a gray bill.

Season: Winter in southern Texas; migrating through the state's northern half

Habitat: Waterways, including ponds and moving streams

Food source: Insects, spiders, invertebrates, small crustaceans and mollusks

Nest: In a dip or hollow in the ground

Call: High-pitched *weet, weet, weet*

Hot spots: Shorebirds of all kinds concentrate around Texas's limited number of lakes and ponds, but you're only likely to see one or a pair in any of these spots. Check your local pond or wetland before traveling out of your way. Brazoria National Wildlife Refuge Auto Loop Tour, Clute, 29.0599843 / -95.267568; Kaufer-Hubert Memorial Park, Loyola Beach, 27.3196959 / -97.6841211; Roy G. Guerrero Colorado River Metro Park, Austin, 30.246172 / -97.7049763; Twin Buttes Reservoir, San Angelo, 31.3774555 / -100.5366611; Fort Peña Colorado Park, Marathon, 30.152997 / -103.2874735.

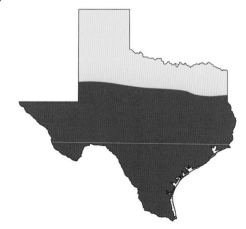

GREATER YELLOWLEGS
Tringa melanoleuca

Near-constant foraging behavior can make it tough to tell the two yellowlegs species apart. Look for dark barring on the flanks and underside to pick out the greater yellowlegs.

Field marks: Black, gray, and white mottling overall; black streaks on head and neck, slightly upturned bill, white underside with black barring, yellow legs, white rump. In nonbreeding plumage, back and wings are browner.

Size: L: 14", WS: 23"–28"

Similar species: Lesser yellowlegs is shorter, has a straight bill, and has whiter flanks with no barring.

Season: Winter in most of the state; migrating along the edges and up the middle

Habitat: Beaches, mudflats in salt- and freshwater marshes, open fields, pools, lakeshores

Food source: Small invertebrates, fish, frogs, seeds

Nest: In the open on a mudflat; northern Canada

Call: Lyrical, continuous *pew-yoo, pew-yoo, pew-yoo*; also a three-note *tew-tew-tew* in flight

Hot spots: Yellowlegs of both varieties are among the most common shorebirds in Texas. Your favorite shorebird location is sure to have at least a few individuals, if not large flocks, so it's safe to plan your birding excursion around less-common birds, knowing that you will find yellowlegs as well.

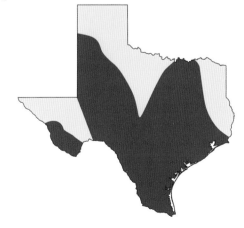

LESSER YELLOWLEGS
Tringa flavipes

The lesser yellowlegs' straight bill, clear underside, and shorter stature sets it apart from its greater counterpart.

Field marks: Gray and white–streaked head and neck; mottled black and white breast, back, and wings; white underside, white rump, yellow legs. Mottling and streaking is muted in nonbreeding plumage.

Size: L: 10"–11", WS: 20"–24"

Similar species: Greater yellowlegs is up to 4 inches taller, has an upturned bill, and is barred with black on its underside in breeding season.

Season: Winter in the southeast; migrating through the rest of the state

Habitat: Beaches, fresh- and saltwater marshes, mudflats, open fields

Food source: Insects, invertebrates, seeds, tiny fish

Nest: On a pile of vegetation near water; northern Canada and west to Alaska

Call: *Tu-du* song singly and in pairs; also high-pitched, continuous notes as an alarm

Hot spots: Yellowlegs of both varieties are among the most common shorebirds in Texas. Your favorite shorebird location is sure to have at least a few individuals, if not large flocks, so it's safe to plan your birding excursion around less-common birds, knowing that you will find yellowlegs as well.

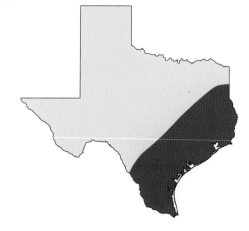

WILLET
Tringa semipalmata

The willet's white wing stripe makes it easy to spot as it arrives and lands on a beach or mudflat.

Field marks: Gray head, nape, wings, and back; long, straight gray bill with black tip; buffy breast with darker brown mottling, white underside with brownish barring, gray legs, wide white stripe on wings visible in flight. Nonbreeding adult is grayer overall with no barring.

Size: L: 15"–16", WS: 25"–30"

Similar species: Greater yellowlegs is darker, smaller, and has yellow legs.

Season: Year-round on the ocean and Gulf coasts; spring and fall migration inland

Habitat: Coastline beaches and lagoons, tidal mudflats, sandy shorelines on larger lakes

Food source: Small crustaceans, insects, invertebrates, tiny fish

Nest: On a clump of grass or on open ground

Call: A continuous *willa-will-willa, willa-will-willa*

Hot spots: Just about every beach on the Gulf coast has a winterlong population of willets. Plan to see this bird while you are searching for scarcer shorebirds on Gulf beaches, inlets, and bays.

QUAIL AND TURKEY

NORTHERN BOBWHITE
Colinus virginianus

More likely heard than seen, the bobwhite is considered exotic in northeast and far western Texas, but is a permanent resident throughout most of the state.

Field marks: Male is small and rotund, with a distinctive white face patterned in rufous and black, reddish breast and shoulders, white underside with bold rufous lines and streaks, brown and buff wing pattern, short tail. Female has a buff face and a more muted facial pattern.

Size: L: 9"–10", WS: 13"

Similar species: Common ground dove also has some ruddy coloring, but lacks the bright facial pattern.

Season: Year-round

Habitat: Forests, farms, marshes; under feeders near these habitats

Food source: Seeds of many kinds

Nest: On the ground among tall grasses and other vegetation

Call: The onomatopoeic *bob-WHITE, bob-WHITE*

Hot spots: Choke Canyon State Park—Calliham Unit, 28.4717282 / -98.3394384; Canyon Lake 6, Lubbock, 33.5676571 / -101.8033202; San Angelo State Park—South Unit, San Angelo, 31.4669145 / -100.5013617; Salineño Wildlife Preserve, Roma, 26.5148584 / -99.116206; Bentsen–Rio Grande Valley State Park/World Birding Center, Mission, 26.1849709 / -98.3793885.

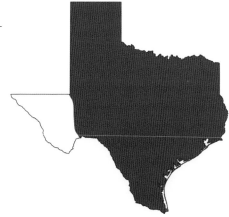

PLAIN CHACHALACA
Ortalis vetula

This large, long-tailed, social ground bird announces its approach, and then appears under feeders with a cadre of friends.

Field marks: Warm brown body with a lighter tan-to-buff belly; long, gray and tan tail tipped in white; a grayer head; small, chicken-like bill.

Size: L: 19"–23", WS: 26"

Similar species: Wild turkey is taller, larger, and bulkier, with a thinner neck, smaller head, and darker brown body; males have large, showy tails they can fan out during mating display.

Season: Year-round

Habitat: Brushy areas, including south Texas forests with a healthy understory

Food source: Fruit, insects, and plant matter

Nest: In the fork of a tree or large shrub

Call: Very loud *chuck, chuck, chuck*, followed by a noisy, rising cackle: *kak-kak-kak-kak-kak*, continuing for some time

Hot spots: Laguna Atascosa National Wildlife Refuge, Brownsville, 26.2338009 / -97.3643036; Sabal Palm Sanctuary, Brownsville, 25.85233 / -97.4176839; Resaca de la Palma State Park/World Birding Center, Brownsville, 25.9965839 / -97.5690513; Estero Llano Grande State Park World Birding Center, Llano Grande, 26.1268335 / -97.9578167; Hugh Ramsey Park, Harlingen, 26.1857402 / -97.6641657.

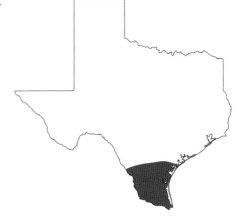

DOMINIC SHERONY

SCALED QUAIL
Callipepla squamata

Watch for males perching on top of a bush in spring, showing off their elegant, scaly feathers to attract a mate.

Field marks: Brown head with bright white, peaked crest, rows of scaly-looking grayish feathers on neck and down the breast to the belly, soft brown back and wings, short gray tail.

Size: L: 10"–12", WS: 15"

Similar species: Gambel's quail female is grayer overall and has a single black plume rising from the forehead, as well as striking dark brown wings. Male Gambel's quail has a bold black face with white markings and a chestnut crest.

Season: Year-round

Habitat: Desert shrubland and grasslands

Food source: Insects, leaves, and seeds found on the ground

Nest: On the ground in dense clusters of cactus or other tall desert plants

Call: A rhythmic, barking, repeated *ah-choo*; also a squealed single note

Hot spots: Big Bend National Park, Dugout Wells, 29.2712002 / -103.1352997; Christmas Mountains Oasis, Alpine, 29.4917768 / -103.4670389; Seminole Canyon State Park, Comstock, 29.6935703 / -101.3185787; Sibley Nature Center, Midland, 32.0349286 / -102.0706594; Balmorhea Lake, Balmorhea, 30.9583956 / -103.7123108.

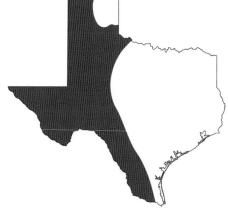

WILD TURKEY
Meleagris gallopavo

The nation's largest ground bird usually appears in flocks in grassy meadows.

Field marks: Large, heavy, iridescent body and thin, fleshy neck; rufous tail, orange legs. Male acquires long red wattles and a bright blue face and neck during breeding season, when he is often seen with his tail spread out in a fan shape.

Size: L: 44"–46", WS: 60"–64"; female much smaller: L: 37", WS: 50"

Similar species: Turkey vulture is smaller, has an all-red head and a much shorter tail. Black vulture is also smaller and has a short, squared-off tail.

Season: Year-round

Habitat: Oak and pine forests adjacent to open grassland

Food source: Plants, nuts, seeds, fruit, small invertebrates

Nest: On the ground at the base of a tree, or hidden in masses of tall grasses and weeds

Call: A comical *gobble-gobble-gobble*, like a chuckle. Females have a *cluck-cluck* alarm call.

Hot spots: Farm fields, suburban backyards, roadsides from the rural hills to the interstate, and even city neighborhoods now have their own wild turkeys, so no hot spot is required to see them. The spectacular success of the turkey's reintroduction in the late 1960s and early 1970s is in evidence all around us—and some would say that it has long since gotten out of hand. If you'd like to see some, take a drive down a country road and scan the fields for a healthy flock.

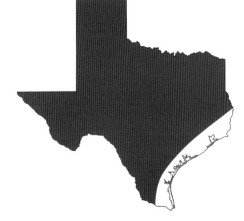

VULTURES

TURKEY VULTURE
Cathartes aura

Soaring in kettles over virtually any landscape, this very large bird is easily recognized by its flight pattern.

Field marks: Large, black body; red featherless head, gray flight feathers for the entire length of each wing, rectangular tail. This vulture glides with wings held in a distinctive dihedral V.

Size: L: 26"–30", WS: 67"–72"

Similar species: Black vulture has gray head, black wings with gray-white "fingers" at the outer ends. Immature bald eagle has black-feathered head and all-black or mottled wings, which it holds flat.

Season: Year-round in east and south Texas, summer in central and west Texas

Habitat: Soaring over open areas, including farmland, forests, ocean dunes, and plains

Food source: Carrion

Nest: In a crevice or dead tree

Call: Usually silent

Hot spots: Turkey vultures soar over open lands, suburban areas, and even at the edges of cities in every part of Texas, often in kettles of thirty or more birds. In the right seasons, you should have no trouble seeing them gliding over interstate highways as they search for the roadkill that drivers graciously provide for their daily repast.

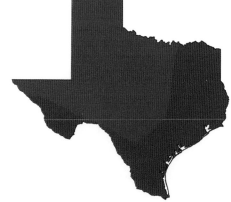

BLACK VULTURE
Coragyps atratus

This large, dark raptor is usually spotted in the company of turkey vultures.

Field marks: Large, uniformly black body; gray featherless head, whitish feather "fingers" at the outer tips of wings, squared-off tail.

Size: L: 24"–27", WS: 55"–60"

Similar species: Turkey vulture is larger and has a red, featherless head and gray flight feathers.

Season: Year-round

Habitat: Usually found soaring over wide-open landscapes, including farmland, plains, marshland, and forests

Food source: Carrion, though this vulture sometimes kills its own prey.

Nest: In a hollow tree, cave, or stump, in woodlands or even inside buildings

Call: Generally silent

Hot spots: Black vultures are as prevalent as turkey vultures in east Texas. Check your local landfill, and watch the skies over the interstate highways for both black and turkey vultures waiting for some yummy roadkill.

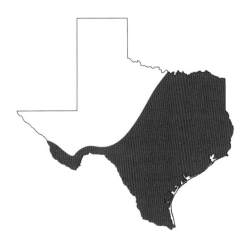

HARRIER AND ACCIPITER

NORTHERN HARRIER
Circus hudsonius

A slim, sleek hawk with long wings, the harrier is usually spotted as it glides over open fields.

Field marks: Male is gray above and white below, with a spotted breast, black wing tips, a black trailing edge on its wings, and a gray and white–striped tail. Its most distinctive field mark is a white patch at the rump, easily visible in flight. Female and juvenile are brown above and buff below with brown streaks, also with the obvious white rump.

Size: L: 18"–22", WS: 41"–46"

Similar species: Cooper's hawk is smaller, with a rusty breast and longer tail. Snail kite also has a white rump, but the male is smaller, sleeker, and more uniformly gray; both male and female kites have a bright yellow bill and red legs.

Season: Winter

Habitat: Open fields, plains, meadows, desert, and marshes

Food source: Rodents, small birds, frogs, reptiles, insects

Nest: On the ground, often in colonies, throughout Canada and the subarctic region

Call: A sharp *vee-yah, vee-yah* in flight

Hot spots: Every wildlife refuge and open area has at least one harrier hunting for rodents over its fields throughout the winter. Stormwater treatment facilities are among the best places to find this bird as it soars along the edges of pools or perches on a fence post. Look up as you scan the landscape for birds on the ground, and watch for a soaring bird with a white rump.

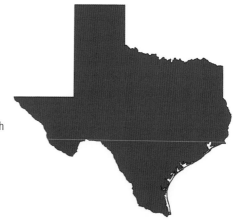

COOPER'S HAWK
Accipiter cooperii

If there's a hawk hunting the birds that come to your feeders, chances are good it's a Cooper's hawk.

Field marks: Larger than a sharp-shinned hawk but very similar in appearance: gray above, white underside with heavy rufous barring, long white tail with black bars. The female is larger than the male and a paler gray. White nape between head and breast helps with identification in flight or perched in a tree or on a fence post.

Size: L: 15"–20", WS: 28"–34"

Similar species: Sharp-shinned-hawk is smaller and lacks the white nape.

Season: Winter on the Gulf coast and along the southern border; year-round in the rest of Texas

Habitat: Woodlands and forests

Food source: Birds, small mammals

Nest: High in a tree, usually above 20 feet

Call: Squeaky, continuous *kek-kek-kek-kek*; single *keh-hek* calls between male and female

Hot spots: Mitchell Lake Audubon Center, San Antonio, 29.3105956 / -98.4996938; San Antonio Botanical Garden, San Antonio, 29.4601113 / -98.4572897; Prairie Creek Park, Richardson, 32.9872119 / -96.7180109; Jenna Welch Nature Center I-20 Pond, Midland, 31.9630947 / -102.1210903; Rincon del Diablo (near Magnolia and Barron Streets), Del Rio, 29.350534 / -100.8931965.

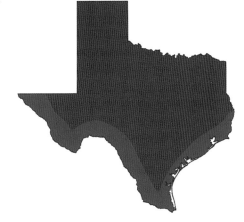

BUTEOS AND EAGLE

DOMINIC SHERONY

RED-SHOULDERED HAWK
Buteo lineatus

Look on the edges of wooded areas near water for this year-round east Texas resident.

Field marks: Reddish-brown head, red patches at shoulders, white chest heavily barred with orange, chunky body, square black tail with narrow white bands. In flight, pale underneath with rusty orange chest and shoulders, wings lightly barred in black with light area at the wing tips. Juvenile may be streaked in brown instead of orange.

Size: L: 17"–24", WS: 35"–45"

Similar species: Red-tailed hawk is larger and has a red tail. Broad-winged hawk is smaller and nearly all white underneath.

Season: Year-round in east Texas; a winter resident along the Lower Rio Grande Valley

Habitat: Forests and wooded areas near lakes, ponds, and ocean

Food source: Reptiles, amphibians, small mammals and birds, some insects

Nest: In a tree

Call: Repeated *kee-yah, kee-yah, kee-yah*; more rapidly when agitated

Hot spots: This ubiquitous hawk is one of the easiest raptors in east Texas to spot, and it's likely to linger in place while you get a good look. You can find them in any wooded area near water, and they are often seen in trees along highways and perched above less-traveled roads through forested land. Many national wildlife refuges and national parks have their own populations of red-shouldered hawks, so you should have no trouble locating at least one.

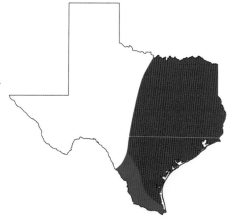

DOMINIC SHERONY

WHITE-TAILED HAWK
Geranoaetus albicaudatus

This grassland hawk's dark plumage, chestnut shoulders, and bright white tail make it easy to identify as it glides over flat, open land.

Field marks: Dark gray head and wings, white chest and belly, rufous shoulders, white rump and tail with a single black band at the end.

Size: L: 18"–20", WS: 50"–52"

Similar species: Swainson's hawk has a dark throat, barred belly, and several stripes across the tail. Short-tailed hawk is smaller with several tail stripes. Ferruginous hawk (rarely in the same territory) is larger and whiter under the wings, and has an all-white tail with no stripes.

Season: Year-round

Habitat: Prairie, grasslands, pastures

Food source: Mostly rodents, as well as some birds and insects

Nest: In a tree or shrub, about 6 to 10 feet up

Call: One long, open note, followed by several two-syllable calls: *ket-a, ket-a, ket-a, ket-a, ket-a*

Hot spots: Hazel Bazemore Park Hawkwatch Platform, Corpus Christi, 27.8660551 / -97.6427346; Palo Alto Battlefield National Historical Park, Brownsville, 26.0191488 / -97.4760676; Bentsen–Rio Grande Valley State Park/World Birding Center, Mission, 26.1849709 / -98.3793885; Santa Ana National Wildlife Refuge, San Juan, 26.0787993 / -98.1330503; Resaca de la Palma State Park/World Birding Center, Brownsville, 25.9965839 / -97.5690513.

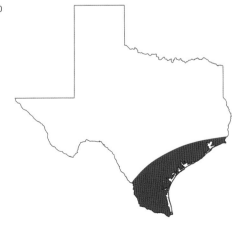

COMMON BLACK HAWK
Buteogallus anthracinus

Remarkably uncommon regardless of its name, this hawk brings in birders from all over the country to see it at its nesting site in Big Bend National Park.

Field marks: Large, all-dark hawk with a yellow bill and a broad wide stripe across its black tail.

Size: L: 17"–22", WS: 46"–47"

Similar species: Zone-tailed hawk is a little smaller and has longer wings, and the white band on its tail is narrower.

Season: Summer

Habitat: Desert riparian areas along a river or stream

Food source: Fish, reptiles, rodents, large insects

Nest: In a large tree, close to the trunk, often overhanging a river

Call: A high, rising and falling *klee-klee-klee-klee-KLEE-KLEE-KLEE-klee-klee*

Hot spots: This bird nests in a cordoned-off area of Big Bend National Park, Rio Grande Village, 29.1809226 / -102.9557133, where it can be seen fairly easily in the last three weeks of May. In spring, individuals are often seen in and around the primitive area of Davis Mountains State Park, Fort Davis, 30.60079 / -103.92579, or over the TX 118 rest area, 7 miles southeast of Fort Davis, 30.5276479 / -103.8233033.

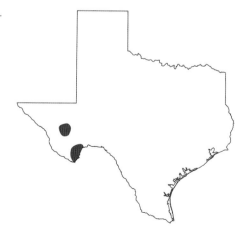

HARRIS'S HAWK
Parabuteo unicinctus

With its chocolate-brown body and primary wing feathers and rufous patches from shoulder to coverts, this hawk of Texas scrublands is grand and distinctive.

Field marks: Brown head, body, and wing primaries; chestnut marginal and secondary wing coverts and thigh feathers, white rump and undertail coverts with white tail edge, bright yellow legs and bill.

Size: L: 18"–23", WS: 40"–45"

Similar species: Common black hawk is all charcoal with a shorter tail. White-tailed hawk is predominantly white in flight and has longer wings that taper to a point.

Season: Year-round

Habitat: Low desert with cactus and short shrubs, usually at the base of mountains, rock formations, or even power poles that can provide perches and wide views.

Food source: Larger rodents like rabbits, ground squirrels, and marmots, as well as ground birds like quail

Nest: In cacti or trees (native and introduced species), on power poles, on cliff ledges, or on man-made structures

Call: A loud, high, piercing *eerp*, sometimes repeated several times

Hot spots: In addition to these known spots for Harris's hawk sightings, watch the skies and the tops of utility poles along any highway in southeastern Texas. Hazel Bazemore Park Hawkwatch Platform, Corpus Christi, 27.8660551 / -97.6427346; TX 4/ Boca Chica Boulevard, Brownsville, 25.9543404 / -97.3196411; Estero Llano Grande State Park World Birding Center, Llano Grande, 26.1268335 / -97.9578167; Concan Frio Bat Cave area, Concan, 29.4350096 / -99.6843734; Mitchell Lake Audubon Center, San Antonio, 29.3105956 / -98.4996938.

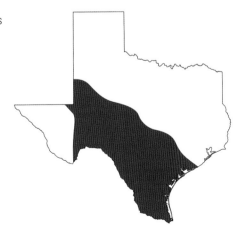

SWAINSON'S HAWK
Buteo swainsoni

The hawk with the dark bib soars all summer over prairies in west Texas, its wings held in a dihedral position as it hunts for meaty rodents and large bugs.

Field marks: The light morph has long wings with dark flight (outer) feathers, dark head with white throat, dark breast forming a distinctive bib, light body, and fanned tail with white and dark bands. The darker morph can be uniformly dark from chest to belly, but with some chestnut to the underwing.

Size: L: 19"–22", WS: 49"–51"

Similar species: Red-tailed hawk lacks the dark bib, has a dark, jagged belly band and a rufous tail. White-tailed hawk has no bib, and its tail is solid white with a single wide black band.

Season: Summer

Habitat: Open prairie and farmland

Food source: Small mammals, large insects

Nest: At the top of a tree, usually near a water source

Call: A hoarse, short, repeated *kree*

Hot spots: Jenna Welch Nature Center I-20 Pond, Midland, 31.9630947 / -102.1210903; Canyon Lake 6, Lubbock, 33.5676571 / -101.8033202; Fort Peña Colorado Park, Marathon, 30.152997 / -103.2874735; Big Bend National Park, Cottonwood Campground, 29.1366997 / -103.5220032; Max A. Mandel Golf Course, Laredo, 27.660146 / -99.66685.

ZONE-TAILED HAWK
Buteo albonotatus

The white stripe across the tail helps differentiate this hawk from the very similar turkey vulture in flight.

Field marks: Very dark brown overall with a white bill; in flight, the underwing appears white but is heavily barred. Tail is barred in white, with a wide white stripe visible near the end of the tail in flight.

Size: L: 19"–22", WS: 47"–54"

Similar species: Turkey vulture has no barring on the tail, and has a featherless red head. Gray hawk is lighter-colored overall with smaller, more-rounded wings. Common black hawk is shorter and bulkier, with more-rounded wings.

Season: Summer

Habitat: Deserts and other wide-open spaces, as well as higher elevations with cliffs and canyons

Food source: Vertebrates, including reptiles, small mammals, and birds

Nest: In willow or cottonwood trees in riparian areas, such as along the Rio Grande

Call: Long, high-pitched, descending *kraaaaay*

Hot spots: Devils River State Natural Area, Del Rio, 29.9406182 / -100.9710073; Seminole Canyon State Park, Comstock, 29.6935703 / -101.3185787; Davis Mountains State Park, primitive area, Fort Davis, 30.60079 / -103.92579; Johnson Ponds area, Alpine, 30.3660623 / -103.6742771; Big Bend Ranch State Park, Aqua Adentro Spring, Redford, 29.4943714 / -104.1020015.

RED-TAILED HAWK
Buteo jamaicensis

The nation's most common hawk is often seen near roadways, soaring over fields, or sitting at the tops of trees.

Field marks: Brown head and body with bright reddish-orange tail, usually visible in flight or at rest; white underside with brown streaks around the middle, forming a distinctive bellyband. Juvenile may be paler underneath and lack the red tail.

Size: L: 19"–25", WS: 46"–55"

Similar species: Broad-winged hawk is much smaller and has a black and white tail. Red-shouldered hawk has orange-banded chest, black tail with white stripes.

Season: Year-round

Habitat: Open fields, meadows, and marshes that have tall trees or other high perches

Food source: Primarily small mammals, but with a preference for red-winged blackbirds

Nest: In large trees

Call: A loud, hoarse *kee-e-e-r-r-rh*—the quintessential hawk call used in countless movies and television shows (and often attributed to the bald eagle)

Hot spots: Red-tailed hawks are the most common and widespread hawks in Texas—and across the United States. You will see them standing atop utility poles and lampposts along state and interstate highways, watching fields from perches at the tops of trees, and being mobbed by starlings or crows when the hawks venture too close to a nest. Look for the white chest and underside with a jagged gray-to-brown bellyband, as well as the bright rufous tail.

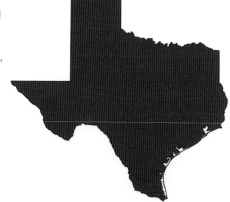

BALD EAGLE
Haliaeetus leucocephalus

This unmistakable raptor is the national bird of the United States.

Field marks: Adult has white head, yellow bill, all-brown body, white tail. Juvenile may be all brown or mottled brown and white.

Size: L: 30"–43", WS: 75"–95"

Similar species: Turkey vulture and black vulture are often mistaken for eagles, but they have featherless heads. The bald eagle soars while holding its wings flat, while the turkey vulture makes a wide V shape with its wings in flight. Osprey has a completely white underside, a white cap with a black band through its eye, and a dark tail.

Season: Winter throughout the state, year-round in east Texas

Habitat: Areas with open water, including rivers, lakes, ponds, and ocean

Food source: Fish, road-killed carrion (especially deer)

Nest: Near the top of a large tree that can support a big nest made of twigs

Call: A very high series of notes and squeaks, ending in a rapid *wee-ee-ee-ee-ee-o*

Hot spots: Any habitat near a sizable body of water may provide a home for bald eagles, and they have become a common sight in their year-round habitat in east Texas. Here are some very reliable spots to see them: Mad Island Marsh Preserve and Wildlife Management Area, Palacios, 28.6475113 / -96.0950947; Archbishop Fiorenza Park, Eldridge Retention Basin, Houston, 29.7193575 / -95.6289482; Lakeside Park, The Woodlands, 30.2011339 / -95.5413902; San Bernard NWR Moccasin Pond Loop, Cedar Lake, 28.884594 / -95.562815; Richland Creek Wildlife Management Area, Cayuga, 31.9832577 / -96.0818564.

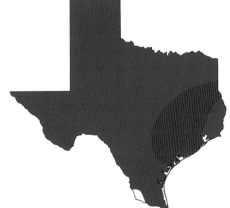

OSPREY AND FALCONS

OSPREY
Pandion haliaetus

This fish-eating raptor is easily spotted near major waterways, especially in winter in southeastern Texas.

Field marks: White head and face with black band from eye to shoulder, dark body and tail, white underside with streaky black breastband. Juvenile has buff-colored upper breast.

Size: L: 21"–24", WS: 56"–72"

Similar species: Bald eagle, often seen in the same habitat, is larger and has an all-white head and white tail.

Season: Year-round

Habitat: Areas with open water that supports a healthy fish population; high perches

Food source: Fish

Nest: At the top of a tree, or on a platform or crosspiece at the top of a utility pole or lamppost

Call: Very high *pip-pip-pip-pip*

Hot spots: Despite their wide range, ospreys are most easily seen in wetlands near the Gulf shore or near large lakes with ample fish. Aransas National Wildlife Refuge Wildlife Drive, 28.2403924 / -96.818819; Cape Valero Drive, Rockport, 28.0421467 / -97.1168125; South Padre Island Birding and Nature Center, 26.1374628 / -97.1739367; San Benito Wetlands, Harlingen, 26.1739485 / -97.6235167; TX 100 aplomado viewing area, Brownsville, 26.0913939 / -97.3272438.

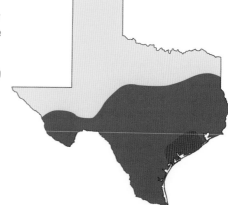

CRESTED CARACARA

Caracara plancus

A bird of open desert, this falcon shows up along roadsides throughout south-central Texas in its search for a roadkill meal.

Field marks: Dark brown cap extended to the nape, orange facial skin extending to bill, gray bill tip, white neck and throat, white breast mottled with brown, brown back and wings with white outer feathers, white undertail coverts, white tail with brown trailing edge, yellow legs and feet. Large white patches on wing tips in flight.

Size: L: 22"–24", WS 49"–50"

Similar species: Black vulture is much larger and is all black with white outer wing "fingers."

Season: Year-round in a concentrated area

Habitat: Open land, including farm fields, prairie, and pastures; often seen perching on a fence post

Food source: Carrion, as well as fish, reptiles, birds, rodents, and amphibians

Nest: In the tallest tree or shrub they can find

Call: Generally silent; sometimes a rattling sound of warning

Hot spots: The vast majority of caracara sightings are along roadways, where the birds watch for carrion, but here are some dependable preserves: Lake Findley, Alice, 27.7888887 / -98.0641977; Katy Prairie Conservation Area Indiangrass Preserve, Cypress. 29.9288434 / -95.9256542; Laguna Atascosa National Wildlife Refuge, Brownsville, 26.2338009 / -97.3643036; Brownsville Landfill, Brownsville, 25.9380025 / -97.3939785; Estero Llano Grande State Park World Birding Center, Llano Grande, 26.1268335 / -97.9578167.

MERLIN
Falco columbarius

An aggressive hunter, this adaptable falcon may prey upon the small birds at your feeder.

Field marks: Dark, streaked head with white stripe through the eye and grayish vertical stripes; dark back; mottled gray, white, and rusty chest and underside; long, dark tail with light gray stripes. Wings are short and tapered.

Size: L: 10"–13", WS: 23"–25"

Similar species: American kestrel is much redder overall. Peregrine falcon is much larger, with pronounced black vertical stripes on its face.

Season: Winter through most of Texas; a migrant in northern areas

Habitat: Coniferous forest, often near an adjoining housing tract or farm where small birds are plentiful

Food source: Small birds and occasional small mammals, reptiles (including snakes), dragonflies

Nest: A tree cavity, high ledge, or abandoned bird's nest

Call: A single, high-pitched *heee*; repeated rapidly when used as an alarm call

Hot spots: Katy Prairie Conservation Area Indiangrass Preserve, Cypress. 29.9288434 / -95.9256542; Hornsby Bend, Austin, 30.2181988 / -97.6458054; San Angelo State Park, San Angelo, 31.4677918 / -100.5033213; Guadalupe Mountains National Park, Pine Springs, 31.9074905 / -104.8013279; Clapp Park, Lubbock, 33.5550145 / -101.8639944.

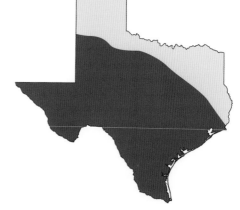

AMERICAN KESTREL
Falco sparverius

Our smallest falcon stands out for its reddish wings and body, as well as its uncanny ability to hover while hunting.

Field marks: Gray cap, white face with gray vertical stripes, bright rust back and tail. Male has gray wings, a buff breast with black streaks, and a buff patch on the back of the head. Female has rusty streaks on chest and lacks the buff patches.

Size: L: 9"–11", WS: 20"–24"

Similar species: Merlin is larger and has no rusty areas. Peregrine falcon is much larger and darker.

Season: Year-round in northern and westernmost Texas; winter in central and south Texas

Habitat: Farmland, open fields and meadows, as well as city parks and housing developments

Food source: Grasshoppers and other large insects, small mammals, birds, frogs and other amphibians

Nest: In a tree cavity

Call: High-pitched, gargled *klee-klee-klee-klee-klee*

Hot spots: Any farmer's field, marshland, airfield, open area in a neighborhood, or very large backyard may attract a kestrel to consider it as a hunting ground. These robin-sized hawks are fairly easy to identify because of their bright plumage and their ability to hover; they perch on the tops of utility poles and on wires, fence posts, and fences along roadsides. The vast majority of sightings are along major roads and over open fields, desert, and grasslands.

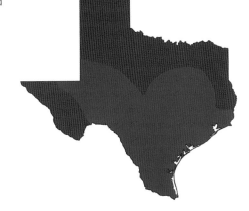

109

PEREGRINE FALCON
Falco peregrinus

After being nearly wiped out by the pesticide DDT, this large falcon has returned to its accustomed habitat across the country.

Field marks: Black and white head with vertical black stripe through the eye, dark gray back and wings, white breast with heavy, dark barring from mid-breast to undertail coverts; long gray tail with darker gray barring. Juvenile is very similar, but browner.

Size: L: 16"–20", WS: 41"–45"

Similar species: Merlin and American kestrel are both smaller, and both have rusty barring on their breasts. Kestrel is more reddish overall.

Season: Winter in south Texas, migrating through the rest of the state; summer in the Davis Mountains

Habitat: Open spaces, including mountains and rocky coastlines with cliffs. Peregrines are renowned for their ability to nest and breed on top of tall buildings in major cities.

Food source: Birds, especially rock pigeons and doves, small reptiles

Nest: Up high, near the top of a cliff or on the ledge of a city skyscraper

Call: A rapid, repeated, cackled *ka-ka-ka-ka-ka*, sometimes for several minutes

Hot spots: Davis Mountains State Park, primitive area, Fort Davis, 30.60079 / -103.92579; Big Bend National Park, Chisos Mountains area trails, 29.2699985 / -103.3004522; Hornsby Bend, Austin, 30.2181988 / -97.6458054; San Jacinto Battleground, Deer Park, 29.7506484 / -95.0770891; Progreso Lakes grain silos, Progreso, 26.0740159 / -97.9425523.

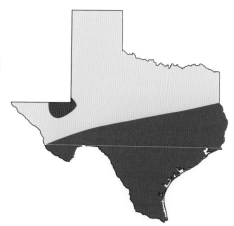

APLOMADO FALCON
Falco femoralis

The bold facial markings, dark body, and long wings make this falcon stand out among raptors in Texas. Its endangered status makes it one of the most sought-after sightings for birders.

Field marks: Black and white–striped face, yellow bill, dark mantle and wings, white breast with fine streaks, dark bellyband and rufous underparts, darkly banded tail.

Size: L: 15"–17", WS: 35"

Similar species: American kestrel is smaller and more boldly patterned with rusty cap and back, buff breast, and white undertail coverts. Peregrine falcon is heavily barred across the chest and belly, with no bellyband.

Season: Year-round in a very limited area between Corpus Christi and Brownsville

Habitat: Grasslands along the Gulf coast, open desert with mesquite trees

Food source: Small mammals, insects, birds, reptiles

Nest: In stick nests left behind by other birds; also human-provided platforms on tall poles supplied for this purpose or atop utility poles

Call: One-syllable, high-pitched *kik*, sometimes repeated

Hot spots: Several parks along the Gulf coast provide nesting platforms for aplomado falcons, making this rare bird fairly easy to see. Mustang Island State Park, aplomado falcon viewing platform on TX 361, Corpus Christi, 27.692173 / -97.16353; Kleberg County Beach, Corpus Christi, 27.5512938 / -97.2363746; TX 100 aplomado viewing area, Brownsville, 26.0913939 / -97.3272438; Laguna Atascosa National Wildlife Refuge—Bahia Grande Unit, Brownsville, 26.041662 / -97.282077.

KITES

WHITE-TAILED KITE
Elanus leucurus

Watch the skies over south Texas's open fields for this sleek, white rodent hunter with black shoulders.

Field marks: White face, amber eyes rimmed in black; white throat, breast, and underside; light gray wings with black shoulders, long white tail extending past dark wing tips when standing. Juvenile has buff breast for first few weeks. Flies with wings held in dihedral position.

Size: L: 14"–16", WS: 39"–40"

Similar species: Mississippi kite is uniformly gray with a dark tail.

Season: Year-round

Habitat: Open grassland and savanna

Food source: Rodents, snakes and other small reptiles, some insects

Nest: In tall trees at forest edges, or in a lone tree in an open area

Call: A crackling grunt, like metal rubbing a rough surface

Hot spots: Bolivar Flats Shorebird Sanctuary, Galveston, 29.3711371 / -94.7287083; Sabal Palm Sanctuary, Brownsville, 25.85233 / -97.4176839; San Benito Wetlands, Harlingen, 26.1739485 / -97.6235167; Estero Llano Grande State Park World Birding Center, Llano Grande, 26.1268335 / -97.9578167; Resaca de la Palma State Park/World Birding Center, Brownsville, 25.9965839 / -97.5690513.

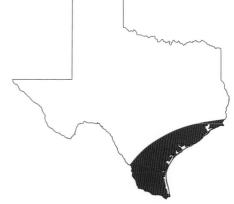

MISSISSIPPI KITE
Ictinia mississippiensis

This light gray kite's long, slender wings make it easy to mistake for a falcon.

Field marks: Adult is light gray overall with dark eye patch, gray wings with white secondary feathers, darker fan tail. Juvenile has a brown and white breast and underside, brown underwings at the shoulders, and faint stripes in tail.

Size: L: 14"–15", WS: 31"–32"

Similar species: Peregrine falcon has a boldly patterned face and a black and white, horizontally striped breast and underside. White-tailed kite is whiter overall with a bright white tail.

Season: Breeding in the panhandle and in central Texas, spring and fall migration in the rest of east Texas, with a small breeding population on the Gulf coast

Habitat: Forests with mature trees

Food source: Large insects, reptiles, amphibians, small mammals, sometimes bats

Nest: In trees in lowland forests

Call: A wispy *PEW-phew*, dropping in pitch at the end

Hot spots: Palo Duro Canyon State Park, Lake Tanglewood, 34.9651086 / -101.671257; Thompson Park, Amarillo, 35.2382514 / -101.8330479; Canyon Lake 6, Lubbock, 33.5676571 / -101.8033202; Mae Simmons Park, Lubbock, 33.5752826 / -101.8240776; Cedar Creek Trail, Abilene, 32.4523433 / -99.7214315.

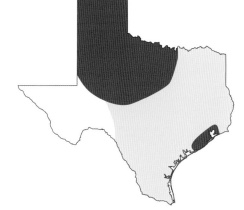

OWLS

DOMINIC SHERONY

BARN OWL
Tyto alba

Like a gray ghost in the night, this nocturnal bird is very difficult for birders to see clearly and well.

Field marks: Male has heart-shaped white face, black eyes, light pink bill; pale tan head, nape, back, and wings; white breast and underside, mottled gray and light brown wings with pure white underside visible in flight, dark legs. Female has a tawny breast.

Size: L: 16"–20", WS: 42"–44"

Similar species: Barred owl has vertical barring on its chest and horizontal barring around its neck.

Season: Year-round

Habitat: Structures or wooded areas near open grasslands

Food source: Primarily rodents; also rabbits and bats

Nest: In a barn, church steeple, or other building; in a hollow tree, a crevice on a rocky cliff, or on a ledge

Call: A chilling screech that sounds uncannily like an ill-fated Alfred Hitchcock heroine; also a high-pitched *kik-kik-kik* by the male approaching the nest

Hot spots: Many of the most reliable places to see barn owls are on private property, making them tricky to access. These parks also have frequent sightings: El Franco Lee Park, Houston, 29.594929 / -95.2589295; Estero Llano Grande State Park World Birding Center, Llano Grande, 26.1268335 / -97.9578167; Katy Prairie Conservation Area Indiangrass Preserve, Cypress. 29.9288434 / -95.9256542; Anahuac National Wildlife Refuge, Bolivar Peninsula, 29.609066 / -94.535253; Village Creek Drying Beds, Arlington, 32.7842795 / -97.1266181.

GREAT HORNED OWL
Bubo virginianus

A year-round resident throughout Texas, this large owl often perches in the open as evening approaches.

Field marks: Orange face with brown forehead and yellow eyes, large "horn" tufts, rufous and buff chest and underside with strong brown barring, brown back and wings with some rufous tint, buff underside of wings, brown tail.

Size: L: 20"–25", WS: 36"–44"

Similar species: Barred owl is smaller, with dark eyes and no ear tufts. Barn owl has a white face and no ear tufts, a ruddy-brown back and wings.

Season: Year-round

Habitat: Woodlands, swamps, farmland with wooded areas

Food source: Larger mammals and birds other than owls (ducks, quail, geese), rabbits, groundhogs, skunks; also squirrels and rats

Nest: In a large nest abandoned by another bird

Call: A four- or five-note series: *hoo-HOO, hoo, hoo*; also a shriek not unlike a red-tailed hawk

Hot spots: Just about every wooded area in the state has its own great horned owl, if not a pair. Check the park nearest you before venturing cross-country to find one—try an evening just before twilight or the hour or so before the sun rises, and listen for one calling. Rangers in parks often know where these owls are nesting, and if they have nearly fledged young that may be visible in the nest.

BARRED OWL
Strix varia

The barred owl's familiar "Who cooks for you?" call helps birders narrow its location in the forest after dark.

Field marks: Gray facial disc, black eyes, gray barring around neck and throat, buff breast with heavy brown streaking, mottled brown and white back and wings, buff and brown–barred tail.

Size: L: 18"–23", WS: 42"–50"

Similar species: Great horned owl is larger, has a tawny face and yellow eyes, and has large tufts of feathers that resemble ears or horns.

Season: Year-round in east Texas

Habitat: Forests and woodlands near water

Food source: Rodents and other small mammals, fish, reptiles, amphibians, grasshoppers and other insects

Nest: In a tree cavity or in a nest built by a hawk or squirrel

Call: *Hoo, hoo, huh-hoo, hoo, hoo, huh-hoo-ah*, often defined as "Who cooks for you, who cooks for you all?" with a long descending note at the end

Hot spots: Pecan Valley Park, Arlington, 32.6629339 / -97.451992; Riverside Park, Victoria, 28.8101559 / -97.0273025; San Bernard National Wildlife Refuge, Cedar Lake, 28.884594 / -95.562815; Brazos Bend State Park, Thompsons, 29.3735739 / -95.6230259; Big Thicket National Preserve, Kountze, 30.4621326 / -94.3512954.

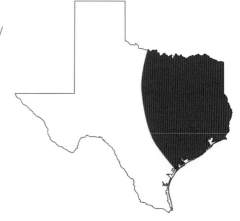

EASTERN SCREECH-OWL
Megascops asio

This year-round resident calls with an eerie, elongated trill that strikes fear in many species, including unsuspecting humans.

Field marks: Two morphs are possible: rufous/brown and gray. Facial disc is brown or gray with a white X from eyebrows to chin; yellow eyes, small ear tufts. Wings are brown or gray with white lines from shoulder. Breast is heavily barred with gray or brown streaks.

Size: L: 7"–9", WS: 18"–22"

Similar species: Western screech-owl looks much like an eastern screech-owl, but their territory only overlaps in central Texas and in and around Big Bend National Park. Listen for the eastern's shrill, descending whinny, while the western's call is shorter (five to ten notes), lower-pitched, and speeds up for the last few notes.

Season: Year-round

Habitat: Mixed deciduous and coniferous forest, parks, woods near streams or marshes, open fields

Food source: Rodents and other small mammals

Nest: In a tree cavity, either natural or excavated by woodpeckers

Call: A long, soprano, descending trill, lasting 3 seconds or more; a trill on one note with no descent, also 3 or 4 seconds long

Hot spots: Prairie Creek Park, Richardson, 32.9872119 / -96.7180109; Cedar Hill State Park, Dallas, 32.6227136 / -96.9800091; Lake Corpus Christi State Park, Lake City, 28.0586183 / -97.8616507; Concan Frio Bat Cave area, Concan, 29.4350096 / -99.6843734; Kickapoo Cavern State Park, Kinney County, 29.61154 / -100.4533.

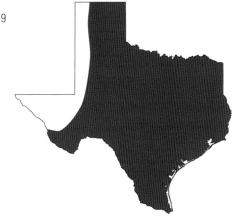

DOMINIC SHERONY

WESTERN SCREECH-OWL
Megascops kennicottii

More likely heard than seen, this nocturnal bird nestles in a tree cavity and emerges at dusk.

Field marks: Small, chunky body, gray overall with thin black streaks; square head with bright yellow eyes, tiny tufts resembling ears.

Size: L: 7.5"–9.5" , WS: 21.5"–24"

Similar species: Eastern screech-owl is nearly identical, but its range only overlaps in a focused area of central Texas and in Big Bend National Park. The two owls are easily differentiated by call.

Season: Year-round

Habitat: Deciduous forests, including mountain forests

Food source: Small mammals are preferred, but they will eat birds and amphibians as well.

Nest: In tree cavities created by woodpeckers

Call: Five to ten notes, lower-pitched than an eastern screech-owl's whinny, speeding up for the last few notes

Hot spots: Big Bend National Park, Dugout Wells, 29.2712002 / -103.1352997; Big Bend National Park, Cottonwood Campground, 29.1366997 / -103.5220032; Big Bend National Park, Chisos Mountains area trails, 29.2699985 / -103.3004522; Lawrence E. Wood Picnic Area and Madera Canyon Trail, Davis Mountains Preserve, 30.7063007 / -104.1054001; Devils River State Natural Area, Del Rio, 29.9406182 / -100.9710073; Davis Mountains State Park, primitive area, Fort Davis, 30.60079 / -103.92579.

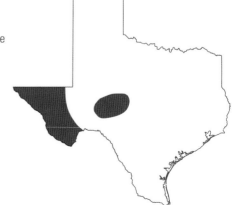

BURROWING OWL
Athene cunicularia

These tiny owls live in colonies in holes in the ground in flat, open plains.

Field marks: Mottled brown head, chest, and body; yellow eyes and bill, long legs, short tail. Males and females are similar.

Size: L: 8"–9", WS: 21"

Similar species: This is the only Texas owl that lives on the ground.

Season: Year-round through most of the state; summer only in the northern panhandle

Habitat: Open grassland, airports, ball fields, and other flat, clear areas

Food source: Insects, small rodents, small reptiles and amphibians

Nest: Burrows dug by other animals, including tortoises, armadillos, prairie dogs, skunks, or ground squirrels, often on a small mound in an otherwise open area

Call: A high-pitched, two-note *cu-COO*

Hot spots: McGee Lake, Amarillo, 35.2810102 / -101.6586828; Buffalo Lake National Wildlife Refuge, Umbarger, 34.9101471 / -102.1138; CR 352, field south of Alligator Road, Bartlett, 30.7531218 / -97.3829198; Granger Lake area, Friendship, 30.7001608 / -97.3597466; fields between TX 35 & FM 774, Austwell, 28.3761091 / -96.871562.

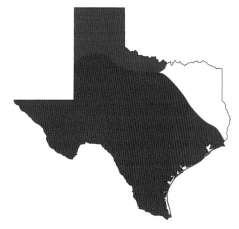

DOVES AND PIGEON

EURASIAN COLLARED-DOVE
Streptopelia decaocto

Larger and lighter than a mourning dove, this widespread species is everywhere that people congregate.

Field marks: Light gray-tan overall with a thin black line around nape of neck; dark primary feathers on wings, gray undertail coverts, red eye, pink legs and feet. White outer tail feathers visible in flight.

Size: L: 13", WS: 21"–23"

Similar species: Mourning dove is slightly smaller, darker tan and gray, and has black spots on its wings. White-winged dove has a bright white line along the outer edge of its wings, most visible when standing.

Season: Year-round

Habitat: Human-populated areas, including cities, suburbs, and farms, especially where bird feeders are found.

Food source: Seeds, some berries and insects

Nest: On buildings or in trees, at least 10 feet off the ground

Call: Repeated *coo-COO coo*, as well as a distinctly different, elongated *waw* when alarmed, not unlike a blue jay

Hot spots: You won't need a specific place to look for this dove. If you don't have a yard with a bird feeder, watch electrical wires or light poles along roadsides and at shopping centers, or scan mowed lawns throughout the state.

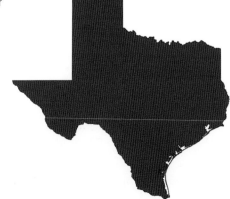

COMMON GROUND DOVE
Columbina passerina

Bright rufous underwings, a scaly head and chest, and mourning dove–like spots make this little dove distinctive, if not easy to find.

Field marks: Scaly-feathered black and white crown and nape; ruddy face, breast, underside and wings; red bill with black tip, light brown back, black spots in lines on wings, short wings, brownish tail.

Size: L: 6"–6.5", WS: 10"–11"

Similar species: Inca dove has a scaly appearance all over its body. Mourning dove is slimmer, twice the size, and has no rufous features or scaly-looking feathers. Eurasian collared-dove is slightly larger than the mourning dove and is lighter gray.

Season: Year-round

Habitat: Open ground, often with very little vegetation, especially under bird feeders

Food source: Seeds from weeds and grass, as well as bird feeders

Nest: On the ground, or low in a shrub or other sturdy vegetation

Call: *Cooo, cooo, cooo*, in a series, each rising at the end

Hot spots: If common ground doves are not coming to your backyard feeders, try some of these parks—some have feeders; others have picnic tables under which doves congregate. Jackson Nature Park, Stockdale, 29.2194894 / -98.0096126; Salineño Wildlife Preserve, Roma, 26.5148584 / -99.116206; Bentsen–Rio Grande Valley State Park/World Birding Center, Mission, 26.1849709 / 98.3793885; Hugh Ramsey Park, Harlingen, 26.1857402 / -97.6641657; Green Hill Cemetery, Hebbronville, 27.3536448 / -98.7504036.

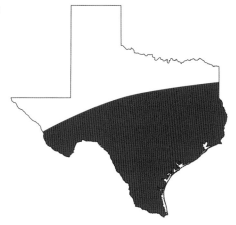

WHITE-WINGED DOVE
Zenaida asiatica

With its rapidly expanding range throughout the state, white-winged dove can be found in any metropolitan area.

Field marks: Gray-brown overall; orange eye with blue ring, black path along jawline, white wing patch that forms a line along the bottom edge of the wing while at rest, becoming visible on upper wing during flight; black flight feathers, square tail with white trailing edge, red legs and feet.

Size: L: 11"–12", WS: 19"–20"

Similar species: Mourning dove has black spots on its wings and no white areas. Eurasian collared-dove has a black line extending around the nape and is paler overall.

Season: Summer in the northern half of the state; year-round throughout central and southern Texas

Habitat: Cities, towns, suburbs, and anywhere else where there are people

Food source: Seeds, both from plants and from feeders

Nest: In the crotch or on a sturdy branch of a large shade tree

Call: *Coo-coo-coo-COO-woo*, very like the "Who cooks for you?" of a barred owl

Hot spots: This ubiquitous bird collects on utility wires, congregates in parking areas, and hangs out in picnic grounds, on beaches, and at feeders; they are particularly numerous at any restaurant with outdoor dining. They are also staples on trails in all of Texas's wildlife refuges, parks, and wildlife management areas.

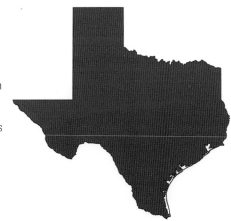

MOURNING DOVE
Zenaida macroura

A resident of suburban yards, parks, and shopping centers, this gentle creature can be seen and heard virtually anywhere in Texas.

Field marks: Light grayish brown overall with a black spot on the cheek and black spots on the wings; short, thin bill; long tail expands in flight to show white tips with a black edge; whitish undertail coverts.

Size: L: 12", WS: 17"–19"

Similar species: Rock pigeon is larger and heavier, and is either light gray and black or a combination of colors due to interbreeding with other dove species. Eurasian collared-dove is lighter in color and has a black line around its nape. White-winged dove lacks the black spots and has a solid white line visible just below its wings. Common ground dove has a scaly appearance on its head, neck, and breast.

Season: Year-round

Habitat: Mowed lawns and platform or ground feeders in suburban areas, parks with trees and shrubs, and other areas frequented by people

Food source: Seeds, leaves, and plant matter found on the ground

Nest: In a tree, shrub, or on the ground

Call: A slow, mournful *ohh-WOO, hoo, hoo*; also a pronounced whistling made by the wings during flight

Hot spots: Mourning doves are among the most common birds in the United States and are easy to locate. Watch utility wires in your area for single birds, pairs, and flocks, and keep an eye on platform feeders, tops of lampposts, and other places where they can stand comfortably.

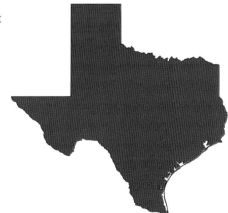

INCA DOVE
Columbina inca

An unobtrusively grayish dove on the ground, the Inca dove surprises in flight with its rufous underwing and white outer tail feathers.

Field marks: Smaller than other doves, with gray-brown feathers in an overall scaly pattern; in flight, rufous under the wings, and white tail feathers appear along the edges of the long tail.

Size: L: 7"–8", WS: 11"

Similar species: Mourning dove is larger, has spots on its wings, and is not scaly. Common ground dove is scaly only on head, nape, and chest.

Season: Year-round

Habitat: Metropolitan areas with parks and people; open areas, including deserts and plains with bare ground

Food source: Seeds and grains; these doves come to feeders in backyards throughout their range.

Nest: In trees and shrubs, as well as anywhere on a house or building that will support a nest

Call: A repeated, low, two-note whistle, often described as "no hope"

Hot spots: If you have a bird feeder or know someone who does, you will have no trouble locating Inca doves in your neighborhood. Beyond the backyard, Inca doves frequent parks, picnic areas, gardens, mowed lawns, plowed fields, and anywhere else they can find seeds and grain.

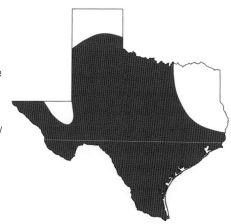

ROCK PIGEON
Columba livia

An introduced species from Europe, this member of the dove family (formerly known as rock dove or feral pigeon) took full advantage of its new territory and is now found on every city street in the country.

Field marks: Original coloring is a purple head, iridescent-blue neck and breast, light gray back and upper wings, darker gray primary flight feathers, black stripe across both wings, black trailing edge; white rump, gray tail with a black tip. Interbreeding with domestic species has produced a variety of alternate plumages in mottled shades of brown, black, gray, and white.

Size: L: 12.5"–14", WS: 26"–34"

Similar species: Mourning dove is smaller, more delicate, and is always grayish-brown with black spots on wings.

Season: Year-round

Habitat: Areas inhabited by humans, including cities, suburbs, buildings, and barnyards in rural areas; also on agricultural lands

Food source: Seeds, berries, and human discards scavenged from streets, yards, and parks

Nest: On man-made ledges—windowsills, bridge girders, eaves, gutters, etc.

Call: Elongated, descending *coo* with a throaty rumble

Hot spots: Rock pigeons are everywhere humans are. Check city streets, gravel driveways, parking lots, rooftops of houses and barns, landfills, dumpsters, restaurants with outdoor dining, fairs and festivals, and other places where people may drop a morsel of food.

PARAKEETS, CUCKOOS, AND ANI

MONK PARAKEET
Myiopsitta monachus

Probably descended from birds released by pet owners as far back as the 1960s, established colonies of these gregarious birds from South America thrive in most cities in Texas.

Field marks: Bright green head with whitish face and orange bill, green back, green wings with bright blue primaries, grayish breast, gray-to-yellow belly, long diamond-shaped green tail.

Size: L: 11"–12", WS: 17"–19"

Similar species: A wide variety of similarly marked parrot and parakeet species have colonized cities in south Texas, but the monk parakeet's pale gray forehead and breast set it apart from most of them.

Season: Year-round

Habitat: City parks and structures with lots of perches, especially power substations

Food source: Seeds, fruits, berries, nuts, flowers, insects

Nest: On top of a tall structure (a building or utility pole), or at the top of a very tall tree. Monk parakeets are the only communally-nesting parakeet in the United States, creating large nests for big groups of birds.

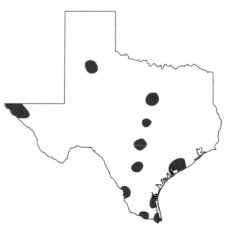

Call: Rattling *chaa, chaa* calls with several syllables in succession; loud screeches

Hot spots: Rio Bosque Park, El Paso, 31.6408997 / -106.3099976; Hidalgo monk parakeet colonies, South 5th Street and Gardenia Avenue and surrounding area, 26.097378 / -98.258218; University of Houston campus, Houston, 29.7214985 / -95.3438187; power station at 306 Mission Road, San Antonio, 29.3972441 / -98.4890494; White Rock Lake & Old Fish Hatchery, Dallas, 32.8156276 / -96.7264652.

RED-CROWNED PARROT
Amazona viridigenalis

The most common of the parrots along the Lower Rio Grande Valley, these showy birds swoop into neighborhoods and parks by the hundreds just before sunset.

Field marks: Green overall with red forehead, blue-gray nape, dull white bill, yellow tail tip, and bright red patches on wings (seen in flight).

Size: L: 13"–14", WS: 25"

Similar species: Monk parakeet has a white face and breast, blue wing tips, and a much longer tail. Parrots of several other species may mix in the same flocks, especially in Brownsville; watch for red-lored parrot, lilac-crowned parrot, and white-fronted parrot.

Season: Year-round

Habitat: City parks and neighborhoods, especially where there are fruit trees

Food source: The fruit of native and non-native tropical trees

Nest: In tree cavities excavated by woodpeckers, usually along the edges of thickly treed areas

Call: A squealy jumble of sounds followed by four or five scratchy, barking caws

Hot spots: Oliviera Park, Brownsville, 25.9374284 / -97.52159; Hugh Ramsey Park, Harlingen, 26.1857402 / -97.6641657; Harlingen Convention Center, Harlingen, 26.1996901 / -97.708261; East Houston Avenue red-crowned parrot roost, McAllen, 26.1952144 / -98.2214856; Pharr Vanguard Academy Nature & Birding Center, Pharr, 26.184073 / -98.182569.

DOMINIC SHERONY

YELLOW-BILLED CUCKOO
Coccyzus americanus

This common cuckoo prefers pastures, meadows with high grass, orchards, and other open areas with trees and shrubs.

Field marks: Brown cap, nape, and back; brown wings with bright reddish primaries; brown tail with white spots on outer tail feathers, large white spots visible on the underside of the tail; white throat, breast, and underside; yellow bill with black upper mandible, yellow eye ring.

Size: L: 11"–12", WS: 16"–18"

Similar species: Black-billed cuckoo, which is only occasional in Texas, has a black bill and white stripes on the underside of the tail instead of large white patches.

Season: Summer

Habitat: Grasslands with trees for roosting, especially willows

Food source: Caterpillars, cicadas, bird eggs, small reptiles, fruit

Nest: In a shrub or young tree

Call: Long, slow, descending rattle: *ki-ki-ki-ki-kow-kow-kow-kow*, a series of single *koo* sounds on one note

Hot spots: Any park or wildlife refuge with open areas and willows provides cuckoo habitat. These spots are particularly dependable: Resaca de la Palma State Park/World Birding Center, Brownsville, 25.9965839 / -97.5690513; Mitchell Lake Audubon Center, San Antonio, 29.3105956 / -98.4996938; Roy G. Guerrero Colorado River Metro Park, Austin, 30.246172 / -97.7049763; Village Creek Drying Beds, Arlington, 32.7842795 / -97.1266181; South Llano River State Park, Junction, 30.4391651 / -99.8128617.

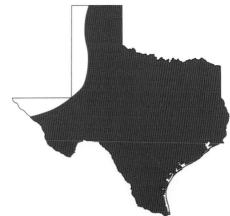

GROOVE-BILLED ANI
Crotophaga sulcirostris

This slimmer of the two anis (and the only one found in Texas) has narrow grooves in its bill.

Field marks: All black, with disheveled feathers and a long tail; short, bulky bill like a parrot. Gray skin extends from the bill to the area around the eye. Grooves on bill may be visible with binoculars or a scope.

Size: L: 13"–14" WS: 17"–18"

Similar species: American crow and fish crow are sleeker with a long, pointed bill. Common raven has a longer, heavier, pointed bill and a shorter tail. Great-tailed grackle is sleeker with a slimmer, pointed bill.

Season: Year-round

Habitat: Fields of low scrub, pastures, savannas

Food source: Insects, small reptiles, fruit, seeds

Nest: In groups in a tree or bush

Call: *Tuck-tuck-tuck-tuck*, slow and steady, with occasional whistles between *tucks*

Hot spots: Salineño Wildlife Preserve, Roma, 26.5148584 / -99.116206; National Butterfly Center, Mission, 26.1796025 / -98.3664483; San Benito Wetlands, Harlingen, 26.1739485 / -97.6235167; Leonabelle Turnbull Birding Center, Port Aransas, 27.8275297 / -97.0789558; Bentsen–Rio Grande Valley State Park/World Birding Center, Mission, 26.1849709 / -98.3793885.

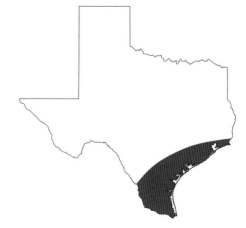

GREATER ROADRUNNER
Geococcyx californianus

No other bird is as synonymous with the American desert as the roadrunner, thanks to decades of Looney Tunes cartoons. But an actual coyote can easily outrun the bird, making it a dangerous predator to roadrunners.

Field marks: Brown overall in several shades; spotted light and dark across the face, throat, back, and wings; creamy belly; high, dark brown crest with lighter spots, light eye line (blue in breeding season) with red spot behind the eye, heavy bill. Long, dark tail serves to balance the bird while running.

Size: L: 20"–22", WS: 19"–20"

Similar species: Female ring-necked pheasant is lighter overall, with no crest, heavier body, and shorter legs. Scaled quail is shorter, stockier, and lacks the long tail.

Season: Year-round

Habitat: Open range: desert, grassland, riparian areas, mountainsides with shrubby landscapes

Food source: Reptiles, amphibians, insects, rodents; will plunder other birds' nests

Nest: In a tree or cactus, usually not more than 10 feet off the ground

Call: Not *beep-beep*, but a slow, descending *whoop, whoop, whooooop*

Hot spots: The majority of roadrunner sightings occur along every interstate, US, or state route throughout Texas, where the birds do indeed run. Beyond chance glimpses while driving, the best places to find this bird are in campgrounds and picnic areas in state and national parks, where they often approach people because visitors feed them. (Please do not feed them—human food is not appropriate for roadrunners.)

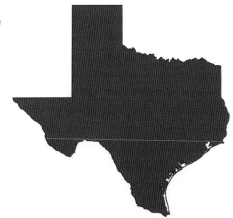

NIGHTJARS

COMMON NIGHTHAWK
Chordeiles minor

Look for this darting hunter just after sunset, often catching bugs by the glow of industrial lighting systems at factories, stadiums, or shopping malls.

Field marks: Adult is mottled gray overall with tiny bill, slightly brown throat, white band across front of throat; brownish and gray back and wings, white feather at side below wing, broad white bar on each wing seen during flight; white stripe across tail just before terminal black stripe.

Size: L: 8"–10", WS: 22"–24"

Similar species: Whip-poor-will is similarly colored but lacks the wing stripe, and habitat does not generally overlap. Lesser nighthawk is similar, but the white stripe on its wings is closer to the wing tip.

Season: Summer

Habitat: Very comfortable in human-populated areas, using buildings as roosting and nesting sites and lights to illuminate prey

Food source: Flying insects

Nest: In a hollow on the ground or on top of a flat-roofed building

Call: A nasal *peent*, not unlike a woodcock

Hot spots: Any developed area may have a population of nighthawks. Here are some very dependable places to see them: Leonabelle Turnbull Birding Center, Port Aransas, 27.8275297 / -97.0789558; Estero Llano Grande State Park World Birding Center, Llano Grande, 26.1268335 / -97.9578167; Balmorhea Lake, Balmorhea, 30.9583956 / -103.7123108; Village Creek Drying Beds, Arlington, 32.7842795 / -97.1266181; Clapp Park, Lubbock, 33.5550145 / -101.8639944.

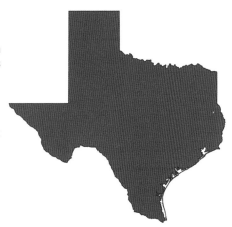

COMMON PAURAQUE
Nyctidromus albicollis

This nocturnal bird virtually disappears by day, as its mottled plumage makes it nearly impossible to distinguish from the woodland floor on which it sleeps.

Field marks: Chunky body covered in several mixed shades of brown and gray, forming a near-complete camouflage, with very large all-black eye, tiny bill, and long tail with white outer tail feathers visible in flight. Wings have a white band, also visible only in flight.

Size: L: 11"–12", WS: 24"

Similar species: Common nighthawk is smaller, and its wings are slimmer in flight. Common poorwill is smaller and grayer overall with a much shorter tail, and it does not have the white wing bar.

Season: Year-round

Habitat: Shrubby or brushy open areas, including farm fields and shrublands adjacent to wooded lots

Food source: Insects that fly or creep at night, caught on the ground or in midair

Nest: Usually under a bush or small tree on the edge of a field

Call: A looping *puh-WEE-er* or more-staccato *woo-whit-woo-wer*, especially after dark

Hot spots: Estero Llano Grande State Park World Birding Center, Llano Grande, 26.1268335 / -97.9578167; Bentsen–Rio Grande Valley State Park/World Birding Center, Mission, 26.1849709 / -98.3793885; Resaca de la Palma State Park/World Birding Center, Brownsville, 25.9965839 / -97.5690513; Laguna Atascosa National Wildlife Refuge, Brownsville, 26.2338009 / -97.3643036; Sabal Palm Sanctuary, Brownsville, 25.85233 / -97.4176839.

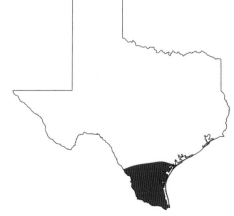

DOMINIC SHERONY

COMMON POORWILL
Phalaenoptilus nuttallii

A small nightjar with the ability to vanish into its surroundings, common poorwill sings its own name after dark.

Field marks: Mottled brown or gray overall with a white throat band that usually is not visible when the bird is on the ground; large dark eye and tiny bill.

Size: L: 7.5"–8.5", WS: 17"

Similar species: Common pauraque is larger and browner overall with a more rufous face. Common and lesser nighthawks have tapered wings and a white band across each wing that is easily seen in flight.

Season: Year-round in El Paso area and along Lower Rio Grande Valley; summer in west Texas

Habitat: Open desert and other areas with low shrubs and no ground cover

Food source: Insects in flight

Nest: On the ground, laying eggs on whatever leaf or needle detritus is there, or at the base of a shrub or cactus

Call: A low, repeated *poorwill*

Hot spots: Amistad National Recreation Area Spur 406 area, Del Rio, 29.5522277 / -101.0230652; Kickapoo Cavern State Park, Kinney County, 29.61154 /
-100.4533; Big Bend National Park, Chisos Mountains area trails, 29.2699985 / -103.3004522; Christmas Mountains Oasis, Alpine, 29.4917768 / -103.4670389; Davis Mountains State Park, primitive area, Fort Davis, 30.60079 / -103.92579.

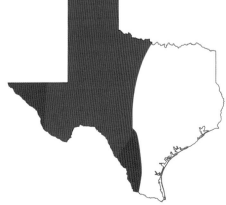

HUMMINGBIRDS

RUBY-THROATED HUMMINGBIRD
Archilochus colubris

The westernmost edge of the breeding region for this hummingbird extends into east Texas.

Field marks: Male has green cap and back, black bar through eye under cap, bright red throat, white breast, green sides, gray wings, gray and black tail with white wing tips. Female lacks the red throat.

Size: L: 3"–3.75", WS: 4.5"

Similar species: Rufous hummingbird has a bright orange throat and underside, orange at base of the tail.

Season: Summer throughout east Texas; spring and fall migration down the center of the state

Habitat: Backyards, parks, other areas with nectar-producing flowers; open woodlands

Food source: Nectar from flowers, including petunias, fuchsia, and cardinal flower; some insects

Nest: Fastened to a tree branch with spiderweb silk

Call: Tiny, squeaky chip note repeated in rapid succession, sometimes in quick triplets

Hot spots: Any east Texas backyard with a hummingbird feeder with clean, fresh nectar may attract this bird, but here are some parks that have sightings throughout the summer: Gulf Coast Bird Observatory, Lake Jackson, 29.0464812 / -95.4757787; Leach Gardens, Texas A&M University, College Station, 30.6069862 / -96.3516867; White Rock Lake & Old Fish Hatchery, Dallas, 32.8156276 / -96.7264652; Tyler State Park, Tyler, 32.4799358 / -95.2991867; Lake Bob Sandlin State Park, Blodgett, 33.0555798 / -95.0936222.

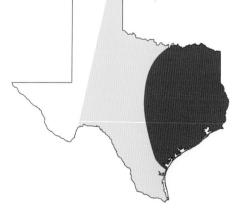

BLACK-CHINNED HUMMINGBIRD
Archilochus alexandri

One of the most common hummingbirds in the Southwest, this male bird's throat glows bright purple under its black chin.

Field marks: Bright green body in both sexes, with slightly decurved bill. Male has dark head, black chin, purple gorget, white chest, grayish-white belly, fan tail with green base, black band, white tips. Female has gray-green head, white throat and chest.

Size: L: 3.75", WS: 4.75"

Similar species: Ruby-throated hummingbird has bright red gorget. Buff-bellied hummingbird has all-green head, green throat, buff-colored belly, red bill with dark tip.

Season: Summer

Habitat: In desert and canyons where there are tall trees

Food source: Flower nectar, sugar water from feeders, small insects

Nest: A tiny cup made from spiderwebs and other fine fibers, usually about 6 feet off the ground in a tree or tall shrub.

Call: A quick, reverberating buzz, repeated while in flight

Hot spots: These hummers come readily to clean feeders with fresh nectar, so look for parks with feeders. Easy places to see them include Estero Llano Grande State Park World Birding Center, Llano Grande, 26.1268335 / -97.9578167; Bentsen–Rio Grande Valley State Park/World Birding Center, Mission, 26.1849709 / -98.3793885; Falcon State Park, Roma, 26.5836148 / -99.1452921; Garner State Park, Concan, 29.587714 / -99.7373199; Davis Mountains State Park, primitive area, Fort Davis, 30.60079 / -103.92579.

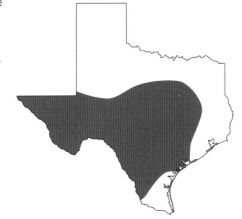

BUFF-BELLIED HUMMINGBIRD
Amazilia yucatanensis

Look for the bright red bill and buff-colored belly of this south Texas specialty.

Field marks: Blue-green back and head, bright blue-green throat and breast in sunlight (otherwise grayish), red bill with dark tip, buff belly, rufous tail. Males and females are similar. Somewhat larger than other local hummers.

Size: L: 4.25", WS: 5.75"

Similar species: Closest to a berylline hummingbird, which is virtually unheard of in south Texas.

Season: Winter along the Gulf coast; year-round in southernmost Rio Grande Valley

Habitat: Parks, gardens, shrubby lowlands

Food source: Flower nectar, feeder nectar, and small insects

Nest: A tiny cup of plant fibers, flower petals, lichen, moss, and spiderwebs; in a tree about 10 feet off the ground

Call: A high-pitched, dry, insect-like *tk, tk* or *tsp*, or a rapid *si-si-si-si-sp*

Hot spots: Hugh Ramsey Park, Harlingen, 26.1857402 / -97.6641657; Quinta Mazatlan World Birding Center, McAllen, 26.176876 / -98.2309932; Bentsen–Rio Grande Valley State Park/World Birding Center, Mission, 26.1849709 / -98.3793885; Frontera Audubon Center, Weslaco, 26.1479755 / -97.9897937; South Padre Island Birding and Nature Center, 26.1374628 / -97.1739367.

RUFOUS HUMMINGBIRD
Selasphorus rufus

This hummingbird is distinctive among Texas birds with the male's orange head, gorget, belly, and tail.

Field marks: Adult male has an orange head, gorget, back, belly, and undertail, with a white chest and green upper wings, tapering to dark wing feathers. Female has a green cap and back, with pale orange flanks, a white throat and chest, and an orange-to-red spot at the base of the throat.

Size: L: 3.75", WS: 4.5"

Similar species: Allen's hummingbird, not usually found in Texas, is nearly identical but slightly smaller, with a shorter tail.

Season: Migration, with some localized overwintering populations in cities in east Texas

Habitat: Parks, yards, areas with low shrubs, some woodlands

Food source: Flower nectar, feeder nectar, some small insects

Nest: A tiny cup made from plant materials and spiderwebs, high up in a conifer or maple tree (not in Texas)

Call: A series of *tchp-tchp-tchp* notes as a warning call, or an insect-like buzz followed by a second of high-pitched chatter. The motor-like sound you may hear is the humming of their wings, one of the loudest among North American hummingbirds.

Hot spots: Big Bend National Park, Chisos Mountains area trails, 29.2699985 / -103.3004522; Christmas Mountains Oasis, Alpine, 29.4917768 / -103.4670389; Davis Mountains State Park, primitive area, Fort Davis, 30.60079 / -103.92579; Lawrence E. Wood Picnic Area and Madera Canyon Trail, Davis Mountains Preserve, 30.7063007 / -104.1054001; San Antonio Botanical Garden (winter only), San Antonio, 29.4601113 / -98.4572897.

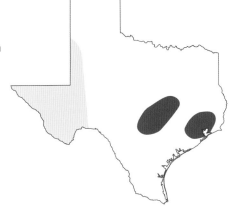

KINGFISHERS

BELTED KINGFISHER
Megaceryle alcyon

Hunting over moving streams, rivers, ponds, and lakes, this easily recognized kingfisher can be fascinating to watch.

Field marks: Male has blue crest and face to just below the long bill, white collar, blue breastband over white breast, blue wings and back, white underside, blue tail with white bands. Female has a rust-colored band below the blue breastband, and some rust on flanks under the wings.

Size: L: 12"–14", WS: 20"–24"

Similar species: Ringed kingfisher is larger with a much longer, heavier bill, and a solid chestnut belly and flanks.

Season: Year-round in northern Texas; winter in far western and south Texas

Habitat: Ponds, lakes, rivers, streams, saltwater waterways

Food source: Fish, mollusks, crustaceans, reptiles, amphibians, small mammals

Nest: Adults dig a tunnel in a riverbank and lay the eggs at the far end.

Call: Long, loud rattling *ak-ak-ak-ak-ak*, often in flight

Hot spots: Just about every pond and lake in Texas has a belted kingfisher in season; if you don't have luck close to home, kingfishers are well known to favor these spots: Roy G. Guerrero Colorado River Metro Park, Austin, 30.246172 / -97.7049763; Village Creek Drying Beds, Arlington, 32.7842795 / -97.1266181; Dallas Southside Wastewater Treatment Plant, Dallas, 32.6456988 / -96.6391754; Mitchell Lake Audubon Center, San Antonio, 29.3105956 / -98.4996938; Hazel Bazemore Park Hawkwatch platform, Corpus Christi, 27.8660551 / -97.6427346.

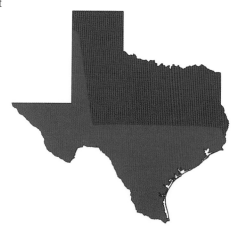

RINGED KINGFISHER
Megaceryle torquata

Much larger than a belted kingfisher, this bird of Central and South America has made the Lower Rio Grande Valley part of its range.

Field marks: Dark blue crest and head; very large, bulky bill; white neckband, dark blue body and tail with all-chestnut underside. Females have dark blue breast above chestnut belly.

Size: L: 11"–14", WS: 25"

Similar species: Belted kingfisher is smaller with a lighter, smaller bill, and a white chest and belly (females have a rusty band across the chest).

Season: Year-round

Habitat: Freshwater lakes, ponds, and rivers with perches above (trees or wires) where they can watch for fish

Food source: Fish, reptiles, amphibians, crustaceans

Nest: Burrowed deep into a riverbank well above the water

Call: A long, low, rapid rattle

Hot spots: University of Texas Resaca Habitat, Rio Grande Valley, Brownsville, 25.8939907 / -97.4889322; Bentsen–Rio Grande Valley State Park/World Birding Center, Mission, 26.1849709 / -98.3793885; Salineño Wildlife Preserve, Roma, 26.5148584 / -99.116206; Las Palmas Trail and Zacate Creek, Laredo, 27.4994356 / -99.4944084; Max A. Mandel Golf Course, Laredo, 27.660146 / -99.66685.

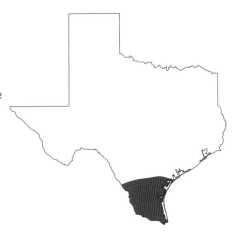

GREEN KINGFISHER
Chloroceryle americana

This small, comparatively quiet kingfisher's green mantle masks it in dense foliage, making it easy to miss.

Field marks: Green above with a dark green head and crest and a large, heavy bill; lines of white spots on wings, white neckband, and a chestnut breast and underside. Female has two green bands across the breast.

Size: L: 11"–12", WS: 11"

Similar species: Belted kingfisher is dark blue with a smaller bill. Ringed kingfisher has the chestnut underside but is much larger and blue overall with a heavier bill.

Season: Year-round

Habitat: Freshwater rivers, lakes, ponds, or streams with tall foliage and plenty of perches for hunting

Food source: Fish

Nest: In a burrow dug in a riverbank, well above the water

Call: A series of high-pitched, rattling clicks, much quieter than ringed or belted kingfishers

Hot spots: Las Palmas Trail and Zacate Creek, Laredo, 27.4994356 / -99.4944084; Salineño Wildlife Preserve, Roma, 26.5148584 / -99.116206; Bentsen–Rio Grande Valley State Park/World Birding Center, Mission, 26.1849709 / -98.3793885; Anzalduas Park, Mission, 26.1384105 / -98.3327866; Hugh Ramsey Park, Harlingen, 26.1857402 / -97.6641657; Estero Llano Grande State Park World Birding Center, Llano Grande, 26.1268335 / -97.9578167.

WOODPECKERS

RED-HEADED WOODPECKER
Melanerpes erythrocephalus

The only woodpecker with an all-red head, this charismatic resident populates Texas's eastern forests.

Field marks: Bright red head, long gray bill, navy blue back and wings with large white patches on wings, white breast and underside, dark blue tail.

Size: L: 8.5"–9.5", WS: 16"–18"

Similar species: Red-bellied woodpecker has a red stripe at the back of the head, a buff face, and black and white–barred wings.

Season: Year-round in the east; winter toward central Texas

Habitat: Open woodlands

Food source: Insects, invertebrates, nuts, seeds, berries

Nest: Cavity in a tree excavated by the woodpecker.

Call: A low rattling trill, followed by a higher one; also a single-note *wurr*

Hot spots: Any east Texas park with mature trees can attract red-headed woodpeckers. Here are some year-round favorites: Tyler State Park, Tyler, 32.4799358 / -95.2991867; Gus Engling Wildlife Management Area, Bethel, 31.9297289 / -95.8876419; Huntsville State Park, Huntsville, 30.6150161 / -95.5333328; Bear Creek Park, Houston, 29.8247288 / -95.6288409; Big Thicket National Preserve, Kountze, 30.4621326 / -94.3512954.

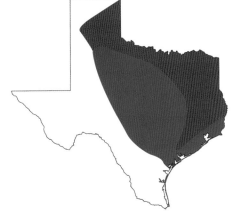

RED-BELLIED WOODPECKER
Melanerpes carolinus

A year-round resident, this midsize woodpecker with a bright red cap readily comes to suet and peanut feeders.

Field marks: Male has red cap extending from bill to shoulder; buff face, breast, and underside; black and white–barred back and wings, black trailing edge and wing primaries, white rump, black and white tail. Female's cap begins at the top of the head, leaving a buff forehead.

Size: L: 9"–10", WS: 16"–18"

Similar species: Yellow-bellied sapsucker has red cap, but its nape is white and it has a distinctive black and white facial pattern. Northern flicker has brown back with black barring, considerable spotting on buff breast, black bib, and gray cap with small red spot.

Season: Year-round in east Texas

Habitat: Open woodlands, parks, backyards

Food source: Insects, seeds, fruit, suet, tree sap

Nest: In a tree cavity excavated by the pair or used in previous years by other woodpeckers

Call: Simple, mid-pitched *quirr* is most familiar; also chattering *kik-kik-kik-kik-kik*

Hot spots: Red-bellied woodpeckers are everywhere in east Texas. Any wooded area has at least a family of woodpeckers, and a morning walk along a forest trail may reveal half a dozen individuals or more. Active and expressive, they make themselves known with considerable movement up tree trunks and with their easily recognizable calls. If you feed birds with suet or peanuts in your yard, you are nearly certain to attract these birds.

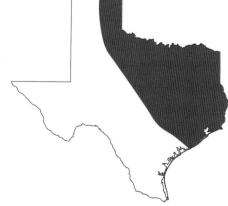

YELLOW-BELLIED SAPSUCKER
Sphyrapicus varius

A winter resident, this is the only sapsucker in its Texas range—so there's no confusion with the very similar red-naped sapsucker, which is found in far west Texas.

Field marks: Male has red forehead, bold black and white facial pattern, red throat with black border, black and white–barred back and wings, wide white stripe on wings, white rump, black and white–barred tail. Female has a white throat and some buff color on nape and breast.

Size: L: 8"–9", WS: 16"–17"

Similar species: Red-bellied woodpecker has a buff face and breast, and more red on the back of the head. Downy woodpecker is smaller and has a wide white area on its back. Hairy woodpecker is slightly larger and has a wide white stripe on its back.

Season: Winter

Habitat: Deciduous woods

Food source: Tree sap, berries, insects

Nest: In a tree cavity the pair excavates (not in Texas)

Call: High, nasal, single note: *pee-ow*; a rapid rattling *wikka-wikka-wikka* when confronted

Hot spots: Sapsuckers may be found in any leafy woods, but the areas noted here have multiple birds that remain throughout the winter: Lewisville Lake Environmental Learning Area, Lewisville, 33.0662579 / -96.9750008; Jesse H. Jones County Park, Houston, 30.024 / -95.295; Cullinan Park, Sugar Land, 29.6355459 / -95.6603193; San Antonio Botanical Garden, San Antonio, 29.4601113 / -98.4572897; Abilene State Park/Lake Abilene, Buffalo Gap, 32.2316256 / -99.8920619.

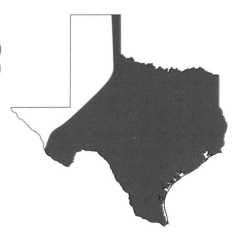

DOWNY WOODPECKER
Dryobates pubescens

The smallest woodpecker in North America is also one of the most common, coming readily to feeders and nesting in neighborhoods with large trees.

Field marks: Male has black and white head with red spot on back of crown, small bill with white tuft at its base, black wings barred in white, large white patch on back, white breast and underside, dark tail. Female is identical but lacks the red spot.

Size: L: 6.75", WS: 11"–12"

Similar species: Hairy woodpecker is larger and has bill about twice the length.

Season: Year-round in northeast Texas and in the panhandle

Habitat: Deciduous forests, parks and backyards with leafy trees

Food source: Seeds, suet, nuts, insects

Nest: In a natural or excavated hole in a tree

Call: Elongated, descending *ti-ti-Tl-ti-ti-ti-ti-ti*; alternate is a high-pitched, one-note *tik*.

Hot spots: Downy woodpeckers are very common and easily spotted in any area with a healthy stand of trees. Look for them in your local parks, woodlands, or backyards with mature trees in your neighborhood, or attract them to your own backyard with a suet or peanut feeder.

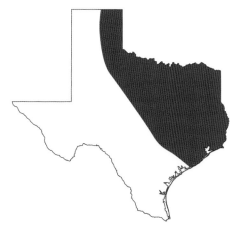

HAIRY WOODPECKER
Dryobates villosus

Larger than a downy with a longer bill, hairy woodpeckers are otherwise nearly identical to the smaller bird. Vocal cues can help determine which is which.

Field marks: Male has black and white head with red spot on back of crown, long bill, black wings barred in white, large white patch on back, white breast and underside, dark tail. Female is identical but lacks the red spot.

Size: L: 9"–10", WS: 15"–17"

Similar species: Downy woodpecker is smaller and has a shorter bill, scattered black spots on the white outer tail feathers.

Season: Year-round

Habitat: Deciduous forests, parks, and neighborhoods with stands of mature trees

Food source: Spongy moth caterpillars, spiders, insects, berries, seeds, nuts, suet

Nest: In a natural or excavated hole in a tree

Call: A single *pik*, followed by a long, high-pitched rattle; also *weeka, weeka, weeka*, like a squeaky wheel

Hot spots: Tyler State Park, Tyler, 32.4799358 / -95.2991867; Lewisville Lake Environmental Learning Area, Lewisville, 33.0662579 / -96.9750008; Clear Creek Natural Heritage Center, Denton, 33.2591514 / -97.0633574; Daingerfield State Park, Daingerfield, 33.0060723 / -94.6959043; Lake McClellan, Alanreed, 35.2114047 / -100.8720016.

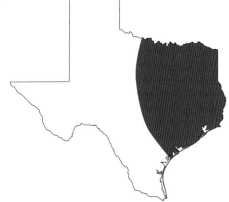

RED-COCKADED WOODPECKER
Dryobates borealis

Once common, this southeastern specialty now confines itself to the few areas in east Texas that have stands of healthy old-growth longleaf, loblolly, and slash pine.

Field marks: Black cap and bold black and white facial pattern with a bright white cheek, dark bill, black and white ladder pattern on back and wings, mottled black and white breast, white underside with faint streaks, black tail. Males have a nearly indistinguishable red line at the top of the white cheek.

Size: L: 8"–9", WS: 14"–14.5"

Similar species: Downy and hairy woodpeckers have a red dot on the back of the head (males), and a wide white stripe down the back. Yellow-bellied sapsucker has a red stripe on top of the head and a black stripe through the eye, dividing the white facial pattern.

Season: Year-round in a limited area of east Texas

Habitat: Old-growth pine forests with a clear understory from repeated fires

Food source: Insects that live under the bark on pine trees

Nest: In colonies in clusters of pine trees in excavated holes in the trees

Call: A tumble of rapid, squeaky chatter when it arrives in its nesting area, as well as a high, one-syllable *chit*

Hot spots: Sam Houston National Forest, Lone Star Trailhead #6, Conroe, 30.5270811 / -95.6301433; W. G. Jones State Forest, Conroe, 30.235563 / -95.4852676; Boykin Springs, Jasper County, Beans, 31.0595928 / -94.2749289; Angelina National Forest, Westwood, 31.0796493 / -94.1645694; Fairchild State Forest, Maydelle, 31.7817362 / -95.3628731.

LADDER-BACKED WOODPECKER
Dryobates scalaris

The ladder-backed is one of only a few woodpeckers found living in the desert and using cacti and arid-land shrubs as its home.

Field marks: Bright red cap, sometimes rising to form a crest (black in females); black and white–striped face with long, straight, pointed bill; black and white horizontal stripes across the back, wings, and tail; white underside with fine black streaks. Female nearly identical, but with no red.

Size: L: 6"–7", WS: 13"

Similar species: Downy woodpecker is smaller, has a shorter bill, and does not have the ladder of stripes across its back. Hairy woodpecker is larger and, like the downy, has a wide white patch on its back instead of the ladder of stripes.

Season: Year-round in central and west Texas

Habitat: Desert scrub and arid forests; also some pine and piñon-juniper woodlands

Food source: Insect larvae or adult insects dug out of tree or cactus branches and trunks

Nest: In a cavity the bird excavates in a tree, usually at least 10 feet off the ground

Call: A single *pik*, or a series of fast *piks* in one phrase

Hot spots: Ladder-backs come to feeders, especially where suet is served, so try attracting them to your yard if you live in their range. Most arid landscapes with cacti and mesquite will provide great looks at this bird, but here are some very dependable spots: Big Bend National Park, Cottonwood Campground, 29.1366997 / -103.5220032; Fort Peña Colorado Park, Marathon, 30.152997 / -103.2874735; South Llano River State Park, Junction, 30.4391651 / -99.8128617; Aquarena Springs, San Marcos, 29.8932402 / -97.9297458; Mae Simmons Park, Lubbock, 33.5752826 / -101.8240776.

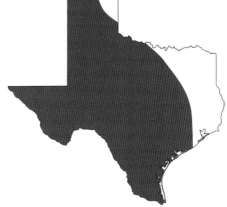

GOLDEN-FRONTED WOODPECKER
Melanerpes aurifrons

A gold dot at the base of the bill, another on the nape, and a brush of gold on the belly give this striking woodpecker its name.

Field marks: Tawny gray head, chest, and underside; red eye, yellow patch at base of strong bill, red forehead patch on males (absent in females), yellow nape; black and white back and wings with slim horizontal stripes, stiff black tail; white rump visible in flight.

Size: L: 9"–10", WS: 16.5"–17.5"

Similar species: Red-bellied woodpecker has an all-red cap (in males) and a pink wash over its belly. Gila woodpecker lacks the yellow patches on its head, but the male has a red forehead patch; the Gila has a black and white–striped rump patch. Northern flicker (red-shafted race) has a pronounced black chest patch, a spotted breast and underside, no forehead or crown patches, and a red stripe from throat to bill (males).

Season: Year-round in central and southwest Texas

Habitat: Arid woodlands and brushy areas with low trees; also riparian areas and parks

Food source: Insects, nuts, fruits, spiders, small reptiles

Nest: In a tree cavity, at least 6 feet off the ground

Call: A descending *churrrrr*, or a single or repeated series of *chuk* calls

Hot spots: Widespread and very common the farther south you go, this woodpecker is easy to find. Not only are its numbers large wherever there are trees, but it comes readily to feeders serving seed, fruit, or suet. Any park or wildlife refuge in south Texas will have its own population.

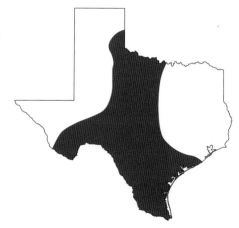

ACORN WOODPECKER
Melanerpes formicivorus

The clownish facial markings and acorn-gathering behavior of these gregarious birds makes them a stand-out among woodpeckers.

Field marks: Black and white face with a bright red cap (black in females, with red on the back of the head only), white eye and sturdy black bill; black back, tail, and breast; white underside with fine black streaks.

Size: L: 7.5"–9", WS: 14"–17"

Similar species: While acorn woodpeckers are distinctive in their limited region in Texas, yellow-bellied sapsucker may overlap in winter; this bird has a black and white mottled back, black and white stripes on the face instead of a clown mask, and a red throat.

Season: Year-round in Big Bend National Park and the area just north

Habitat: Woodlands with plenty of oaks, from which they gather acorns throughout the year; they also gather piñon pine nuts and other tree nuts when available.

Food source: Nuts, especially acorns, and also come to feeders; suck the flowing sap from trees in spring

Nest: In cavities they excavate in living or dead trees. They will return to the same holes for years.

Call: A loud, repeated, rising, squeaky *whokka-whokka-whokka*; also some chattering calls

Hot spots: Big Bend National Park, Chisos Mountains area trails, 29.2699985 / -103.3004522; Christmas Mountains Oasis, Alpine, 29.4917768 / -103.4670389; Davis Mountains Preserve, Tobe Canyon, 30.6461274 / -104.1792727; Davis Mountains State Park, primitive area, Fort Davis, 30.60079 / -103.92579; Kokernot Municipal Park, Alpine, 30.3712753 / -103.6620871.

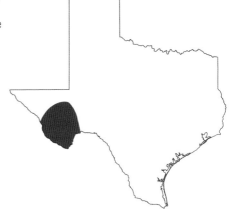

NORTHERN FLICKER
Colaptes auratus

Of the two races of northern flickers found across the country, the Texas variety is the yellow-shafted flicker. The yellow underwing offers proof of this.

Field marks: Yellow-shafted male has gray head, light brown face, red spot on back of head, black malar stripe, black eye, long bill. Red-shafted race has brown and gray head, a red streak from bill to throat. Both have a buff breast with many black spots, black bib at throat; back and wings are light brown and heavily barred with black; white rump is visible in flight. Tail is black with white barring. Female lacks red spot and black malar. Red-shafted race shows red underside of tail; yellow-shafted race has a golden undertail.

Size: L: 12"–14", WS: 19"–21"

Similar species: Yellow-bellied sapsucker has red throat and no brown areas. Golden-fronted woodpecker has no spots on the chest or belly, a bright yellow spot at the base of the bill, and a yellow spot at the nape; males have a red spot over the yellow bill spot.

Season: Year-round in northeast Texas and the panhandle; winter otherwise

Habitat: Open woodlands and edges, parks with mature trees, neighborhoods

Food source: Ants and other insects, fruit and berries, suet, nuts, sunflower seed from feeders

Nest: In a tree cavity or a hole in a utility pole; also in man-made birdhouses

Call: A rapid, repeated *flicker-flicker-flicker-flicker*, also a squeakier *wikka-wikka-wikka* call while interacting with other birds

Hot spots: Nearly every forest, park with mature trees, and neighborhood has a pair or colony of flickers within it. Flickers come to suet and nut feeders, especially platform feeders that allow them to stand horizontally and eat rather than perching or grabbing the mesh of a cage feeder. They are also seen frequently feeding on the ground after a rain, when ants are forced out of their nests.

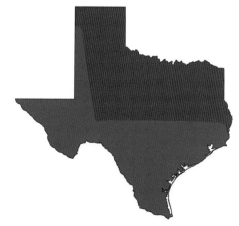

PILEATED WOODPECKER
Dryocopus pileatus

When a pileated woodpecker arrives, it feels like an event. This large, colorful, charismatic bird entertains onlookers as it aggressively excavates a hole in a tree or dines at a suet feeder.

Field marks: Bright red crest, extending down the forehead in males; black and white face with black line through the eye, red malar stripe in males, white throat, black breast with white line extending from head, black underside, black wings with white secondaries, black tail.

Size: L: 16.5"–19.5", WS: 28"–30"

Similar species: No other woodpecker is as large. Acorn woodpecker has a more clownish appearance and lacks the long neck and giant crest.

Season: Year-round

Habitat: Forests of mature trees

Food source: Insect larvae, ants, fruit, nuts

Nest: In a large, excavated hole in a tree, usually about 10 to 15 feet up

Call: Loud *fluk-fluk-fluk-fluk-fluk*, much like a flicker but slower and lower-pitched

Hot spots: These big, striking birds frequent suet feeders in backyards and announce themselves in wooded areas throughout east Texas. Here are five places where you'll find the search particularly easy: Rochester Park, Texas Buckeye Trail, Dallas, 32.7333097 / -96.7529165; Tyler State Park, Tyler, 32.4799358 / -95.2991867; Angelina National Forest, Westwood, 31.0796493 / -94.1645694; Davy Crockett National Forest, Ratcliff Lake, 31.3883733 / -95.1549911; Mitchell Nature Preserve, The Woodlands, 30.1612322 / -95.5199432.

FLYCATCHERS

EASTERN WOOD-PEWEE
Contopus virens

This common summer resident breeds in hardwood forests as far south as San Antonio, and passes through southeast Texas during migration. Listen for the call that gives the bird its name.

Field marks: Gray head with crest, thin eye ring, gray back, black wings with clearly visible white wing bars, grayish breast resembling a vest, yellowish underside, white undertail coverts, long dark tail.

Size: L: 6.25", WS: 10"

Similar species: Eastern phoebe is darker and stockier overall. Willow and alder flycatchers are smaller with brighter wing bars and whiter underside. Western wood-pewee is nearly identical, but the two birds' ranges barely overlap in Texas.

Season: Spring through fall in east Texas; spring and fall migration along the southeastern coast

Habitat: Hardwood forests, parks, suburban neighborhoods with mature trees

Food source: Flying insects

Nest: Built on the end of a tree branch

Call: A single *peeeoowee*, or repeated *peee-wee*, rising at the end

Hot spots: Lake Bob Sandlin State Park, Blodgett, 33.0555798 / -95.0936222; Lake o' the Pines, Rock Springs, 32.7984553 / -94.5892366; Tyler State Park, Tyler, 32.4799358 / -95.2991867; Fairchild State Forest, Maydelle, 31.7817362 / -95.3628731; Russ Pitman Park and Nature Discovery Center, Bellaire, 29.6995225 / -95.4516547.

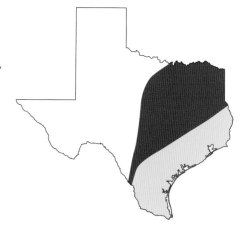

EASTERN PHOEBE

Sayornis phoebe

Like a flycatcher but larger, phoebes make themselves known with their tail-flicking behavior and distinctive song.

Field marks: Dark gray head, black bill, lighter gray nape and back, gray-smudged breast, pale yellowish underside, gray wings with no wing bars; long, straight tail.

Size: L: 7", WS: 10.5"–11.5"

Similar species: Eastern wood-pewee is smaller and lighter colored. Eastern kingbird has a darker head, back, and wings, and a white band at the end of the tail. Black phoebe has an all-black head, back, throat, breast, and tail. Say's phoebe is grayer overall, with a peach wash over the belly.

Season: Year-round in northeast and north-central Texas; winter in west and south Texas, as well as along the southeastern shore

Habitat: Woodlands near open grasslands, pastures, or farms; suburban neighborhoods

Food source: Flying insects, berries, small fish caught from the water's surface

Nest: Glued with mud to the side of a building, or in a tree on top of an old nest

Call: A high, hoarse *PHEE-bee*, or quieter *tu-oo*

Hot spots: Eastern phoebe is among the most common birds in Texas woodlands and pastures. Any walk in the woods will yield at least one phoebe sighting, especially in the hill country or in city parks in heavily populated areas; a focused birding day may turn up several.

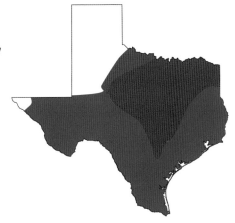

BLACK PHOEBE
Sayornis nigricans

Remarkably easy to see, this phoebe sits on fence posts and low in dead snags and shows off its black breast and bright white belly.

Field marks: All-black head, eye, bill, back, wings, breast, and tail; bright white belly and undertail coverts.

Size: L: 6"–6.5", WS: 11"

Similar species: Eastern phoebe is grayer overall and has a white breast and belly. Say's phoebe is grayer and has a peach-colored underside.

Season: Year-round

Habitat: Stream and riverbanks, beaches, and other shorelines

Food source: Insects of many kinds

Nest: A cup made of mud. They prefer to build low in a tree or against a rock face turned away from wind, but they have adapted to nest in man-made structures, so they can often be observed in the eaves of park shelters or under bridges.

Call: Repeated, wheezy *tee-who, tee-wee* notes; also a short, dry *zip*, especially in flight

Hot spots: Ewald Kipp Way, El Paso, 31.785065 / -106.527189; Lawrence E. Wood Picnic Area and Madera Canyon Trail, Davis Mountains Preserve, 30.7063007 / -104.1054001; TX 118 rest area, 7 miles southeast of Fort Davis, 30.5276479 / -103.8233033; Fort Peña Colorado Park, Marathon, 30.152997 / -103.2874735; Big Bend National Park, Rio Grande Village, 29.1809226 / -102.9557133.

SAY'S PHOEBE
Sayornis saya

It's easy to distinguish a Say's phoebe from other gray songbirds—look for the long tail and orangey underparts.

Field marks: Soft brown above from bill to rump, with a larger head than other local phoebes; grayish breast and peach-colored belly and undertail coverts; long tail in a darker brown than the body.

Size: L: 6.5"–7.5", WS: 13"

Similar species: Eastern phoebe is grayer with a white breast and underside. Black phoebe is black above with a black breast and bright white underside. Female vermilion flycatcher is smaller and darker above with a white eyebrow, white breast, and rosy belly.

Season: Year-round in southwest Texas; winter in central Texas and the Lower Rio Grande Valley; migrating through the panhandle with some summer residents in the north

Habitat: Arid, flat areas with low vegetation or none at all, often at high elevations up to 9,000 feet

Food source: Insects, caught on the ground and in the air

Nest: A sheltered spot on a ledge or in a cave, or on a man-made structure—under a bridge or inside a shed or barn

Call: A drawn-out whistle like a dial telephone, or a series of chattery notes, often repeated for some time

Hot spots: Say's phoebes are common in south and southwest Texas, so you are likely to see them in any park. Here are some places where they congregate: Keystone Heritage Park, El Paso, 31.8209406 / -106.5630008; Davis Mountains State Park, Fort Davis, 30.60079 / -103.92579; Fort Peña Colorado Park, Marathon, 30.152997 / -103.2874735; Salineño Wildlife Preserve, Roma, 26.5148584 / -99.116206; Anzalduas Park, Mission, 26.1384105 / -98.3327866.

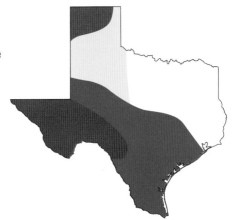

VERMILION FLYCATCHER
Pyrocephalus rubinus

The most brilliantly colored western flycatcher breeds in west Texas and lives year-round along the Rio Grande Valley.

Field marks: Male has a bright crimson head, throat, breast, and underside; a black band through the eye and a thin black bill; black back, wings, and tail. Female has a gray crown and cheek with a white face and thin black eye band, white breast streaked with gray, pink vent and undertail coverts, gray back and wings, black tail. Juvenile looks like female, but with no pink.

Size: L: 6", WS: 10"

Similar species: Scarlet tanager is larger and all red with black wings; only crosses paths with vermilion flycatcher briefly during migration. Summer tanager has no black areas. Northern cardinal is larger and all red with a black area around the bill.

Season: Year-round in some areas of the Rio Grande, winter in southeast Texas, summer in southwest Texas

Habitat: Open grassland with streams, near deciduous trees

Food source: Flying insects

Nest: In trees near streams

Call: A series of tiny notes, speeding up and ending in a brisk trill, *pi-pi-pi-piiiitashee*

Hot spots: Campgrounds and parks with water features and leafy trees attract lots of vermilion flycatchers. Here are some very dependable spots: Big Bend National Park, Rio Grande Village, 29.1809226 / -102.9557133; Cook's Slough Nature Center, Uvalde, 29.1873567 / -99.7886572; University of Texas Rio Grande Valley, Resaca Habitat, Brownsville, 25.8939907 / -97.4889322; Estero Llano Grande State Park World Birding Center, Llano Grande, 26.1268335 / -97.9578167; Bentsen–Rio Grande Valley State Park/World Birding Center, Mission, 26.1849709 / -98.3793885.

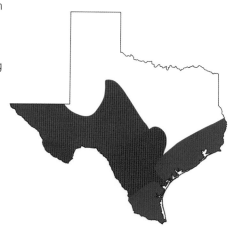

ASH-THROATED FLYCATCHER
Myiarchus cinerascens

This bird of brushy habitats is nearly indistinguishable from brown-crested flycatcher except by song.

Field marks: Brownish-gray head and back, gray bill, grayish "ashy" throat and breast, very pale yellow wash on underside, light brown wings with pale beige-to-white wing bars and rufous primaries, rufous stripe down center of the tail with a grayish tail tip.

Size: L: 8.5", WS: 12"

Similar species: Brown-crested flycatcher is nearly identical, but slightly larger with a heavier bill and less gray in the throat. Where these two birds' territory overlaps in southernmost Texas, song is the best way to tell them apart.

Season: Summer

Habitat: Wide-open areas like dry scrublands and deserts

Food source: Insects, spiders, some fruit and berries

Nest: In holes that occur naturally in trees or left behind by other birds and animals

Call: Sharp, high-pitched, trilling *ka-cheer*, also a single *pritt*

Hot spots: Falcon State Park, Roma, 26.5836148 / -99.1452921; Las Palmas Trail and Zacate Creek, Laredo, 27.4994356 / -99.4944084; Joshua Springs Park, Nelson City, 29.8846717 / -98.8185453; Devils River State Natural Area, Del Rio, 29.9406182 / -100.9710073; Balmorhea Lake, Balmorhea, 30.9583956 / -103.7123108.

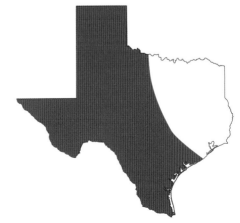

BROWN-CRESTED FLYCATCHER
Myiarchus tyrannulus

Difficult to tell from an ash-throated flycatcher, this brown, white, and yellow bird is most easily differentiated by its song.

Field marks: Brown crest, back, and wings; heavy bill, whitish throat and breast, light yellow wash on the underparts, rufous wing primaries and tail.

Size: L: 8"–9", WS: 13"

Similar species: Ash-throated flycatcher has less rufous in the tail, more gray at the throat, and is slimmer. Great-crested flycatcher has a gray face and throat, brighter yellow on the belly.

Season: Summer

Habitat: Deserts with saguaro cactus and wooded areas along rivers and streams

Food source: Insects caught in flight

Nest: In a natural tree cavity or one excavated by large woodpeckers (In their Texas range, they share territory with golden-fronted woodpeckers to use their abandoned cavities.)

Call: A trilled *whid-de-whid-de-woo*, spiraling down at the end; also a one-note raspy *beer*, repeated in a slow descent, and a single *whit*, rising at the end

Hot spots: Hugh Ramsey Park, Harlingen, 26.1857402 / -97.6641657; Lower Rio Grande Valley National Wildlife Refuge, Linn, 26.5127827 / -98.0463192; Rincon del Diablo (near Magnolia and Barron Streets), Del Rio, 29.350534 / -100.8931965; Mitchell Lake Audubon Center, San Antonio, 29.3105956 / -98.4996938; Riverside Park, Victoria, 28.8101559 / -97.0273025.

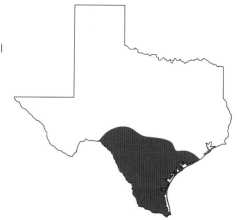

WESTERN KINGBIRD
Tyrannus verticalis

This western bird of open lands shows up on utility wires and fence posts throughout the summer.

Field marks: Gray head and back, small bill, grayish-white throat and breast, yellow underside, greenish-gray back, gray wings and tail with white tail edges in fresh adult plumage.

Size: L: 8.5"–9", WS: 15"–16"

Similar species: Tropical kingbird is slightly larger and has a large, heavy bill. Cassin's kingbird has a darker gray head and chest, white-tipped tail feathers. Couch's kingbird has a yellow chest all the way to the neck, no white on the tail.

Season: Summer

Habitat: Open grassland near woodlands, often seen perched on a fence post or rail

Food source: Insects, some fruit

Nest: In deciduous trees

Call: Tiny *pit-pit-pit*, followed by a rapid burst: *de-WEE-di-ti-ti*

Hot spots: Western kingbirds are everywhere on the Texas plains, sitting on fences and grasping overhead wires as they watch for likely prey. Watch for them behaving like flycatchers, launching from a perch to grab insects in midair.

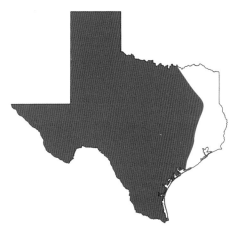

EASTERN KINGBIRD
Tyrannus tyrannus

A black, gray, and white bird of open grasslands, this kingbird is easily identified by the white tip of its tail.

Field marks: Black head, gray back, white throat, grayish breast, white underside, dark gray wings, long black tail with white tip.

Size: L: 8.5", WS: 14"–15"

Similar species: Eastern phoebe is smaller, darker, has a yellowish wash on its underparts; has no white tip on its tail.

Season: Summer in northeast Texas; migration in southeast

Habitat: Open grasslands, meadows, and farmland, where it often perches on fences and posts

Food source: Insects, berries, fruit

Nest: On a tree branch, or inside a barn or other structure

Call: Very high-pitched *dit-dit-dit-dit-dit-dit-derWEE, derWEE*; also a single *chee* note

Hot spots: Eastern kingbirds make themselves easy to see by perching on fences and fence posts, wires, the tops of buildings, and on top of shrubs, bobbing their white-tipped tails and singing almost continuously, especially in spring. Any drive through a rural area or a visit to a sanctuary or wildlife refuge with open fields will yield at least one sighting, probably a number of them.

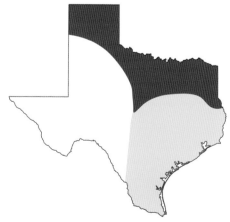

COUCH'S KINGBIRD
Tyrannus couchii

With its bright yellow underside extending all the way to its throat, Couch's kingbird can be sorted out from its western cousins.

Field marks: Gray head with heavy bill, olive back, brown wings and tail, solid yellow underside extending to the throat; long tail with pronounced notch.

Size: L: 7.5"–9.5", WS: 15"–16"

Similar species: Tropical kingbird is nearly identical, usually differentiated by song. Western kingbird has a gray chest, white outer tail feathers visible in flight.

Season: Year-round

Habitat: Riparian areas, woods with high perches along the edges of farm fields or pastures, areas with plenty of fruit trees

Food source: Insects and fruit

Nest: In twig and moss nests in trees, at least 20 feet up

Call: A series of *kweer* notes, followed by a chatter of several syllables

Hot spots: Devils River State Natural Area, Del Rio, 29.9406182 / -100.9710073; Lake Findley, Alice, 27.7888887 / -98.0641977; Hugh Ramsey Park, Harlingen, 26.1857402 / -97.6641657; Estero Llano Grande State Park World Birding Center, Llano Grande, 26.1268335 / -97.9578167; Bentsen–Rio Grande Valley State Park/World Birding Center, Mission, 26.1849709 / -98.3793885.

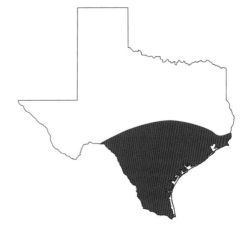

SCISSOR-TAILED FLYCATCHER
Tyrannus forficatus

Unique among North American flycatchers for its luxuriously long tail, this Southwestern bird graces nearly all of Texas throughout the summer.

Field marks: Pale gray overall with brown wings, pinkish flanks and undertail; very long, forked, black tail (longer than its body) with white edges. Pink underwing patches are visible when flying.

Size: L: 14"–15", WS: 14"–15"

Similar species: No other Texas species has this coloring or lengthy tail.

Season: Summer

Habitat: Open grassland with occasional trees and brush

Food source: Insects, some fruit during the winter

Nest: In a lone tree or shrub

Call: Squeaky chatter, sometimes continuous and sometimes in phrases

Hot spots: The way to see a scissor-tailed flycatcher is to drive through areas of open plains, agricultural fields, or other areas with utility poles and wires and low vegetation. These flycatchers perch on wires and other high structures and fly over fields all day as they catch insects on the wing. The majority of sightings of these birds are from a rural road, so drive slowly and keep an eye out.

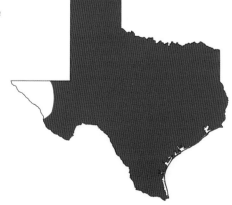

GREAT KISKADEE
Pitangus sulphuratus

The boldly patterned flycatcher with the onomatopoetic name is one of the most desired sightings for birders visiting south Texas.

Field marks: White face with a black cap and a wide black stripe from bill to nape; large, heavy bill; brown back, wings, and tail with rufous wash; bright yellow front from throat to undertail.

Size: L: 9"–10", WS: 15"

Similar species: Western and Couch's kingbirds lack the bold facial markings.

Season: Year-round in south Texas

Habitat: Several different kinds of forest, always near water; also suburban areas with fruit trees

Food source: Insects caught on the wing and foraged from the ground, small fish and other aquatic animals, small rodents, fruit on trees, cat and dog food in outdoor dishes, fruit from feeders

Nest: In the fork of a tree, usually on the edge of a forested area

Call: A three-syllable *WOW-wulla-wow*, which some early recorders described as *KISS-ka-dee*; also a high-pitched, one-syllable *yah*.

Hot spots: Kiskadees are a common sight in south Texas, with virtually guaranteed sightings at all the most productive Lower Rio Grande Valley stops: Bentsen–Rio Grande Valley State Park/World Birding Center, Mission, 26.1849709 / -98.3793885; Resaca de la Palma State Park/World Birding Center, Brownsville, 25.9965839 / -97.5690513; Hugh Ramsey Park, Harlingen, 26.1857402 / -97.6641657; Estero Llano Grande State Park World Birding Center, Llano Grande, 26.1268335 / -97.9578167; Salineño Wildlife Preserve, Roma, 26.5148584 / -99.116206.

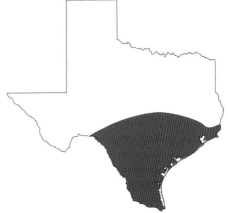

SHRIKE

LOGGERHEAD SHRIKE
Lanius ludovicianus

Common in Texas, this little bird of prey perches on fence posts and wires for easy viewing.

Field marks: Gray cap, wide black mask from ear to ear, white throat, grayish-white breast and underside, gray shoulders and back, black wings with conspicuous white spot, long black tail. Black bill has an obvious hook.

Size: L: 8.5"–9.5", WS 12"

Similar species: Northern mockingbird has a small black bill and no mask.

Season: Year-round

Habitat: Open areas with some trees and shrubs; usually found in or near farmlands and orchards

Food source: Insects, reptiles, amphibians, rodents, some birds

Nest: In trees or shrubs with thorns, or in large piles of brush or weeds

Call: Several variations: a harsh, buzzy *pffft*, a squeaky two-syllable *pi-TEET*, or a note filled with harmonics, followed by a high-pitched squeak.

Hot spots: Every agricultural area and wildlife refuge has its population of shrikes, making this one of the most common birds of prey in Texas. Watch the electrical wires for it when you drive along agricultural fields, open pastures, plains, or desert scrub. You should have little trouble getting a good look at this bird.

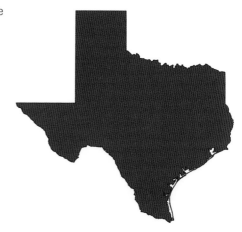

VIREOS

RED-EYED VIREO
Vireo olivaceus

The most common and widespread member of the vireo family is the only one in the area with a red eye.

Field marks: Gray cap with black border, white eyebrow, red eye with dark gray line through it, white throat and breast, light olive green back, pale yellow undertail coverts, olive tail.

Size: L: 6", WS: 10"

Similar species: Plumbeous vireo has distinct white "spectacles" around its black eyes. White-eyed vireo has yellow rings around its white eyes. Warbling vireo is smaller, and while it has similar but less prominent facial markings, it has a black eye and is more muted in color overall.

Season: Spring migration in southeast Texas and up the center of the state, summer throughout east Texas

Habitat: Deciduous woodlands

Food source: Insects, spongy moth caterpillars

Nest: On a tree branch, very close to the ground or as much as 60 feet up

Call: Repeated three-note phrases with a brief pause after each: *Here I am . . . where are you?*

Hot spots: Any woodland area with leafy trees is sure to contain at least one pair of red-eyed vireos. Try these forested areas: Big Thicket National Preserve, Kountze, 30.4621326 / -94.3512954; Davy Crockett National Forest, Ratcliff Lake, 31.3883733 / -95.1549911; Sam Houston National Forest, Conroe, 30.5270811 / -95.6301433; Boykin Springs, Jasper County, Beans, 31.0595928 / -94.2749289; Daingerfield State Park, Daingerfield, 33.0060723 / -94.6959043.

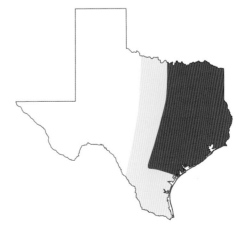

PLUMBEOUS VIREO
Vireo plumbeus

This is the least colorful of the three birds formerly known collectively as "solitary vireo," and the only one that breeds in west Texas.

Field marks: Small and uniformly gray overall with a white throat, breast, and underside; white eye rings that give the appearance of spectacles; two white bars on each wing, long tail.

Size: L: 4.5"–5.5", WS: 10"

Similar species: Cassin's vireo has yellow-tinged flanks and underbelly. Gray vireo lacks the spectacled look, and its wing bars are less noticeable.

Season: Spring and summer

Habitat: Forests at higher elevations in dry climates, starting at about 3,000 feet, as well as in riparian woodlands

Food source: Insects and fruit

Nest: A cuplike nest in a tree, usually tucked into a forked branch

Call: Like most vireos, the song is in short phrases with pauses between them: *tee-oo-wee* (pause), *tu-woo* (pause), with considerable variation.

Hot spots: Guadalupe Mountains National Park, Pine Springs, 31.9074905 / -104.8013279; Davis Mountains Preserve, Tobe Canyon, 30.6461274 / -104.1792727; Davis Mountains State Park, primitive area, Fort Davis, 30.60079 / -103.92579; Big Bend National Park, Chisos Mountains area trails, 29.2699985 / -103.3004522; Big Bend National Park, Cottonwood Campground, 29.1366997 / -103.5220032.

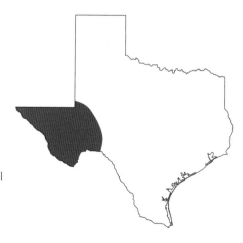

WHITE-EYED VIREO
Vireo griseus

Look for the bright yellow spectacles and white iris to make a positive identification of this small vireo.

Field marks: Gray head, yellow eye ring and lores, small black bill, white throat, yellow flanks, grayish underside, olive back and wings, two bright white wing bars.

Size: L: 5", WS: 7.5"–8"

Similar species: Plumbeous vireo has white spectacles and a blue head. Yellow-throated vireo also has yellow spectacles, but it has a bright yellow throat.

Season: Year-round in the southeast; spring and summer in central and northeastern Texas

Habitat: Ponds, dense woodlands, thickets

Food source: Insects, spiders, small reptiles, berries

Nest: In thickets, no more than 8 feet up

Call: Buzzy, wheezy *wink-doodly-do-a-vee*; variations of this

Hot spots: One of the dominant vireos throughout much of Texas, white-eyed vireo makes itself easy to find. Listen for its call on trails in any wooded area, and keep an eye out for it as it mingles with chickadees and kinglets. Closer to the Gulf coast, mixed flocks of overwintering songbirds almost always include at least one of these birds.

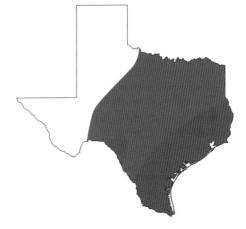

BLACK-CAPPED VIREO
Vireo atricapilla

This showy vireo is a local specialty, found only in scrub oak woodlands in east-central Texas.

Field marks: Black head with broad white stripe around the red eye, olive green back, green and black wings with white wing bars, white underside from under the bill to undertail, greenish tail. Female has the same white eye stripe, but is more muted overall with a dark olive hood.

Size: L: 4"–4.5", WS: 7"

Similar species: Plumbeous vireo is gray overall instead of olive, and it lacks the black hood.

Season: Spring and summer

Habitat: Arid woodlands of scrub oak and other low vegetation

Food source: Insects and insect larvae, as well as spiders

Nest: On a forked branch in a low tree, usually about 3 feet off the ground

Call: A continuous string of twitters, each with two or three syllables followed by short pauses; considerable variety

Hot spots: Balcones Canyonlands National Wildlife Refuge, Shin Oak Observation Deck, Bertram, 30.6600596 / -98.0494916, and Doeskin Ranch, Bertram, 30.6190048 / -98.0728912; Colorado Bend State Park, Bend, 31.0221933 / -98.4426498; South Llano River State Park, Junction, 30.4391651 / -99.8128617; Lost Maples State Natural Area, Vanderpool, 29.8166679 / -99.5721388.

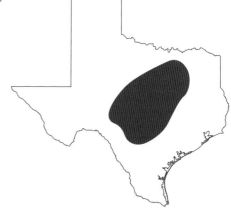

JAYS

BLUE JAY
Cyanocitta cristata

Brightly colored, loud, and aggressive, the blue jay dominates bird feeders, neighborhoods, wooded parks, and forests throughout eastern Texas.

Field marks: Blue crest, black and white face, black bill, black ring across chest, white throat and underside, grayish breast, blue back and wings with one bright white wing bar, white tips on secondary flight feathers, long blue tail with white outer tips.

Size: L: 11", WS: 16"

Similar species: Eastern bluebird is smaller and has an all-blue mantle and ruddy breast. Woodhouse's scrub-jay has no crest or black facial markings, has white streaks over a blue throat, and its flanks and belly are grayer than the blue jay's.

Season: Year-round throughout the eastern half of the state

Habitat: Wooded areas in neighborhoods and parks, forest edges, backyards

Food source: Seeds, nuts, fruit, berries, insects, very small rodents and reptiles, eggs from birds' nests. Blue jays come to backyard feeders filled with seed.

Nest: In trees, often close to the trunk; most likely in conifers

Call: A harsh *jaaaay*, singly or repeated four or five times; also mimic calls (mewing catbird, red-tailed hawk, and others) and a descending warble often compared to a rusty hinge

Hot spots: A popular and often numerous backyard bird, blue jays can be found in any yard with a feeder stocked with sunflower seeds or peanut pick-outs, as well as in neighborhood parks or random stands of mature trees.

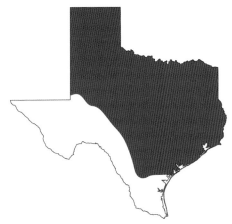

WOODHOUSE'S SCRUB-JAY
Aphelocoma woodhouseii

You won't mistake this for a blue jay—the lack of crest or necklace easily sets this bird apart.

Field marks: Blue head and nape, gray back, blue wings and tail, flurry of white dots at the throat, gray underside and flanks.

Size: L: 11"–12", WS: 15"–15.5"

Similar species: Blue jay is strikingly different, with a high crest, white face, bold black necklace, and boldly patterned wings and tail. Mountain bluebird is smaller and more solidly blue overall, with a white underside.

Season: Year-round

Habitat: Areas forested with piñon, oak, or juniper; also suburban areas with feeders

Food source: Insects and fruit when available; seeds and nuts in the offseasons

Nest: In a tree at least 6 feet up

Call: Scrub-jays have a wide and varied vocabulary, from a squawky *harry-umph* to a piercing single syllable to a chattery series of ten or more syllables

Hot spots: Davis Mountains State Park, primitive area, Fort Davis, 30.60079 / -103.92579; Lawrence E. Wood Picnic Area and Madera Canyon Trail, Davis Mountains Preserve, 30.7063007 / -104.1054001; Devils River State Natural Area, Del Rio, 29.9406182 / -100.9710073; Kickapoo Cavern State Park, Kinney County, 29.61154 / -100.4533; Lost Maples State Natural Area, Vanderpool, 29.8166679 / -99.5721388.

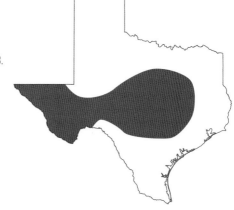

GREEN JAY
Cyanocorax yncas

This beautiful creature is the Lower Rio Grande Valley bird everyone wants to see.

Field marks: Bright blue head with black mask and wide black bib with yellow lower edge, green body and wings, blue-green tail with yellow outer feathers and yellow underside.

Size: L: 11"–11.5", WS: 13.5"

Similar species: Red-crowned parrot has red on its head and a distinctly parrotlike bill.

Season: Year-round

Habitat: Wooded areas, usually near rivers and streams

Food source: Insects, fruit, seeds

Nest: Deep in vegetation above 8 feet

Call: A clear, repeated *cha-cha-cha-cha*; plus a number of different clicking, buzzing, ringing sounds

Hot spots: Numerous at refuges and parks with feeders, green jays are easy to see along the Lower Rio Grande Valley. Bentsen–Rio Grande Valley State Park/World Birding Center, Mission, 26.1849709 / -98.3793885; Estero Llano Grande State Park World Birding Center, Llano Grande, 26.1268335 / -97.9578167; Resaca de la Palma State Park/World Birding Center, Brownsville, 25.9965839 / -97.5690513; National Butterfly Center, Mission, 26.1796025 / -98.3664483; Hugh Ramsey Park, Harlingen, 26.1857402 / -97.6641657.

CROWS

AMERICAN CROW
Corvus brachyrhynchos

Easily spotted in neighborhoods and parking lots, on buildings and beaches, and in large flocks in parks, crows are among the most common birds in America.

Field marks: All black with a long, solid black bill; wide wings, a short tail that fans in flight. Crows flap their wings continuously in flight.

Size: L: 17.5", WS: 35"–40"

Similar species: Fish crow is virtually identical but has a higher, nasal call. Common raven is larger, scruffier, and has a heavier bill and longer wings, as well as a wedge-shaped tail.

Season: Year-round in east Texas, winter only in central Texas and in the western panhandle

Habitat: Farm fields, woods, ocean coastline, areas inhabited by humans

Food source: Carrion, scraps scavenged from human discards, fruit, seeds, small animals and birds, bird eggs, insects

Nest: High in a tree, often more than 90 feet up

Call: The familiar *caw, caw*; also a rhythmic *caw-haw, cah-caw-haw* and a staccato series of clicks

Hot spots: Look in any parking area, on any beach, or on any city street to find this ubiquitous bird, as well as in your own backyard if you feed birds with a platform or ground feeder. Crows compete with great-tailed grackles for perches on utility wires and other high places, and gather in flocks to roost in groves of trees in city parks.

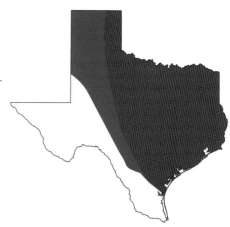

COMMON RAVEN
Corvus corax

The big, black, scruffy bird with the heavy bill can be seen atop rock formations, in forested areas, or occasionally in sparse neighborhoods.

Field marks: Large and black with a thick neck, large bill, a disheveled appearance (especially around the neck), and a wedge-shaped tail.

Size: L: 22"–27", WS: 45"–48"

Similar species: American crow is not as large, is sleeker, and has a thinner bill. Great-tailed grackle is iridescent and has a more erect posture, a much smaller bill, and a very long tail.

Season: Year-round

Habitat: Forests, mountains, deserts, open country with sagebrush or chaparral, farm fields, human-inhabited rural areas

Food source: Carrion, birds, insects, small mammals, reptiles, amphibians, grains, fruit, human leavings, trash

Nest: High in a tree or on a rocky outcropping, usually sheltered by an overhang or higher branches

Call: A hoarse croak, a rattling *caw* (lower in pitch than a crow), and a much higher-pitched, elongated *caw*

Hot spots: Big Bend National Park, Chisos Mountains area, 29.2699985 / -103.3004522; Davis Mountains Preserve, 30.6461274 / -104.1792727; Davis Mountains State Park, Fort Davis, 30.60079 / -103.92579; Kerr Wildlife Management Area, Kerr County, 30.0769673 / -99.5034742; James Kiehl Riverbend Park, Comfort, 29.9723717 / -98.8338447.

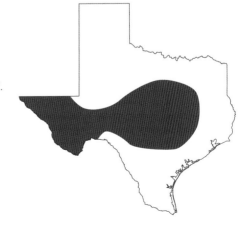

CHIHUAHUAN RAVEN
Corvus cryptoleucus

This all-black bird of desert habitats is larger than a crow but smaller than a common raven.

Field marks: All black with a heavy bill and a diamond-shaped tail in flight. If there's a breeze, you may see the white bases of the neck and body feathers, one of the best ways to tell a Chihuahuan raven from a common one.

Size: L: 18"–21", WS: 41"–44"

Similar species: Common raven is larger, and the base of its feathers is gray rather than white.

Season: Year-round

Habitat: Deserts and other dry areas, specifically those with yucca, mesquite, and other low foliage; also prairies bordered with utility poles for nesting

Food source: Carrion, insects, small mammals, spiders, fish, reptiles, amphibians, birds, plants, grains, nuts, some fruits, human leavings, trash

Nest: High in a tree, on a cliff, or on a man-made structure like a utility pole

Call: A raspy *caw*, much like a common raven, but lower-pitched than a crow

Hot spots: The vast majority of Chihuahuan raven sightings are along west Texas highways that run through open land. Watch utility poles, cliff faces, oil derricks, and windmills for ravens sitting on top of them, and keep an eye out for the flash of white when their feathers move in the wind. Despite their preference for desert landscapes, these ravens are frequently seen near west Texas lakes, where they may gather in small groups.

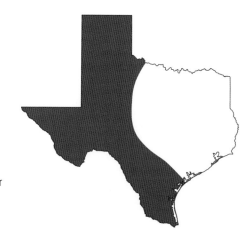

SWALLOWS AND SWIFT

PURPLE MARTIN
Progne subis

This colony nester often lives in man-made martin houses, near a convenient water feature or open beach.

Field marks: Male is deep purple-blue overall, with a small black bill and wings as long as its slightly forked tail. Female has deep blue cap, back, wings, and tail; gray forehead and collar, gray-smudged breast and underside.

Size: L: 7.5"–8.5", WS: 16"–18"

Similar species: All swallow species are smaller. Tree swallow has bright white underparts. Cliff swallow has an orange face and grayish underparts with a rufous wash.

Season: Summer in east and central Texas; migration through parts of west Texas

Habitat: Woodlands, neighborhoods, and open fields near a prominent water feature (ocean, bay, lake, river)

Food source: Flying insects

Nest: In colonies in a man-made martin house, or in a series of tree cavities in a woodland area

Call: A series of whistles and gurgles, differing between male and female birds; also a simple *seet, seet, seet*

Hot spots: Many coastal and lake neighborhoods have martin houses that can be viewed from residential streets, making them the easiest places to see purple martins—but these are private property, so I can't list them here. Here are some public areas that also host martin colonies: Mitchell Lake Audubon Center, San Antonio, 29.3105956 / -98.4996938; Leonabelle Turnbull Birding Center, Port Aransas, 27.8275297 / -97.0789558; Mills Pond at Wells Branch, Austin, 30.45 / -97.68012; Lewisville Lake Environmental Learning Area, Lewisville, 33.0662579 / -96.9750008; Hugh Ramsey Park, Harlingen, 26.1857402 / -97.6641657.

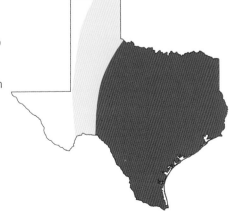

TREE SWALLOW
Tachycineta bicolor

The bright blue tree swallow often nests or roosts in boxes meant for bluebirds.

Field marks: Male has bright blue head, back, and rump with white undertail coverts; bright white throat, breast, and underside; black wings and tail; tail is slightly forked. Female is gray above and white below.

Size: L: 5.75", WS: 12.5"–14.5"

Similar species: Cliff swallow has a rufous face, dark throat, and a grayish-white breast with rufous streaks. Barn swallow has a darker blue back, an orange face and lighter orange underside, and a deeply forked tail.

Season: Winter along the Gulf coast; spring and fall migration throughout the state

Habitat: Open fields with stands of trees near marshes, swamps, lakeshores, rivers, or ponds

Food source: Flying and crawling insects, spiders

Nest: In boxes usually meant for bluebirds; also in tree cavities (not in Texas)

Call: High-pitched, buzzy, chattery *cheet-cheet-cheet* calls with variations in speed and pitch; also simple *treet* note in flight

Hot spots: When you visit any salt marsh, riverside, lakeshore, or other body of water in winter, tree swallows will be very much in evidence. Darting back and forth over the water to catch mosquitoes and other flying insects, they rarely stop to allow you a long look, but you will have the chance to admire their bright blue backs and wings as they glide by you. Try High Island Smith Oaks Sanctuary, Bolivar Peninsula, 29.573681 / -94.3898535, or Anahuac National Wildlife Refuge, Bolivar Peninsula, 29.609066 / -94.535253, in spring to witness large flocks as they migrate through.

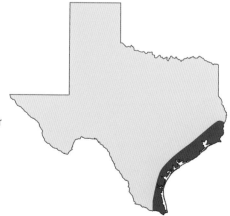

CLIFF SWALLOW
Petrochelidon pyrrhonota

This colony nester builds closely packed, volcano-shaped mud cylinders and raises its young within a community.

Field marks: Dark blue cap, orange face, dark blue throat, small black bill, buff collar, grayish underside with some light rufous streaking, light rufous rump, dark wings and tail.

Size: L: 5.5", WS: 12"–13.5"

Similar species: Barn swallow has an orange face and throat, a lighter orange underside, and a deeply forked tail.

Season: Summer through most of the state; spring and fall migration on the Gulf coast and in the Lower Rio Grande Valley

Habitat: Open farm fields, meadows, or lakes near buildings or cliffs

Food source: Flying and crawling insects

Nest: In colonies, building adjoining mud cylinders on the sides of cliffs or buildings

Call: A repeated, descending *peeer*; also a crackling series of calls like the sound of crumpling plastic wrap

Hot spots: Kirby Lake, Abilene, 32.3724227 / -99.7345734; Hagerman National Wildlife Refuge, Sherman/Denison, 33.7385706 / -96.7527511; Richland Creek Wildlife Management Area, Cayuga, 31.9832577 / -96.0818564; Lake Waco, Woodway Park, 31.5236784 / -97.2314501; Dallas Southside Wastewater Treatment Plant, Dallas, 32.6456988 / -96.6391754.

BARN SWALLOW
Hirundo rustica

The bird that gives all swallowtails their name, this brightly colored migrant and summer resident often follows working farm machinery to catch insects unearthed by plows and harvesters.

Field marks: Male has dark blue cap, mask, back, wings, and tail; orange face and throat, lighter orange breast and underside; long, deeply forked tail. Female has a somewhat whiter underside.

Size: L: 6.75"–7.5", WS: 13"–15"

Similar species: Cliff swallow has a gray collar and underside, a duller orange face, and a dark blue throat.

Season: Summer

Habitat: Farm fields with barns, neighborhoods, lakes, wetlands

Food source: Insects of open fields: grasshoppers, crickets, moths, and others

Nest: In colonies, in the corners of barns and garages or under bridges

Call: High-pitched, constant chatter in groups of three or four notes; also a *chee-deep* chip note

Hot spots: The most common swallow in the region, barn swallows can be found in season in any area of open land, especially if there is a structure—a bridge, pavilion, barn, or porch—under which they can build nests. A summer drive through agricultural lands or through your favorite wildlife management area will almost certainly yield views of barn swallows hunting down insects. Watch the utility wires along these roadsides for rows of swallows (which may include tree swallows in the proper seasons).

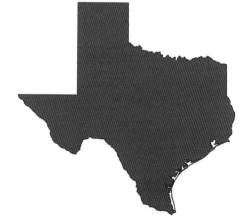

CAVE SWALLOW
Petrochelidon fulva

Small colonies of these birds have developed in cities, but the caves of central Texas attract larger colonies.

Field marks: Small, flat head with dark blue cap; dark patch over eye, rufous head, blue back, brown wings and tail, buff chest, white underside. Juveniles have more brown and are less vibrant.

Size: L: 5"–6", WS: 12"–13"

Similar species: Cliff swallow has a buff collar and rump, and its rufous areas are darker. Barn swallow has a blue hood and a deeply forked tail.

Season: Summer and early fall

Habitat: As there are few caves in Texas, these birds nest under bridges, especially in cities.

Food source: Flying insects

Nest: Mud packed onto cement walls under bridges or on cave walls

Call: A repeated *sreet*—continuous, disorganized notes

Hot spots: Frio Bat Cave area, Concan, 29.4454534 / -99.6648976; Choke Canyon State Park—South Unit, Three Rivers, 28.472577 / -98.2512474; Ascarate Park/Lake, El Paso, 31.7532135 / -106.4023923; Roy G. Guerrero Colorado River Metro Park, Austin, 30.246172 / -97.7049763; Aquarena Springs, San Marcos, 29.8932402 / -97.9297458.

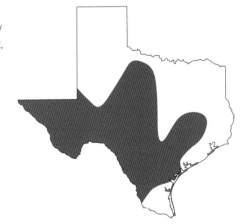

CHIMNEY SWIFT
Chaetura pelagica

Noting its elongated oblong shape in flight, birders refer to this swift as "a cigar with wings."

Field marks: Gray and black overall, paler at the throat; rounded at the head and tail, sometimes with the tail fanned in flight. Wings extend well beyond the tail when in repose (clinging to the side of a building, for example).

Size: L: 5.25"–5.5", WS: 12"–14"

Similar species: Bank swallow is brown above and white below. Northern rough-winged swallow is brown overall with bright rufous wing bars. Tree swallow is distinctly blue above and white below; juvenile tree swallows also have a white face, breast, and underside.

Season: Summer and early fall

Habitat: Buildings with tall chimneys: schools, churches, industrial structures; also open habitat for feeding on the wing

Food source: Insects, captured entirely in flight

Nest: In a nest made from twigs and the bird's saliva, stuck to the inside of a chimney or belfry

Call: A high, rapid, continuous chattering in flight

Hot spots: Chimney swifts are rarely seen perched or clinging to a wall; they are nearly always seen best when they congregate around a smokestack or chimney before they roost for the night. College campuses, the tops of parking garages, and small town squares are often the best places to see them shortly before dusk. During the day, these swifts can be seen catching insects over bodies of water or any area with a lot of bugs. Every wildlife refuge, park, and wetland in east and central Texas has its own summer population.

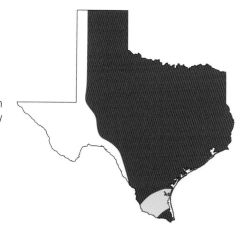

TITMICE AND CHICKADEE

TUFTED TITMOUSE
Baeolophus bicolor

From forests to feeders, this friend of chickadees is a dependable sighting on any east Texas woodland outing.

Field marks: Gray crest, back of head, back, wings, and tail; white face with large black eye and black forehead; grayish-white throat, breast, and underside; light orange flanks, white undertail coverts.

Size: L: 6.5", WS: 9.75"–10.75"

Similar species: Blue-gray gnatcatcher is smaller and bluer, has no crest, and has a white eye ring and a black tail. Black-crested titmouse is paler and has a distinctive black crest.

Season: Year-round

Habitat: Deciduous forests, neighborhoods with mature trees, parks, backyards

Food source: Insects, spiders, nuts, seeds, suet

Nest: In a tree cavity or birdhouse

Call: A musical *peter, peter, peter, peter*; also a rough, scolding *shrii, shrii, shrii* and a series of very high *ti, ti, ti* sounds

Hot spots: Tufted titmouse is one of the most common birds of east Texas woodlands and neighborhoods, and virtually every backyard feeder filled with sunflower seeds receives daily visits from this bird. The titmouse often associates with Carolina chickadees, so if you're on a woodland walk and you haven't detected a titmouse, watch groups of chickadees to see which of their many allies they have with them.

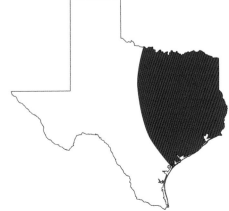

BLACK-CRESTED TITMOUSE
Baeolophus atricristatus

This dapper little gray songbird has a pronounced black crest, making it easy to differentiate it from tufted titmouse.

Field marks: Gray overall with a whiter face and chest, black eyes, a nearly vertical black crest, rosy flanks, and white underside.

Size: L: 5.5"–6", WS: 9"–9.8"

Similar species: Tufted titmouse is darker gray and lacks the black crest. Carolina chickadee has a black cap but no crest, and a black throat.

Season: Year-round in central and south Texas

Habitat: Woodlands of all kinds, as well as any neighborhood or park with feeders

Food source: Small insects, larvae, seeds, small fruits, acorns

Nest: Cavities left behind by woodpeckers; also nest boxes with a 2-inch hole

Call: The familiar *peedle-peedle-peedle-peedle* of a tufted titmouse, as well as a trill like a chipping sparrow, but slower

Hot spots: Anywhere in central or south Texas with feeders will attract black-crested titmouse. These birds are very common in forested areas as well, with no preference for conifers or deciduous trees—everything with foliage is good for these busy little birds.

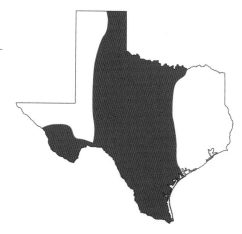

CAROLINA CHICKADEE
Poecile carolinensis

Texas's only chickadee is just a little drabber than its black-capped cousin, but their range does not overlap this far south.

Field marks: Black cap dipping below the eye, black throat, white face and breast, buffy underside; gray wings and tail.

Size: L: 4.5"–5", WS: 7"–8"

Similar species: Black-capped chickadee is nearly identical with a little whiter edging on its wings, but its range does not extend to Texas. White-breasted nuthatch is larger, with a black hood that does not extend to the eye, and a bluish back and wings with striking black and white detail. Black-crested titmouse has a pronounced vertical crest.

Season: Year-round through east and central Texas

Habitat: Wooded areas, including forests, swamps, parks; residential neighborhoods with trees

Food source: Insects, as well as seeds from bird feeders

Nest: In a hole they excavate or find in a tree

Call: A descending four-note whistle: *TOO-dee-di-di;* also as a high-pitched twiddle followed by a raspy *dee-dee-dee-dee-dee-dee* series

Hot spots: Any birding outing in a wooded park or neighborhood east of Abilene and north of Corpus Christi should yield at least one chickadee, and probably many more. Sightings are more numerous in human-populated areas where feeders are plentiful and kept filled. These busy feeder birds are easiest to spot wherever there are sunflower seeds or peanuts to plunder.

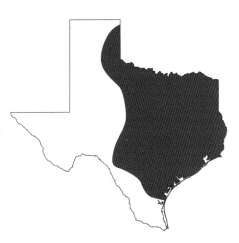

HORNED LARK
Eremophila alpestris

Look for flocks along roadsides, on airstrips, in parking lots, or on winter beaches.

Field marks: Male has yellow face with bold black pattern, black "horn" feathers at top of head, small bill, black throat, white underside, pale rufous back and rump, sand-colored wings and tail. Female lacks the horn feathers; the face, breast, and back are grayer.

Size: L: 7"–8", WS: 12"–14"

Similar species: American pipit lacks the horn feathers and the black and yellow facial pattern. Common yellowthroat is smaller and has a full black mask and a yellow throat.

Season: Year-round

Habitat: Open flatland, roadsides, beaches, dunes, arid landscapes

Food source: Insects, seeds, small shellfish

Nest: In a hollow on the ground

Call: Continuous, high-pitched *cheet-cheet-cheet* on rising and falling pitches; also single *chit* chip note

Hot spots: Any area with flat, open land is likely to attract horned larks. Look along roadsides in agricultural areas to find them gritting in flocks of thirty or forty at a time. Superior Turf Farms/Weaver Road, Rangerville, 26.1039435 / -97.7723229; Sims Lane/Sims Lane Cutoff intersection, Bryan, 30.6766552 / -96.5113794; Marathon Prairie Dog Town, Marathon, 30.296425 / -103.1334686; Buffalo Lake National Wildlife Refuge, Umbarger, 34.9101471 / -102.1138; Bison Road Playa, Levelland, 33.5576789 / -102.3385777.

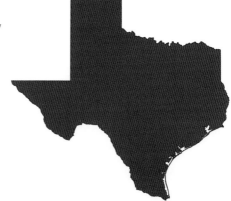

NUTHATCHES

RED-BREASTED NUTHATCH
Sitta canadensis

This little winter visitor prefers wooded areas throughout much of Texas.

Field marks: Male has black cap and eye stripe, white eyebrow and throat, sharp black bill, red-orange underparts, gray-blue back and tail, white stripes on outer tail feathers. Female is slightly less brightly colored.

Size: L: 4.5", WS: 8"–8.5"

Similar species: White-breasted nuthatch is larger, lacks the eye stripe, and has a white breast.

Season: Winter

Habitat: Mixed forests of deciduous and coniferous trees; also backyards and feeders in neighborhoods

Food source: Nuts, seeds, insects, spiders, clusters of insect eggs

Nest: In a tree cavity (not in Texas)

Call: *Toot, toot, toot,* like a toy horn; also an extended trill

Hot spots: Any wooded area may provide a winter home for this nuthatch. In areas often frequented by families, some red-breasted nuthatches have become accustomed to hand-feeding and will let you know by flying at you in hopes of a seed from your palm. Boykin Springs, Jasper County, Beans, 31.0595928 / -94.2749289; Tyler State Park, Tyler, 32.4799358 / -95.2991867; Hornsby Bend, Austin, 30.2181988 / -97.6458054; Lawrence E. Wood Picnic Area and Madera Canyon Trail, Davis Mountains Preserve, 30.7063007 / -104.1054001; Lubbock Cemetery, Lubbock, 33.5632959 / -101.8073516.

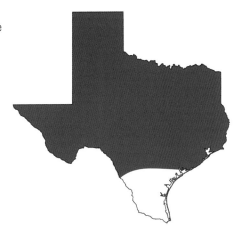

WHITE-BREASTED NUTHATCH
Sitta carolinensis

Feeding upside down on a tree trunk, the larger local nuthatch frequents feeders as well as mature trees.

Field marks: Black cap, white face, black eye; long, upturned bill; gray back and wings, white breast and underparts, rufous-tinted undertail coverts (white in female), gray tail.

Size: L: 5"–6", WS: 10"–11"

Similar species: Red-breasted nuthatch is smaller, has a black eye stripe, and has reddish underparts.

Season: Year-round in east Texas and part of the panhandle; winter in central Texas

Habitat: Mixed forests with oak trees, neighborhoods with mature trees, parks

Food source: Insects, seeds, nuts, suet

Nest: In a nest box, tree cavity, or hole abandoned by woodpeckers

Call: A honking *waah, waah, waah, waah*, all on one note; also a faster series of a single higher note

Hot spots: Tyler State Park, Tyler, 32.4799358 / -95.2991867; Fairfield Lake State Park, Fairfield, 31.7820618 / -96.0662653; W. G. Jones State Forest, Conroe, 30.235563 / -95.4852676; Palo Duro Canyon State Park, Lake Tanglewood, 34.9651086 / -101.671257; Oak Point Park and Nature Preserve, Plano, 33.0560833 / -96.6711473; Huntsville State Park, Huntsville, 30.6150161 / -95.5333328.

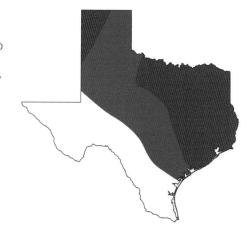

WRENS

CAROLINA WREN
Thryothorus ludovicianus

Don't be deceived by the name—this expressive wren's range extends southward to the border with Mexico.

Field marks: Brown cap, bright white eyebrow edged in black, brown eye line, buff cheek, white throat; buff-orange chest, flanks, and underside; brown back, brown wings barred in black, white undertail coverts with black barring, short brown tail.

Size: L: 5.5", WS: 7.5"

Similar species: All other local wrens are smaller. Marsh wren has white eyebrow, but its crown is black.

Season: Year-round in east and south Texas, with a few birds in populated areas of the panhandle

Habitat: Edges of woodlands with lots of brushy shrubs

Food source: Insects, spiders

Nest: In a crack between rocks, or in a crevice or hole in a building

Call: Often transcribed as *teakettle, teakettle, teakettle*; sometimes very quick, but often slower

Hot spots: Carolina wrens are widespread and numerous in east and central Texas, and they should be fairly easy to find because of their enthusiastic and highly recognizable song. Before you cross the state looking for one, check the brushy areas in your own neighborhood or the shrubs and thickets in your nearest park. These wrens are fond of residential areas and sometimes visit suet feeders in winter.

187

HOUSE WREN
Troglodytes aedon

Tiny birds with a lot to say, house wrens spend the winter in the southern half of Texas. Check parks, woodlands, and brushy areas of your own backyard for this fierce little migrant.

Field marks: Light brown (or light gray) head and body with buff or pale gray throat and breast; faint white eyebrow and long, downward-curving yellow bill; brownish (or grayish) wings with darker horizontal barring. Warm brown undertail coverts and tail with black barring; tail is often held upright at a nearly 90-degree angle from the body.

Size: L: 4"–5", WS: 6"–7"

Similar species: Carolina wren is larger, more rufous, and has a bright white eyebrow extending from bill to nape.

Season: Winter through most of the state; spring and fall migration in the northern region

Habitat: Wooded areas in parks, neighborhoods, and along farm fields; also in forest thickets and shrubs

Food source: Insects found on trees and shrubs, caterpillars, spiders

Nest: In a sheltered opening in a shrub, a tree cavity, or a man-made nest box

Call: One of the most exuberant in the avian kingdom: a series of musical trills, whistles, and song phrases sung without breaks and repeated note-for-note at regular intervals

Hot spots: If you don't have house wrens in your residential area, here are some spots where birders see them regularly, and often in quantity: Colleyville Nature Center, Colleyville, 32.8763434 / -97.1664548; Tyler State Park, Tyler, 32.4799358 / -95.2991867; Leach Gardens, Texas A&M University, College Station, 30.6069862 / -96.3516867l; Mills Pond at Wells Branch, Austin, 30.45 / -97.68012; San Antonio Botanical Garden, San Antonio, 29.4601113 / -98.4572897.

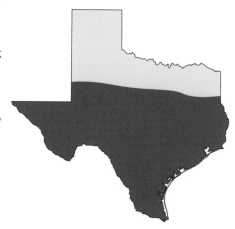

BEWICK'S WREN
Thryomanes bewickii

Larger than a house wren with a bold white eyebrow, Bewick's wrens take an interest in backyard seed feeders in winter.

Field marks: Brown head, back, and wings with a bold white stripe over the eye; slightly decurved bill, white throat and grayish-white underbody, long tail with dark stripes; tail is often held upright.

Size: L: 5", WS: 7"

Similar species: House wren is smaller and lacks the white eye stripe. Carolina wren has a ruddy breast and underside. Cactus wren is much larger and has a black-spotted throat and a ruddy underside with black streaks.

Season: Year-round in most of the state; winter to spring in the east

Habitat: Open scrubland and sparse woodlands; also forests of mixed conifers

Food source: Insects, caterpillars, and other small invertebrates, switching to seeds and fruits in winter

Nest: In cavities in trees, crevices in rock faces, and nest boxes; also in man-made structures like sheds

Call: A sequence of single notes, a buzz, and a high trill, sometimes with additional notes; also a chattery *chee-chee-chee* call, or a longer raspy single-note *chaaah*

Hot spots: While Bewick's wren is common in Texas, they are easier to see in areas with expanses of open country with low shrubs. These are reliable spots: South Llano River State Park, Junction, 30.4391651 / -99.8128617; Davis Mountains State Park, primitive area, Fort Davis, 30.60079 / -103.92579; Canyon Lake 6, Lubbock, 33.5676571 / -101.8033202; Lewisville Lake Environmental Learning Area, Lewisville, 33.0662579 / -96.9750008; Lady Bird Johnson Wildflower Center, Austin, 30.1853476 / -97.8745151.

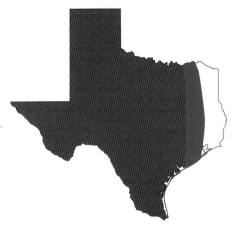

MARSH WREN
Cistothorus palustris

Living up to their name, these tiny wrens fill low marshland with their chip notes and rattling song.

Field marks: Black cap, white eyebrow, brown cheek, long gray bill, whitish throat and breast, rufous back and wings, light rufous flanks and undertail coverts, darker wing primaries, rufous tail barred in black and held at a nearly 90-degree angle from body.

Size: L: 5", WS: 6"–7"

Similar species: Carolina, winter, and house wrens all prefer woodland habitat.

Season: Spring and fall migration in east Texas north of the Gulf coast; winter in the rest of the state

Habitat: Open freshwater marshes with tall vegetation, wetlands near the Gulf coast

Food source: Insects, tiny invertebrates

Nest: Near the ground and built to be entered from the side, toward the base of tall grasses and reeds

Call: Buzzy but musical elongated trill, repeated at intervals; also one- or two-syllable *chut* note

Hot spots: High Island Smith Oaks Sanctuary, Bolivar Peninsula, 29.573681 / -94.3898535; Aransas National Wildlife Refuge Wildlife Drive, 28.2403924 / -96.818819; Aquarena Springs, San Marcos, 29.8932402 / -97.9297458; Big Bend National Park, Rio Grande Village, 29.1809226 / -102.9557133; Thompson Park, Amarillo, 35.2382514 / -101.8330479.

ROCK WREN
Salpinctes obsoletus

As gray as the landscape it inhabits, this busy little wren can be difficult to spot as it dips into crevices to search for bugs.

Field marks: Grayish-brown back, wings and head, with a spray of dots over the wings; faint buffy eyebrow, slim bill, white throat and breast streaked with gray, slightly buff flanks and underside, long tail with checkered look.

Size: L: 5"–6", WS: 8.5"–9.5"

Similar species: Canyon wren is darker brown with a chestnut tail and a ruddy underside, white throat, and longer bill.

Season: Year-round in some parts of west Texas; winter only in some areas; spring and fall migration through parts of the panhandle and central Texas

Habitat: Arid landscapes with plenty of rocks, from Big Bend's low desert to the Guadalupe Mountains

Food source: Insects and spiders; some seeds

Nest: In between rocks in a crevice

Call: A variety of songs in succession like a mockingbird, but with pauses between phrases

Hot spots: Guadalupe Mountains National Park, Pine Springs, 31.9074905 / -104.8013279; Davis Mountains Preserve, Tobe Canyon, 30.6461274 / -104.1792727; Big Bend National Park, Chisos Mountains area trails, 29.2699985 / -103.3004522; Fort Lancaster Overlook, Sheffield rest area, 30.6780349 / -101.6727483; San Angelo State Park—South Unit, San Angelo, 31.4669145 / -100.5013617.

DOMINIC SHERONY

CANYON WREN
Catherpes mexicanus

Find this bird wherever there are rock faces to be climbed, with cracks and crevices for gathering insects.

Field marks: Brown head and nape blending into chestnut back, downcurved bill, white throat, chestnut underside, and ruddy tail with dark bars

Size: L: 4.5"–6", WS: 7"–8"

Similar species: Rock wren uses much of the same habitat, but is grayer overall with no chestnut areas.

Season: Year-round in west Texas

Habitat: Canyons, cliffs, rocky areas

Food source: Insects and spiders

Nest: Among rocks in sheltered areas, often with an overhang

Call: A long, descending phrase of clear notes, two on a pitch at a time, ending in a buzzing note or two

Hot spots: Big Bend National Park, Chisos Mountains area trails, 29.2699985 / -103.3004522; Davis Mountains Preserve, Tobe Canyon, 30.6461274 / -104.1792727; Heart of the Hills Fishers Center, Mountain Home, 30.1574845 / -99.34811; Lake Travis, Bob Wentz Windy Point Park, Austin, 30.4128174 / -97.9008651; Fort Lancaster Overlook, Sheffield rest area, 30.6780349 / -101.6727483.

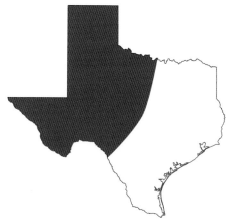

CACTUS WREN
Campylorhynchus brunneicapillus

Living up to its name, this cheeky little bird lives in deserts, does not require drinking water, and stands atop cacti to announce its presence.

Field marks: Brown back with white spots, brown cap, bold white stripe over the eye, black throat with streaks extending to the breast, white breast with brown streaks, buffy underside and flanks; long, striped tail.

Size: L: 7"–8.5", WS: 11"

Similar species: Canyon wren is smaller and has chestnut mantle and underside, bright russet tail. Bewick's wren is smaller and more solid brown overall, with a whitish underside.

Season: Year-round in southwest Texas

Habitat: Open desert with cacti, yucca, cholla, and other desert plants

Food source: Insects and spiders

Nest: In a cactus or other tall desert plant as much as 10 feet off the ground. The nest is distinctive: football-sized with a side entrance.

Call: Often compared to a car that won't start, the raspy *chaw, chaw, chaw* continues for 4 or 5 seconds, pauses, and begins again

Hot spots: Big Bend National Park, Chisos Mountains area trails, 29.2699985 / -103.3004522; Fort Davis National Historic Site, Fort Davis, 30.5985609 / -103.8923299; Lawrence E. Wood Picnic Area and Madera Canyon Trail, Davis Mountains Preserve, 30.7063007 / -104.1054001; Heart of the Hills Fishers Center, Mountain Home, 30.1574845 / -99.34811; Fort Lancaster Overlook, Sheffield rest area, 30.6780349 / -101.6727483.

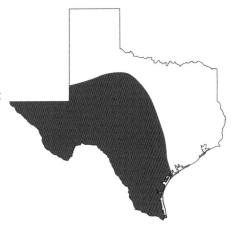

KINGLETS AND GNATCATCHERS

RUBY-CROWNED KINGLET
Corthylio calendula

Always in motion, the tiny kinglet make it very difficult to get a good look at its ruby crown.

Field marks: Male has light olive-green head and back, white eye ring, bright red crest (visible only in breeding season), olive-washed breast, lighter flanks, whitish undertail coverts, dark wings with one white wing bar, dark tail. Female is identical but lacks the ruby crown.

Size: L: 4.25", WS: 6.5"–7.5"

Similar species: Golden-crowned kinglet has a bright orange and yellow crown in all seasons. Tennessee warbler is larger and has a gray head and bright white underparts.

Season: Winter

Habitat: Woodlands and forests with both deciduous and coniferous trees

Food source: Insects, seeds, fruit

Nest: Hidden in a tree, suspended from a high branch

Call: Three to five *tsee-tsee-tsee* notes, followed by an exuberant series of musical chirps and trills

Hot spots: Ruby-crowned kinglets are plentiful throughout the winter months, and just about any grove of trees, thicket, nature center, or park will have its own population. Their preference for dense vegetation makes them more prevalent in the eastern half of the state, but they don't shy away from desert landscapes. They are early migrants, heading north by the end of March and vanishing from the panhandle in the first few days of April.

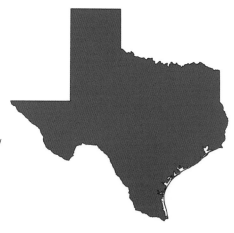

GOLDEN-CROWNED KINGLET
Regulus satrapa

Watch for constant motion in woodlands with conifers to find this tiny bird, the smaller of the two local kinglets.

Field marks: Bright orange and yellow cap outlined in black, white eyebrow, black eye line, white throat, greenish-gray back and breast, grayish-white underparts, black and greenish wings with white bar across secondaries, greenish tail with dark gray end.

Size: L: 3.5"–4", WS: 6.5"–7"

Similar species: Ruby-crowned kinglet is slightly larger and lacks bold facial pattern; males have a raised red crest during breeding season. Golden-winged warbler is larger and grayer overall, with bright yellow patches on wings.

Season: Winter

Habitat: Mixed woodlands with conifers, boreal woodlands

Food source: Insects, tree sap, seeds

Nest: On a branch in a conifer, generally 30 feet up or more

Call: Very high-pitched *tsee* or *tsee-tsee-tsee*; also a song that begins with high *tsee-tsee* notes and ends in a tumbling warble

Hot spots: Golden-crowned kinglets' love of conifers limits their habitat to wooded areas of east Texas, but they do congregate in areas of the panhandle and the Davis Mountains. Palo Duro Canyon State Park, Lake Tanglewood, 34.9651086 / -101.671257; Government Canyon State Natural Area, San Antonio, 29.5490104 / -98.7641682; Sam Houston National Forest, Kelly's Pond Road and environs, Conroe, 30.5192994 / -95.6475507; Lake o' the Pines, Cedar Springs Park, Ore City, 32.8402939 / -94.6934795; Lewisville Lake Environmental Learning Area, Lewisville, 33.0662579 / -96.9750008.

VERDIN

Auriparus flaviceps

A flash of fast-moving yellow among desert shrubs can be all you see of a verdin, its gray body blending with its dusty surroundings.

Field marks: All grayish-white body, yellow face, small chestnut patch at the shoulder; short bill, black eye, brownish-gray wings and tail. Juveniles lack the yellow face.

Size: L: 3.5"–4.5", WS: 6.5"

Similar species: No other desert bird of this size has a yellow face. Lucy's warbler has a thinner bill, a chestnut patch on its head, and no yellow. Bushtit is all gray with a smaller bill, and it has no chestnut shoulder patch.

Season: Year-round in southwest Texas

Habitat: Deserts with considerable scrub, especially shrubs with thorns

Food source: Insects, spiders, some fruit and plant nectar; may come to hummingbird feeders

Nest: A ball of twigs that contains a smaller ball of softer material, in a shrub or tree, usually about 5 to 6 feet off the ground

Call: A simple, clear *tseep tseep tseep*

Hot spots: Big Bend National Park, Dugout Wells, 29.2712002 / -103.1352997; TX 118 at Musquiz Creek, Fort Davis, 30.53569 / -103.80343; Jenna Welch Nature Center I-20 Pond, Midland, 31.9630947 / -102.1210903; Salineño Wildlife Preserve, Roma, 26.5148584 / -99.116206; Bentsen–Rio Grande Valley State Park/World Birding Center, Mission, 26.1849709 / -98.3793885.

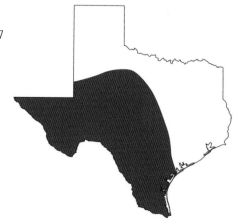

BUSHTIT
Psaltriparus minimus

Tiny gray birds in perpetual motion, bushtits plunder trees in flocks, often in the company of other small birds like chickadees and verdins.

Field marks: Gray overall with a long tail and a very small bill. Females have a strikingly yellow eye.

Size: L: 3"–4.5", WS: 6"

Similar species: Blue-gray gnatcatcher has a white eye ring, a longer black tail with white outer tail feathers, and a longer bill. Golden-crowned kinglet has a yellow crown with a black outline, yellow streaks in the wings and tail, and white wing bars.

Season: Year-round in areas of central and southwest Texas; some near cities in the panhandle

Habitat: Wooded or forested areas; also chaparral and scrub woodlands

Food source: Insects and spiders, some seeds

Nest: Unusual hanging nests as much as a foot long, often in hanging foliage like mistletoe

Call: A three-note, very high-pitched *tiddle-tick*; also a one-note *tssk*, repeated often, and other combinations of wispy notes

Hot spots: Davis Mountains Preserve, Tobe Canyon, 30.6461274 / -104.1792727; Big Bend National Park, Chisos Mountains area trails, 29.2699985 / -103.3004522; Kickapoo Cavern State Park, Kinney County, 29.61154 / -100.4533; South Llano River State Park, Junction, 30.4391651 / -99.8128617; Hill Country State Natural Area, Tarpley, 29.6277682 / -99.1819096.

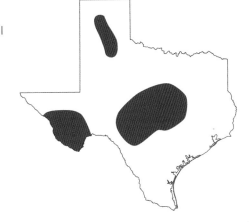

BLUE-GRAY GNATCATCHER
Polioptila caerulea

The unbroken color, bright white eye ring, and long, black tail with white outer feathers will help you identify this frenetic bird.

Field marks: Bright blue-gray cap, nape, and back; black forehead (male only), gray cheek, whitish throat, grayish-white breast and underside, gray wings with white tertials, black tail with white outer feathers and white undertail.

Size: L: 4.25"–4.5", WS: 6"–6.75"

Similar species: Bushtit has a shorter bill and lacks the long, black tail. Black-tailed gnatcatcher has a black cap (in breeding males) and less white in the tail.

Season: Year-round along the southern border and Gulf coast, spring and summer in most of the rest of the state

Habitat: Deciduous woodlands

Food source: Gnats, as well as many other insects, butterflies, spiders, bees, and wasps

Nest: Fastened to a tree branch, with no specific height preference

Call: *Bees, bu-bu-bees, bees*, with a buzzy spiraling downward note on each *bees*; also a *speez, speez, speez* call, all on one note

Hot spots: Just about every area with trees attracts this gnatcatcher, so chances are good you will come across at least one when you go looking for warblers and other passerines in spring, or for resident birds in winter. They often will come close to you in what seems like a deliberate play for attention, hopping from branch to branch as actively as a kinglet and singing their buzzy song.

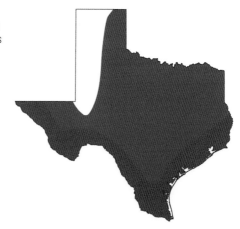

BLACK-TAILED GNATCATCHER
Polioptila melanura

This desert-loving bird shares habitat with blue-gray gnatcatcher, so watch for the strikingly all-black tail as it hops through shrubs.

Field marks: Male is gray overall with a black cap, white eye ring, slightly lighter breast and underside, and solid black tail above and below. Female lacks the black cap.

Size: L: 4.5"–5", WS: 5.5"–6"

Similar species: Blue-gray gnatcatcher lacks the black cap and has white outer tail feathers and a white underside of the tail.

Season: Year-round

Habitat: Desert; this bird avoids water features and gets all the moisture it needs from the insects it eats.

Food source: Insects and the occasional fruit or seed

Nest: A cup nest concealed in a shrub

Call: A combination of unmusical *chk, chk, chk* notes and buzzy, thready squawks

Hot spots: Big Bend National Park, Dugout Wells, 29.2712002 / -103.1352997; Fort Peña Colorado Park, Marathon, 30.152997 / -103.2874735; Seminole Canyon State Park, Comstock, 29.6935703 / -101.3185787; Salineño Wildlife Preserve, Roma, 26.5148584 / -99.116206; Balmorhea Lake, Balmorhea, 30.9583956 / -103.7123108.

THRUSHES

EASTERN BLUEBIRD
Sialia sialis

Bright blue above and bright orange below, this folk symbol of happiness battles all spring and summer to keep its nest box, eggs, and nestlings safe from house sparrows and other aggressive raiders.

Field marks: Male has bright blue head, back, wings, and tail; orange throat, breast, and flanks; white belly and undertail coverts, black primaries. Female has gray head and back, blue leading edge of wing and primaries; light orange throat, breast, and flanks; white belly and undertail, blue tail.

Size: L: 7"–7.75", WS: 12"–13"

Similar species: Western bluebird has a blue throat and a wash of chestnut over its shoulders and upper back (and the two birds' territories barely cross in Texas). Mountain bluebird is blue all over, with a lighter blue chest and underside and no orange or chestnut. Black-throated blue warbler is smaller and has a black face, black stripe on flanks, and no orange. Indigo bunting is solid blue over all of its body. Blue grosbeak is a darker blue with chestnut wing bars and a large bill.

Season: Year-round in east Texas; winter in central and much of west Texas.

Habitat: Open grasslands, farm fields, pastures, parks with grassy areas and trees

Food source: Insects and invertebrates; readily comes to mealworm feeders in backyards

Nest: In a tree cavity, nest box, disused woodpecker hole, or a hole in a utility pole

Call: A short series of syrupy notes and trills, sometimes interlaced with sharp, raspy *chic* notes

Hot spots: Many farm fields and other open areas attract bluebirds throughout the season, so check in your local area before traveling a long distance to find them. Parks with grasslands, agricultural fields, pastures, and other open areas provide birds with the insects and worms they need to thrive.

WESTERN BLUEBIRD
Sialia mexicana

A common sight in open western lands, this bright blue and orange bird uses nest boxes and comes to feeders that offer mealworms.

Field marks: Male has a bright blue head, throat, back and wings, with a chestnut wash over the upper back; orange breast and flanks, white underside, long blue tail. Female is gray where the male is blue, with a more muted rust-colored breast and flanks.

Size: L: 6.5"–7.5", WS: 11.5"–13.5"

Similar species: Eastern bluebird lacks the chestnut upper back and has a chestnut throat (and does not overlap much with western bluebird in Texas). Mountain bluebird is blue overall with no chestnut. Blue grosbeak is larger and chunkier and has a much larger, heavier bill, and chestnut wing bars.

Season: Winter in southwest Texas

Habitat: Open farmland, woodlands with space between trees, backyards

Food source: Insects and spiders, supplementing with seeds and fruit in winter

Nest: In a tree cavity formed naturally or excavated by other birds; also in nest boxes provided by humans

Call: A breathy series of soft *pew* notes, rising and falling; also a rapid, harsh *chuh-chuk* alarm call

Hot spots: Guadalupe Mountains National Park, The Bowl, 31.9225171 / -104.8287964; Lawrence E. Wood Picnic Area and Madera Canyon Trail, Davis Mountains Preserve, 30.7063007 / -104.1054001; Big Bend National Park, Rio Grande Village, 29.1809226 / -102.9557133; Big Bend National Park, Chisos Mountains area trails, 29.2699985 / -103.3004522; Cedar Hill Cemetery, Ozona, 30.6928402 / -101.2059045.

MOUNTAIN BLUEBIRD
Sialia currucoides

Arrestingly blue, this thrush is easy to spot as it flits through open areas like prairies, pastures, and meadows.

Field marks: Bright blue above and paler blue below, tapering to a white underside; with a black eye and small bill. Female is gray overall with some blue in the wings and tail.

Size: L: 6.5"–8", WS: 11"–14"

Similar species: Western and eastern bluebirds have an orange chest and flanks. Blue grosbeak is uniformly dark blue overall with chestnut wing bars and a very large bill.

Season: Winter

Habitat: Open country: prairie, meadow, grassland, agricultural fields

Food source: Insects, some fruit and berries

Nest: Cavities, especially nest boxes

Call: A chirrupy, liquid song very like an American robin, often continuing for some time; also a quick, two-syllable *tu-tu*

Hot spots: As this bird loves open spaces, many sightings are from roadsides, especially where landowners have placed nest boxes on fence posts. Otherwise, here are some very reliable spots: Davis Mountains State Park, Fort Davis, 30.60079 / -103.92579; TX 118, Limpia Crossing, Fort Davis, 30.6153115 / -103.9919472; San Angelo State Park—South Unit, San Angelo, 31.4669145 / -100.5013617; Buffalo Lake National Wildlife Refuge, Umbarger, 34.9101471 / -102.1138; Balmorhea Lake, Balmorhea, 30.9583956 / -103.7123108.

AMERICAN ROBIN
Turdus migratorius

The unofficial harbinger of spring in most of North America, robins actually live year-round in most of Texas, and overwinter in the southernmost parts of the state.

Field marks: Dark gray head, broken white eye ring, yellow bill, thin white lines on throat, bright orange breast and belly, white undertail coverts, gray back and wings, gray tail with white outermost tail feathers. Juveniles have a lighter breast and belly covered in gray spots.

Size: L: 10", WS: 14"–17"

Similar species: Spotted towhee has an all-black head, white breast, and rufous flanks. Female eastern bluebird is smaller, a lighter gray overall, and has blue wing feathers.

Season: Year-round in north, east, and central Texas; winter in the south and westernmost areas

Habitat: Open woodlands, neighborhoods, commercial and industrial areas with mowed lawns, gardens, farm fields, grasslands with trees

Food source: Worms, grubs, berries, fruit, some insects

Nest: In a tree or on a man-made platform under shelter (like the joist of a porch roof), often in full view

Call: Series of musical notes and triplets with brief pauses: *wheedie, wee, wheedio, wheedie, wee*; also a less-melodious five-note phrase: *chi-chi-chi-chi-chi*

Hot spots: Look out any window onto a lawn, and robins will be performing their hop-and-listen behavior as they hunt for invertebrates just under the ground's surface. Every neighborhood and mowed, landscaped open space in Texas becomes a robin magnet, especially once the weather turns colder up north.

WOOD THRUSH
Hylocichla mustelina

The wood thrush's bright rufous cap, nape, and back differentiate it from other thrushes, but its song is the real identifier—one many birders consider the most beautiful in the forest.

Field marks: Bright rufous cap, nape, and back; black and white–striped cheek, white eye ring, black and pink bill, white throat streaked with black; white breast and belly with large, heavy black spots; white undertail coverts, brownish-orange wings and tail. The wood thrush stands taller and more upright than other thrushes.

Size: L: 7.75", WS: 13"–14"

Similar species: Veery has a lighter orange back and light brown spots on its breast, with a clear white underside. Swainson's thrush is light brown with a buff and brown–striped cheek and light yellow spectacles. Hermit thrush has a light brown cap, nape, back, and wings and a bright red tail.

Season: Summer in the easternmost part of the state; spring and fall migration through south and central Texas

Habitat: Deciduous woods with a lush, thriving understory

Food source: Insects, fruit

Nest: In a tree or shrub, at least 6 feet off the ground

Call: A three-part song, often described inadequately as *ee-o-lay*; begins with a series of high piccolo notes, followed by a lower note and ending in a harmonically rich, buzzy trill; also a *wap-wap-wap* call note and a very rapid *bip-bip-bip-bip-bip* clucking call

Hot spots: Tyler State Park, Tyler, 32.4799358 / -95.2991867; Caddo Lake State Park, Karnack, 32.6873809 / -94.1783493; High Island Boy Scout Woods, Bolivar Peninsula, 29.5613445 / -94.3902236; Lafitte's Cove, Galveston, 29.2169006 / -94.9349016; Leonabelle Turnbull Birding Center, Port Aransas, 27.8275297 / -97.0789558.

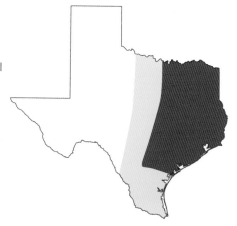

CLAY-COLORED THRUSH
Turdus grayi

It doesn't look like much, but among life-listing birders, this brown bird is one of the most sought-after Texas specialties.

Field marks: Warm brown overall with a lighter breast and underside, with slim brown streaks on the lighter throat; an orange eye and a yellowish bill.

Size: L: 9"–10.5", WS: 14"-16"

Similar species: American robin has a darker back and wings and a red breast and underside. Canyon towhee has a reddish crown, a pinkish underside, and a dark spot in the center of its chest.

Season: Year-round

Habitat: Wooded areas, city parks, places with feeders

Food source: Insects, fruits, small vertebrates

Nest: In the crotch of a tropical tree, usually about 10 feet up; also on a ledge or other structure

Call: Very like the musical song of an American robin, with many twirls and flourishes

Hot spots: Hugh Ramsey Park, Harlingen, 26.1857402 / -97.6641657; Estero Llano Grande State Park World Birding Center, Llano Grande, 26.1268335 / -97.9578167; Resaca de la Palma State Park/ World Birding Center, Brownsville, 25.9965839 / -97.5690513; Quinta Mazatlan World Birding Center, McAllen, 26.176876 / -98.2309932; Bentsen–Rio Grande Valley State Park/World Birding Center, Mission, 26.1849709 / -98.3793885.

HERMIT THRUSH
Catharus guttatus

This common woodland thrush flicks its bright red tail consistently as it rustles through leaves on the forest floor.

Field marks: Olive-brown cap, nape, back, and wings; white eye ring, pink and black bill, white throat and breast covered in black spots, white belly with light brown spots, light rusty flanks, white undertail coverts, red wing primaries, red tail.

Size: L: 6.75", WS: 11.5"

Similar species: Wood thrush has a bright orange-brown cap, nape, back, and tail. Veery has a lighter orange back and light brown spots on its breast, with a clear white underside. Swainson's thrush is light brown with a buff and brown–striped cheek and light yellow spectacles.

Season: Winter except in the panhandle, which is on its migration path

Habitat: Deciduous, coniferous, and mixed woodlands; open woods with a thick understory

Food source: Insects, invertebrates, fruit

Nest: On the ground or in a shrub, usually deep in the forest

Call: A single piccolo note, followed by a harmonically rich, descending trill; also a clucking *chut-chut-chut* and a simple *vee* call note

Hot spots: Hermit thrushes live wherever there's a wooded area with a productive understory, so your favorite forest, park, or nature preserve that has woodland trails is likely to produce a sighting. Watch the ground among the trees for movement among the leaves, especially debris being flung out of the way over the bird's shoulder.

MIMIC THRUSHES

GRAY CATBIRD
Dumetella carolinensis

The catbird's trademark *mew* call is not the only unique thing about it. It's also the only solidly bill-to-tail gray bird in North America.

Field marks: Uniformly gray with a black cap, black eye, rufous undertail coverts, and black tail.

Size: L: 8.5"–9", WS: 11"–12"

Similar species: Northern mockingbird is gray above and whitish below, with large white patches on its wings.

Season: Winter on the Gulf coast, year-round just north of the coast, summer in the rest of east Texas; spring and fall migration through central Texas and the panhandle

Habitat: Forest and marsh edges, wooded edges of farm fields and grasslands, neighborhoods with mature trees

Food source: Insects, spiders, fruit, seeds; sometimes comes to jelly feeders used by orioles

Nest: In the lower branches of a tree or in a shrub

Call: A chattery series of notes that may vary from one bird to the next, derived from the catbird's ability to mimic other birds; also a single *mew* note, very like a cat

Hot spots: Every city park, neighborhood, cemetery, nature center, sanctuary, forest, and farm has its resident catbird, and many of these areas have several. The only places you are not likely to encounter these birds is in areas of dense forests with few discernible edges and in the arid southwestern region.

NORTHERN MOCKINGBIRD
Mimus polyglottos

Nicely adapted to city parks, neighborhoods, cemeteries, and other human-inhabited areas, the mockingbird can incorporate everything from other birds' calls to car alarms in its own song.

Field marks: Gray cap, nape, and back; black eye line, yellow eye, white lores; white throat, breast, and belly; darker wings with two wing bars, large white wing patches, visible during flight; white undertail coverts; long, dark tail often held at an upward angle.

Size: L: 9"–10", WS: 12"–14"

Similar species: Gray catbird is uniformly gray all over. Loggerhead shrike has a black mask, black wings, and a black tail. American pipit is smaller, has a light breast with black streaks, and is found on open ground like beaches and fallow fields.

Season: Year-round

Habitat: Parks, neighborhoods, farmland with hedgerows and wooded areas

Food source: Many kinds of insects, fruit, worms, some small reptiles

Nest: In shrubs or low in trees

Call: Varied phrases that may be different from one bird to the next. Each mimicked call is usually repeated in sets of five or six, and may incorporate the songs of killdeer, Carolina wren, Baltimore oriole, ovenbird, and a wide range of others. Some have learned to imitate car alarms, emergency vehicle sirens, and the beeping of construction vehicles backing up.

Hot spots: Northern mockingbird is one of the most common birds in Texas, especially in residential and commercial areas. While it generally does not come to feeders, it often frequents the wooded edges of backyards, as well as rail-to-trail conversions and other nature trails.

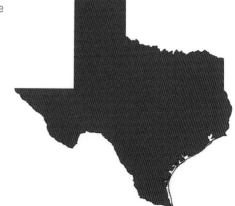

THRASHERS

BROWN THRASHER
Toxostoma rufum

The eastern United States' only thrasher is also a mimic, but its songs are always sung in couplets, so a careful listener can pick it out of a dawn chorus.

Field marks: Bright reddish-brown cap, nape, back, wings, and tail; gray cheek, pink and black bill curving slightly downward, white throat with black malar stripes, light breast and belly striped in black and reddish brown, two black and white stripes on wings, buff undertail coverts, long tail.

Size: L: 11.5", WS: 13"–14"

Similar species: Wood thrush is equally reddish, but its breast is heavily spotted rather than streaked, and its bill is shorter.

Season: Year-round in east Texas, winter in central Texas, summer in parts of the panhandle

Habitat: Shrubby areas, including farm fields with hedgerows, forest edges, parks

Food source: Insects, fruit, grains, some small amphibians

Nest: Close to the ground in a shrub, often one with thorns

Call: A range of distinctly musical phrases, incorporating whistles, rasps, warbles, and other sounds, always sung with one or two repetitions before moving on to the next

Hot spots: Palo Duro Canyon State Park, Lake Tanglewood, 34.9651086 / -101.671257; Sabine Woods, Port Arthur, 29.6984073 / -93.9481795; Cullinan Park, Sugar Land, 29.6355459 / -95.6603193; Clear Creek Natural Heritage Center, Denton, 33.2591514 / -97.0633574; Commons Ford Ranch Metro Park, Austin, 30.3373826 / -97.8930759.

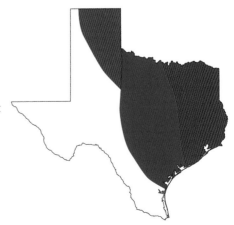

CURVE-BILLED THRASHER
Toxostoma curvirostre

A common bird of the plains, thickets, and low woods, this thrasher's decurved bill allows it to clear debris from the ground to find the insects hidden beneath.

Field marks: Dusty brown overall with an orange eye and longer-than-average, curved bill; lighter breast and underside with brown spots; long tail, and sturdy legs and feet.

Size: L: 10.5"–11", WS: 13"–13.5"

Similar species: Crissal thrasher is gray overall with a longer, more dramatically curved bill. Bendire's thrasher is very similar, but is smaller than a curve-billed, and the two birds' territories do not overlap in Texas.

Season: Year-round in west Texas

Habitat: Open areas with low vegetation, from piñon woods to deserts with multiple cactus species

Food source: Insects, snail, fruit, seeds; often seen on backyard platform feeders filled with sunflower and other seeds

Nest: In a shrub or cactus, usually about 5 feet up

Call: A tumble of notes, squeals, and twitters; a two- or three-syllable *wap-wap* whistle, much like someone hailing a cab. Like all thrashers, curve-billeds can be excellent mimics of other birds' calls.

Hot spots: Estero Llano Grande State Park World Birding Center, Llano Grande, 26.1268335 / -97.9578167; Palo Alto Battlefield National Historical Park, Brownsville, 26.0191488 / -97.4760676; San Antonio Botanical Garden, San Antonio, 29.4601113 / -98.4572897; Sibley Nature Center, Midland, 32.0349286 / -102.0706594; Big Bend National Park, Dugout Wells, 29.2712002 / -103.1352997; Lake Ransom Canyon, Lubbock, 33.5304843 / -101.6825438.

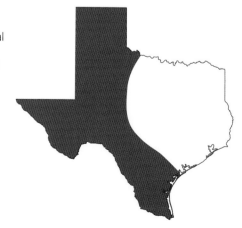

STARLING

EUROPEAN STARLING
Sturnus vulgaris

This introduced species arrived in North America in the 1800s and is now one of the most widespread and numerous birds on the continent.

Field marks: Starlings have three distinct plumages. Breeding adult has iridescent purple head, black eye, yellow bill, greenish back, greenish-black breast and belly, spotted flanks, black wings and short black tail with feathers outlined in brown. Nonbreeding adult has black head with white edges of each feather; black back, breast, belly, and flanks covered with white spots; scaly brownish wings and tail. Juvenile is softly brownish gray with a light gray throat, slightly darker wings.

Size: L: 8.5", WS: 15.5"–16"

Similar species: Purple martin is more uniformly blue-black. Molting indigo bunting is smaller and lacks the spotting of a winter starling.

Season: Year-round

Habitat: Very comfortable in residential and commercial areas; a frequent visitor to backyard feeders

Food source: Insects, invertebrates, spiders, fruit, berries, plants, seeds from feeders, human discards

Nest: In a tree cavity, on a girder under a bridge, in a hole in a building or tree, or in a nest box

Call: Most often a high-pitched, descending *zheeer, zheeer*, a long, chattering phrase of syllables gleaned from other birds' songs. Starlings also have a rasping, nonmusical, one-note *hashhh* call to signify danger.

Hot spots: Any gathering place for people has a population of starlings, whether it's in the middle of a city or along an open beach. Look for them around the edges of shopping malls, on city streets, at fairgrounds or outdoor festivals, in any farm field, along the paths of electrical lines, and in your own backyard if you feed birds regularly. Starlings often form colonies of tens of thousands of birds in winter to scavenge for food together, creating clouds of birds that move in unison to avoid predators. (Search "murmuration" on YouTube for some astonishing examples of this.)

211

BULBUL

RED-VENTED BULBUL
Pycnonotus cafer

This Southeast Asian species came to Texas as a caged bird. Escaped birds have established colonies in the suburbs of Houston.

Field marks: Black head with crest, mottled brown body with darker wings, white rump, bright red vent under the tail, long brown tail.

Size: L: 7", WS: 11"

Similar species: Northern cardinal is all red (male) or all tawny with red highlights (female). Other, more colorful birds with crests in similar habitat include blue jay (predominantly blue and white), several flycatchers (olive or gray overall), and eastern kingbird (solid gray with a bright white tail tip).

Season: Year-round

Habitat: In large gardens, parks, and other areas with exotic vegetation or plants that are not native to Texas

Food source: Fruit (mostly from exotic plant species), nectar, insects

Nest: In dense shrubs

Call: A liquid, musical burble of two or three notes in quick succession

Hot spots: White Oak Bayou Greenway Trail, Houston, 29.781494 / -95.3761943; Tony Marron Park, Houston, 29.7593853 / -95.3269637; University Place, Rice University Campus, Houston, 29.7185728 / -95.3991151; Stude Park, Houston, 29.7785 / -95.3855; Glenwood Cemetery, Houston, 29.765346 / -95.3849316.

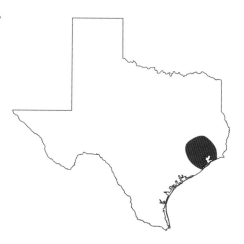

WAXWING

CEDAR WAXWING
Bombycilla cedrorum

Elegant winter visitors, waxwings move among the treetops in flocks as they devour berries in winter, as well as insects when available.

Field marks: Warm yellow-brown crest, neck, breast, and back; black mask outlined in white, white malar stripe against black throat, gray-brown upper wing, darker wing tips with red-tipped secondaries, lighter belly, white undertail coverts, black tail with yellow tip.

Size: L: 7"–7.25", WS: 11"–12"

Similar species: Bohemian waxwing is grayer overall, has white spots and yellow tips on its primaries, reddish undertail coverts, and a reddish forehead (and is almost never found in Texas).

Season: Winter

Habitat: Woodlands, neighborhoods, arboretums, orchards and other areas with many fruit trees

Food source: Insects, caterpillars, berries, fruit, sap, some flowers

Nest: On a branch in a tree with plenty of leaf canopy

Call: A single, high-pitched *pseeet*, often repeated

Hot spots: Waxwings move in large flocks, so any area with many trees may play host to dozens of them at once. Here are some particularly popular spots: Fort Worth Botanic Gardens, Fort Worth, 32.7370212 / -97.3639083; Brackenridge Field Labs, University of Texas at Austin, 30.282121 / -97.7791786; Government Canyon State Natural Area, San Antonio, 29.5490104 / -98.7641682; Davis Mountains State Park, Fort Davis, 30.60079 / -103.92579; Palo Duro Canyon State Park, Lake Tanglewood, 34.9651086 / -101.671257.

WARBLERS

NORTHERN PARULA
Setophaga americana

Look in moist forests with conifers for this small warbler, which prefers woodlands bordering freshwater marshes and streams.

Field marks: Male has gray head, white eye ring, black and yellow bill, yellow throat, rufous and black breast band with yellow below, white underside, greenish-brown back, gray wings with two white wing bars, gray tail. Female has slightly less yellow and may have no breast band.

Size: L: 4.25"–4.5", WS: 7"

Similar species: Nashville warbler has yellow throat and breast with no breast band, olive-green back, and yellow underside (in males). Mourning warbler has gray head, black throat, and mostly yellow underside.

Season: Summer in east Texas; migrating through central Texas in spring and fall

Habitat: Coniferous woods, especially bordering freshwater marshes, streams, and rivers

Food source: Insects, spiders, caterpillars, moths

Nest: Hidden among moss and lichens in trees

Call: An elongated, insect-like trill, terminating in a single staccato chip

Hot spots: Martin Dies State Park, Island Trail, Beech Grove, 30.87 / -94.1761111; Big Thicket National Preserve, Kirby Trail, Kountze, 30.4621326 / -94.3512954; High Island Boy Scout Woods, Bolivar Peninsula, 29.5613445 / -94.3902236; Bear Creek Park, Houston, 29.8247288 / -95.6288409; Kleb Woods Nature Preserve, Cypress, 30.0720853 / -95.7398187.

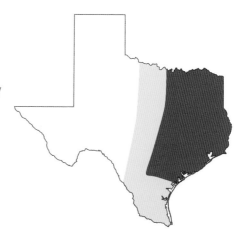

ORANGE-CROWNED WARBLER
Leiothlypis celata

This warbler's orange crown patch is almost never seen in the wild, so don't let this elusive field mark sway your identification.

Field marks: Olive-green above and dull yellow below, with a thin black eye line on the otherwise olive head. Breast and flanks are streaked with lighter yellow and olive, lighter yellow undertail coverts, olive tail.

Size: L: 4.75"–5", WS: 7"–8"

Similar species: Philadelphia vireo is gray above with a white eyebrow and much lighter undersides. Tennessee warbler has a gray head and white undersides.

Season: Winter in most of the state; spring and fall migration in the panhandle and northernmost Texas

Habitat: Deciduous forest edges, thickets, and shrubs, with a preference for willows

Food source: Invertebrates, berries, flower nectar

Nest: Low in a shrub or thicket, or on the ground; breeding in southern Canada and north to Alaska

Call: A high, one-pitch trill, ending on a single *cheet* note

Hot spots: This very common warbler can be found in any wooded area, but these spots are particularly dependable: Hornsby Bend, Austin, 30.2181988 / -97.6458054; San Antonio Botanical Garden, San Antonio, 29.4601113 / -98.4572897; South Texas Botanical Gardens, Corpus Christi, 27.6525275 / -97.4068666; Estero Llano Grande State Park World Birding Center, Llano Grande, 26.1268335 / -97.9578167; White Rock Lake, Dallas, 32.8337313 / -96.7121315.

GIL ECKRICH

GOLDEN-CHEEKED WARBLER
Setophaga chrysoparia

Texas has many localized bird populations, but few are as stunning as this one.

Field marks: Bright yellow face with black stripe through the eye, black cap and nape, black throat and breast, white underside with black streaks on flanks, black wings with two white wing bars, dark tail with white underside. Female is similar but paler, with more white in the throat.

Size: L: 4.5"–5", WS: 7.5"–8.5"

Similar species: Black-throated green warbler has no black cap, and is more olive on the head and back. Townsend's warbler has a black teardrop around the eye and a yellow cheek spot, and its breast is yellow streaked with black.

Season: Spring and fall near the Texas-Mexico border to San Antonio, summer in the hill country

Habitat: In Texas's Edwards Plateau, exclusively in juniper-oak woodlands

Food source: Caterpillars and other soft larvae

Nest: In juniper or oak trees, usually above 15 feet

Call: A high, buzzy *zhu-zhu-zhu-zhu-ZEE-zee*; also a long *zhuuu* ending in a short, upward *zhee*

Hot spots: Fort Cavazos (numerous locations; permit required), Gatesville, 31.3730563 / -97.7176809; Baker Sanctuary, Cedar Park, 30.4826306 / -97.8739357; Balcones Canyonlands National Wildlife Refuge, Doeskin Ranch, Bertram, 30.6190048 / -98.0728912; Pedernales Falls State Park, Cypress Mill, 30.3067833 / -98.2512236; Lost Maples State Natural Area, Vanderpool, 29.8166679 / -99.5721388.

NASHVILLE WARBLER
Leiothlypis ruficapilla

Bright and vocal, Nashville warblers move through during spring and fall migration.

Field marks: Male has gray head with bright white eye ring, small black bill; small reddish patch at top of head may be visible during breeding season; greenish back and wings, bright yellow breast and underside, yellow undertail coverts, short greenish tail. Female does not have the reddish patch and is paler yellow.

Size: L: 4.75", WS: 7.5"

Similar species: Mourning warbler has a gray head and black throat. Tennessee warbler has a gray head, olive-green back, and white underside.

Season: Spring and fall migration, with some individuals remaining through the winter along the Gulf coast

Habitat: Mixed forests with shrubs, wooded areas along edges of wetlands

Food source: Insects

Nest: On the ground, hidden at the base of a shrub or behind grasses

Call: Two-part call: high-pitched *seedle, seedle, seedle, seedle, bit-bit-bit-bit-bit*, also a simple *chit* note

Hot spots: White Rock Lake & Old Fish Hatchery, Dallas, 32.8156276 / -96.7264652; Lake Waco, Woodway Park, 31.5236784 / -97.2314501; Brackenridge Field Labs, University of Texas at Austin, 30.282121 / -97.7791786; San Antonio Botanical Garden, San Antonio, 29.4601113 / -98.4572897; Jenna Welch Nature Center I-20 Pond, Midland, 31.9630947 / -102.1210903.

YELLOW WARBLER
Setophaga petechia

America's most numerous and widespread warbler—with an estimated population of 39 million birds—is also one of its most delightful, with its cheery song and showy plumage.

Field marks: Male has bright yellow head, dull yellow back and tail, black eye and bill, yellow breast and underside with bright reddish streaks. Female is very similar but lacks the red streaks.

Size: L: 5", WS: 7.75"–8"

Similar species: Wilson's warbler has no red streaks, and it has a black cap and a greenish mantle. American goldfinch is lemon yellow with a black cap and black wings.

Season: Spring and fall migration

Habitat: A combination of mixed woodlands and water features, including bogs, marshes, and swamps; also farmland, thickets, and residential areas

Food source: Insects, spiders; berries in a pinch

Nest: On a branch in a young tree

Call: A high-pitched warble, popularly parsed as *sweet-sweet-sweet-sweedle-sweet*; also a series of simple *tsp* notes when alarmed

Hot spots: These warblers are everywhere during migration, including many backyards and gardens, so check your neighborhood parks and wooded areas before traveling to look for this bird. Here are some places that migrating warblers favor: Hornsby Bend, Austin, 30.2181988 / -97.6458054; San Antonio Botanical Garden, San Antonio, 29.4601113 / -98.4572897; South Texas Botanical Gardens, Corpus Christi, 27.6525275 / -97.4068666; Estero Llano Grande State Park World Birding Center, Llano Grande, 26.1268335 / -97.9578167; White Rock Lake, Dallas, 32.8337313 / -96.7121315.

YELLOW-RUMPED WARBLER
Setophaga coronata

Texas sees both the Audubon (left) and myrtle (right) races of this abundant bird—and plenty of them, as the planet hosts more than 90 million of this species.

Field marks: Male has yellow cap, black mask with a white eyebrow and throat; gray back, wings, and tail; white breast and underside with heavy black streaks, yellow flanks, two white wing bars, white undertail coverts, yellow rump. Female is less boldly marked, with a gray cap and more muted mask.

Size: L: 5.5", WS: 9.25"

Similar species: Magnolia warbler has a yellow throat, breast, and underside. Black-throated green warbler has a yellow-green face, olive-green back, and black throat.

Season: Winter, and spring and fall migration through the panhandle

Habitat: Woodlands, thickets, shrubby areas, beach dunes, residential areas, parks, others

Food source: Insects, berries

Nest: Usually high in a conifer, but possibly in lower vegetation in some areas (not in Texas)

Call: A rapid, two part song: *twee-twee-twee-twee-twee, tooey-tooey*; also an irregularly spaced series of very high *tsi, tsi* notes

Hot spots: This common warbler can turn up anywhere, from a national forest to your front yard. Easily confused with a number of other warbler species, yellow-rumpeds require a careful look even if you've already seen a dozen of them that day. Slight variations in plumage between the male, female, and immature are enough to confuse even the most experienced birders, but their "butter butt" nickname is a good reminder to always check for yellow at the base of the tail.

JASON VASSALLO

COLIMA WARBLER
Leiothlypis crissalis

One of the hardest birds to see in Texas, this tiny, drab warbler breeds in the Chisos Mountains in Big Bend National Park.

Field marks: Gray-to-brown head, back, wings, and tail; small rusty patch on head in fresh adults; white eye ring, slightly lighter breast and underside, golden undertail coverts.

Size: L: 5.5"–6", WS: 7.5"–8"

Similar species: Lucy's warbler is smaller, grayer, and has a rust-colored rump. Virginia's warbler has a yellow breast and rump.

Season: Spring; the bird remains in the Chisos Mountains through the summer to breed, but it is nearly impossible to find once it stops singing.

Habitat: Oak woods between 5,500 and 6,400 feet

Food source: Larvae, caterpillars; insects caught in midair

Nest: On the ground on a mountain slope

Call: A long trill, ending in a single *tsp*

Hot spots: Big Bend National Park, Chisos Mountains area trails, 29.2699985 / -103.3004522. When Colima warblers arrive at the end of April, daytime temperatures may already rise above 100 degrees Fahrenheit. See the rangers in the Chisos Basin Visitor Center before you choose a trail to hike to determine where the bird is being seen and how far up the mountains you need to go. You will have the best results if you take advantage of the cooler air before sunrise. Take twice as much water as you think you will need, and bring sweet/salty snacks and lunch.

PINE WARBLER
Setophaga pinus

The pine warbler's yellow plumage stands out for winter birders as this bird mingles with palm warblers.

Field marks: Male has olive head and face with yellow spectacles, yellow dot above bill, yellow throat and breast, olive streaks on breast and flanks, white belly and undertail coverts, olive back, gray wings with two white wing bars, gray tail. Female lacks the streaking on breast but has light streaks on flanks. *Fall plumage:* Gray head and back with white eye ring, pale neck patch, light gray underside with indistinct streaks on flanks, gray wings with white wing bars.

Size: L: 5.5", WS: 8.75"

Similar species: Female Cape May warbler has more distinct dark streaks on the breast and underside. Fall Cape May lacks the eye ring and has a greenish rump. Fall blackburnian warbler has yellow throat.

Season: Year-round in easternmost Texas, winter through the eastern third of the state

Habitat: Mixed or coniferous forests with pine trees

Food source: Insects, seeds, fruit

Nest: At the end of a pine tree branch at least 20 feet up, hidden by needles

Call: A long, melodious trill, similar to a chipping sparrow but slower

Hot spots: Pine warblers are widespread and numerous throughout the winter, usually found feeding in mowed areas near wetlands in the company of palm warblers. Here are some dependable spots: Jesse H. Jones County Park, Houston, 30.024 / -95.295; Lake o' the Pines, Cedar Springs Park, Ore City, 32.8402939 / -94.6934795; Tyler State Park, Tyler, 32.4799358 / -95.2991867; Davy Crockett National Forest, Ratcliff Lake, 31.3883733 / -95.1549911; Sam Rayburn Reserve, San Augustine Park, Pineland, 31.1986329 / -94.0782666.

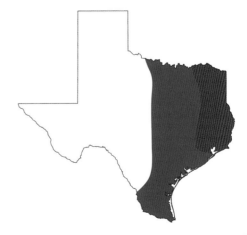

BLACK-AND-WHITE WARBLER
Mniotilta varia

The black-and-white warbler climbs trees like a nuthatch and is comfortable upside down on a tree trunk—a unique quality among eastern warblers.

Field marks: Male has black and white–striped head with wide black eye stripe, patchy black throat, white underside with black stripes from breast to undertail, black and white–striped back and wings, two horizontal white wing bars, black tail. Female has black and white–striped head with thin eye stripe, pale cheek and throat, gray nape, white underside with gray stripes, buff flanks, black and white–striped back and wings with two horizontal wing bars.

Size: L: 5.25", WS: 8.25"

Similar species: Blackpoll warbler has a solid black cap that extends down the head to the eye and a solid gray back.

Season: Winter in the southeast, spring and fall through west and central Texas, summer in the east and south-central area

Habitat: Deciduous forests, parks, residential areas

Food source: Caterpillars, insect eggs found under bark, spiders, insects

Nest: On the ground at the bottom of a tree or stump

Call: A high, wheezy, squeaky song of ten or eleven notes: *ziti-ziti-ziti-ziti-ziti* or *weezee-weezee-weezee-weezee-weezee*; also a single *zeet* chip note

Hot spots: This common warbler may turn up in any park with tall, leafy trees, but these areas are especially productive: Crescent Bend Nature Park, Cibolo, 29.5502272 / -98.2325739; Neches River National Wildlife Refuge, Pierces Chapel, 31.8902629 / -95.429821; Commons Ford Ranch Metro Park, Austin, 30.3373826 / -97.8930759; Colorado Bend State Park, Bend, 31.0221933 / -98.4426498; Granger Lake area, Friendship, 30.7001608 / -97.3597466.

COMMON YELLOWTHROAT
Geothlypis trichas

"Common," in this case, is correct: Every wetland, forest pool, river, stream, or lake in Texas has some of these chatty, bright-colored warblers.

Field marks: Male has tan cap, nape, back, wings, and tail; black mask across eyes to the bill, extending to the throat on either side, with a white upper stripe; dark bill, yellow throat, tan belly and flanks, yellow undertail coverts. Female has tan head, neck, back, wings, tail, and underside; white eye ring, yellow throat and undertail coverts. *Fall plumage:* Male has tan head, back, wings, and tail; brown forehead, nearly black shading along the malars, yellow throat, tan underside, light yellow undertail coverts. Female is similar to male, but without the dark shading along the malar, and with a paler yellow throat.

Size: L: 5", WS: 6.75"

Similar species: Yellow-throated and yellow-rumped warblers have yellow throats, but with black and white heads and bodies. Magnolia warbler has a yellow throat and a black mask, but has a black and white head and body and heavy black streaks on its breast and underside.

Season: Winter in southeast Texas to the Lower Rio Grande Valley, year-round on the northern Gulf coast, summer in east Texas and in the northwest panhandle; spring and fall migration throughout much of the rest of the state

Habitat: Damp woods and fields, wetlands, streambeds, riparian areas, dunes near beaches, or along brushy roadsides with drainage canals

Food source: Spiders, butterflies, dragonflies, beetles, grasshoppers, some seeds

Nest: Near the ground and concealed by high grasses and other vegetation

Call: A musical phrase with the common mnemonic *witchity, witchity, witchity, witt*, sometimes fast and sometimes slower; also a rapid, staccato trill like a rattlesnake and a general unmusical chatter

Hot spots: Any stop at a wetland, coastal dunes, woodland edge near water, or a riparian area can yield at least one common yellowthroat. Listen for its song and calls to determine exactly where it might be, and watch for movement—yellowthroats are usually on the move through their habitat as they forage for food. These birds are also well known for responding to spishing, a birder trick to attract a bird's attention.

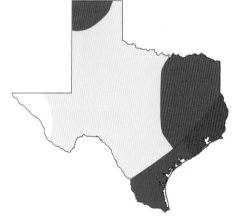

WILSON'S WARBLER
Cardellina pusilla

This small warbler migrates through Texas in spring and fall; a few individuals stay for the winter along the Gulf coast and in the Lower Rio Grande Valley.

Field marks: Male has black oval cap, lemon-yellow face, large black eye, small pink bill; yellow throat, breast, belly, and undertail coverts; solid olive back, wings, and tail. Female is more muted, with a smaller cap that may be olive, black, or with elements of each. *Fall plumage:* Black cap may (or may not) have olive feathers in it during fall and winter.

Size: L: 4.75", WS: 7"

Similar species: Yellow warbler has no black cap. Hooded warbler has a black throat and a black cap that extends from forehead to throat. Common yellowthroat has a substantial black mask. Prothonotary warbler has no cap and has blue-gray wings.

Season: Spring and fall migration except for some areas along the Gulf coast

Habitat: Woodlands with willow and alder trees and water features, including streams, wetlands, and pools

Food source: Insects, spiders

Nest: On the ground among dense vegetation in a thicket or shrubby area (not in Texas)

Call: A two-part series of notes, doubling in speed halfway through: *chi-chi-chi-chi-chichichichichi*; alternately, the song may be just the opposite, with its rapid notes first, slowing to a more languid pace in the middle: *chichichichichi-che-che-che-che-che*. Very high pitched single chip notes are also in the repertoire.

Hot spots: High Island Smith Oaks Sanctuary, Bolivar Peninsula, 29.573681 / -94.3898535; Brazos Bend State Park, Thompsons, 29.3735739 / -95.6230259; Mitchell Lake Audubon Center, San Antonio, 29.3105956 / -98.4996938; Jenna Welch Nature Center I-20 Pond, Midland, 31.9630947 / -102.1210903; Johnson Ponds area, Alpine, 30.3660623 / -103.6742771.

TANAGERS AND ALLIED SONGBIRDS

Tanagers

SUMMER TANAGER
Piranga rubra

North America's only totally red bird and its muted yellow mate love to forage at the tops of trees.

Field marks: Male is entirely bright red, with a heavy gray bill. Female is a dull yellow with olive-yellow wings.

Size: L: 7.5"–8", WS: 11"–12"

Similar species: Northern cardinal has a black facial pattern around the bill, and a pronounced crest (female is soft brown with red accents and an orange bill). Scarlet tanager has black wings. Vermilion flycatcher is smaller and has black wings and tail and a black mask.

Season: Summer

Habitat: Deciduous or mixed forests

Food source: Primarily bees and wasps, as well as a number of other insects

Nest: On a forked tree branch, usually overhanging a waterway or road

Call: A short phrase of five or six sliding whistles, very like an American robin

Hot spots: Village Creek Drying Beds, Arlington, 32.7842795 / -97.1266181; Gus Engling Wildlife Management Area, Bethel, 31.9297289 / -95.8876419; Flat Rock Lake, Kerrville, 30.0092157 / -99.1150153; Government Canyon State Natural Area, San Antonio, 29.5490104 / -98.7641682; South Padre Island Birding and Nature Center, 26.1374628 / -97.1739367.

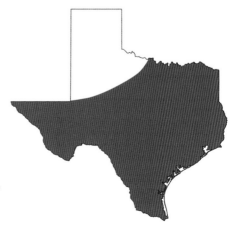

SCARLET TANAGER
Piranga olivacea

The flaming red bird with black wings stands out from any tree it inhabits.

Field marks: Male has red head and body, black wings and tail, gray bill. Female has olive head, back, wings, and tail; black eye, yellow lores and throat, gray bill, olive-yellow underparts. *Fall plumage:* Male has olive head and back, black wings, yellow lores and malars, darker yellow throat and breast, yellow belly, yellow-gray underside and undertail coverts. Female retains the same plumage in nonbreeding season.

Size: L: 7", WS: 11.5"

Similar species: Northern cardinal male has red wings and tail, a pronounced crest, a black face and a red bill. Male summer tanager's wings are red.

Season: Spring and fall migration

Habitat: Deciduous and mixed woodlands, especially those with pine and oak; parks, residential areas

Food source: Insects, fruit, tree leaf and flower buds

Nest: On a tree branch at least 20 feet above the ground (not in Texas)

Call: A sweet, burry *cheet-chip-chureet, churrit, chureet, churitt, chureet*; also a more frequent and recognizable *chick-burr* note

Hot spots: Lafitte's Cove, Galveston, 29.2169006 / -94.9349016; Quintana Neotropical Bird Sanctuary, Quintana, 28.9336226 / -95.3087246; Mills Pond at Wells Branch, Austin, 30.45 / -97.68012; Blucher Park, Corpus Christi, 27.791317 / -97.399174; Valley Land Fund lots, South Padre Island, 26.0988053 / -97.1678612.

Cardinal and Pyrrhuloxia

NORTHERN CARDINAL
Cardinalis cardinalis

The denizen of backyard feeders and neighborhood parks throughout the eastern states, this local resident is one of the first birds that new birders recognize on sight.

Field marks: Male has bright red head with pronounced crest, black face, red bill, red body and tail with darker red wings. Female has brown body, crest with red wash, black face, bright orange bill, red wings and tail.

Size: L: 8.75", WS: 12"

Similar species: Scarlet tanager has no crest, has black wings and a black tail. Summer tanager has no crest, has a dark bill, and no black on the face.

Season: Year-round

Habitat: Deciduous and coniferous woods, residential areas, woodland borders of farm fields and wetlands, parks

Food source: Seeds, insects, fruit, berries

Nest: In a bush or tree with low branches, not more than 5 feet from the ground

Call: Musical and varied, often beginning with a long, plunging pennywhistle note that ends with a *cha-cha-cha-cha-cha* series, or beginning with a *neerEET, neerEET* series and returning to the *cha-cha-cha* notes at the end. Other variations are likely. Also a metallic chip note, often heard just before dusk.

Hot spots: Every neighborhood has several families of cardinals, so you don't need to look far to find them. Draw them into your yard by offering black oil sunflower seed at your feeders, or take a walk in a park or on a converted rail trail to find them just beyond the first trees as you pass. Cardinals perch on the tops of fences or on posts as well as on low tree branches.

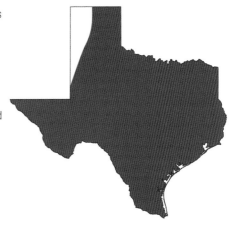

PYRRHULOXIA
Cardinalis sinuatus

With plumage that blends into its desert surroundings, this cardinal-like bird nests in mesquite and other desert shrubs.

Field marks: Gray to sandy brown overall with a red face, red in its crest; blotchy red throat, breast, and belly, and red areas of its wings and tail. Its bright yellow bill is short but bulky for cracking open the shells of seeds.

Size: L: 8"–8.75", WS: 12"

Similar species: Female northern cardinal is browner, with a black frame around its red-to-orange bill.

Season: Year-round

Habitat: Open desert with cactus and low shrubs

Food source: Seeds, cactus fruits and berries, grasshoppers and other large insects

Nest: At least 5 feet off the ground in a mesquite or other desert tree

Call: Clear, simple, repeated *cheer, cheer, cheer, cheer, cheer*; also a high-pitched chip note, softer and breathier than a cardinal's chip

Hot spots: Big Bend National Park, Daniels Ranch Road, 29.1839794 / -102.9645274; Keystone Heritage Park, El Paso, 31.8209406 / -106.5630008; Lake Colorado City State Park, Lake Colorado City, 32.3289899 / -100.931139; Davis Mountains State Park, Fort Davis, 30.60079 / -103.92579; Sibley Nature Center, Midland, 32.0349286 / -102.0706594.

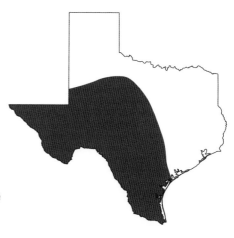

Grosbeaks

BLUE GROSBEAK
Passerina caerulea

The largest of the predominantly blue birds in Texas prefers open areas with low brush and few trees.

Field marks: Male is royal blue with darker wings and two rufous wing bars; a very large, light gray bill. Female is light brownish gray with darker wings and one rufous wing bar.

Size: L: 6.5"–7", WS: 11"–12"

Similar species: Indigo bunting is smaller and solid blue with no wing bars. Eastern bluebird has an orange breast, a white underside, and a smaller bill. Mountain bluebird is smaller and has a lighter blue underside, no wing bars, and a much smaller bill.

Season: Summer

Habitat: Shrubby areas with low, dense vegetation, like fallow farm fields, edges of woodlands, power line right-of-way corridors, and other overgrown lots

Food source: Mostly insects, with some snails

Nest: Low in a tree, shrub or tangle of vines

Call: A series of bubbly musical notes like a shortened finch song, usually about 3 seconds

Hot spots: Any open field throughout the state may invite blue grosbeaks to perch on fence posts or wires. Here are some very dependable places to see them: Jenna Welch Nature Center I-20 Pond, Midland, 31.9630947 / -102.1210903; Hornsby Bend, Austin, 30.2181988 / -97.6458054; Village Creek Drying Beds, Arlington, 32.7842795 / -97.1266181; Corps Woods, Galveston, 29.3289668 / -94.7689354; South Llano River State Park, Junction, 30.4391651 / -99.8128617.

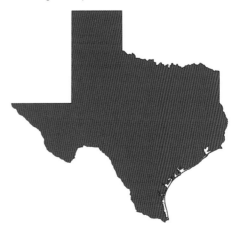

BLACK-HEADED GROSBEAK
Pheucticus melanocephalus

This orange and black bird with the very large bill comes to backyard feeders to feast on sunflower seed—though insects are their preferred diet.

Field marks: Male has all-black head, very large gray bill, mostly orange body, black and white wings, white undertail coverts, black tail. Female has a brown head with a strong white eyebrow stripe, peach and white underside, sometimes with fine brown streaks; brown back and wings with white wing bar, brown tail. First-year birds of both genders look more like female.

Size: L: 7"–7.5", WS: 12"–12.5"

Similar species: Bullock's oriole is thinner and brighter orange overall, with an orange face, black cap and chin, a much smaller bill, and a black back. Spotted towhee has an all-black head and breast, a red eye, a much smaller bill, and a white underside with solid chestnut flanks. Female blue grosbeak is tawnier overall with no white markings on the head or face.

Season: Summer in westernmost Texas; spring and fall migration throughout central Texas and the panhandle

Habitat: Areas with lots of different plants and water nearby, including wooded areas with a healthy understory, riparian areas, gardens with water features, botanical gardens, suburban neighborhoods

Food source: Insects, snails, berries, grains, seeds

Nest: High on a tree branch generally about 25 feet off the ground

Call: A burble of many notes, varied like a finch, but sweeter and clearer; also a single *pik* call

Hot spots: Davis Mountains Preserve, Tobe Canyon, 30.6461274 / -104.1792727; Big Bend National Park, Chisos Mountains area trails, 29.2699985 / -103.3004522; Big Bend National Park, Rio Grande Village, 29.1809226 / -102.9557133; Jenna Welch Nature Center I-20 Pond, Midland, 31.9630947 / -102.1210903; Memorial Park, El Paso, 31.7894117 / -106.4571601.

Buntings

LARK BUNTING
Calamospiza melanocorys

The black bird with white wing patches is unmistakable as it flies over grassy fields.

Field marks: Male is sparrow-sized bird with black head and body, chunky gray bill, black wings with white wing patches visible at rest as well as in flight. Female has a brown head with thin white eyebrow and malars, large bluish bill, white throat; brown and black sparrowlike plumage with brown and white chest, white belly with fine brown streaks; brown tail.

Size: L: 5.5"–7", WS: 10"–11"

Similar species: No other Texas bird is all black with white wings. Female can be confused with many other sparrows, but the large bill is very different from the typical, thinner sparrow bill.

Season: Summer in the northwestern panhandle, year-round in the southern panhandle, winter throughout central and western Texas

Habitat: Grasslands and prairies

Food source: Insects, fruit, seeds

Nest: Deep in the grass at the base of a shrub

Call: A song of several parts in succession, including a rattling call, clear notes like a cardinal, a high trill not unlike a rotary-dial phone, and more clear notes. A *wooWHEET* call note may also be heard.

Hot spots: Buffalo Lake National Wildlife Refuge, Umbarger, 34.9101471 / -102.1138; Seminole Canyon State Park, Comstock, 29.6935703 / -101.3185787; Rolling Plains Quail Research Ranch, Midway, 32.7366061 / -100.5719376; Ballinger City Lake, Ballinger, 31.7326203 / -100.0375557; Boles Road/CR 2800, Lubbock, 33.5559996 / -101.7664164.

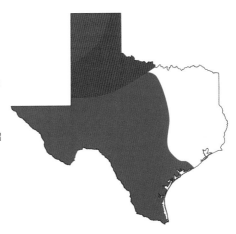

INDIGO BUNTING
Passerina cyanea

This gorgeous all-blue bird raises its young near open woodlands, meadows, and farm fields.

Field marks: Male has bright blue head, body, and tail; whitish bill, black wings with blue shoulders. Female has light brown head and body with a white throat, fine brown streaks on its breast, slightly darker brown wings, whitish undertail coverts, and a light brown tail with a bluish hue. *Fall plumage:* Male has mottled blue and brown head and body, brown wings with a bluish cast, white undertail coverts, and a bluish tail. Female has rosy brown head with white throat, pinkish breast with faint streaks, whitish belly and undertail, rosy-brown wings and tail.

Size: L: 5.5"–5.75", WS: 8"–9"

Similar species: Blue grosbeak has dark wings with two rufous wing bars. Eastern bluebird has an orange breast and belly and white undertail coverts. Cerulean warbler has a white throat, breast, and belly and two white wing bars. Black-throated blue warbler has a black throat and white belly.

Season: Summer through east and central Texas and the panhandle; migration through the west-central region

Habitat: Scrubby fields, pastures with wooded edges, cleared gaps between woodlands

Food source: Seeds, berries, insects

Nest: Well-concealed in a shrub or small tree, not far from the ground

Call: A musical *pitty-pitty-cheeRAH-chee-chee-peeyu*, with longer and shorter variations. A single sharp *chit*, repeated frequently, is the chip note.

Hot spots: Armand Bayou Nature Center, Pasadena, 29.5956627 / -95.07195; Lost Maples State Natural Area, Vanderpool, 29.8166679 / -99.5721388; Trinity River Audubon Center, Dallas, 32.703804 / -96.705555; South Llano River State Park, Junction, 30.4391651 / -99.8128617; Mitchell Lake Audubon Center, San Antonio, 29.3105956 / -98.4996938.

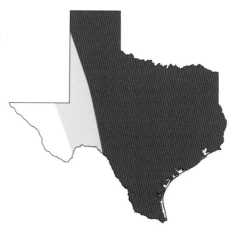

PAINTED BUNTING
Passerina ciris

One of the most beautiful and sought-after birds in North America makes most of Texas its breeding grounds.

Field marks: Male has a purple head with a red eye ring; red throat, breast, underside, and rump; green back and darker wings with a vague red wing bar. Female is olive above and muted yellow below.

Size: L: 5"–6", WS: 8.5"–9"

Similar species: Indigo bunting is solid blue. No other Texas bird has this striking color pattern.

Season: Summer

Habitat: Fields near sparse woods, such as rows of trees between farm fields; roadsides, backyards with feeders

Food source: Seeds, as well as some insects on the ground; also comes to feeders

Nest: In scrub or other dense foliage, usually about 6 feet above the ground (often higher)

Call: A jumble of rising and falling notes, like a house finch but shorter; also a simple *twik* note

Hot spots: Painted buntings are quite common in Texas, regularly visiting backyard feeders and speeding across open fields from one lone tree to another. Whether you keep an eye out in a suburban neighborhood or venture into wildlife refuges and preserves, you are nearly certain to come across this brightly colored bird and its less-flamboyant mate.

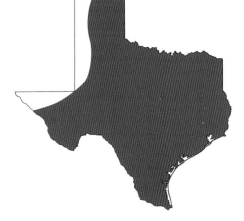

Dickcissel

DICKCISSEL
Spiza americana

A Midwestern bird of open grasslands, this sparrowlike visitor breeds throughout much of Texas and migrates north through the Lower Rio Grande Valley.

Field marks: Male has gray head and nape, white and yellow eyebrow, yellow patch on sides of throat, black V-shaped patch at throat, yellow breast, gray belly and flanks, gray back streaked in black, brown and gray wings with rufous shoulders, gray tail. Female has brownish-gray head with dull yellow eyebrow, darker gray cap, white malar stripe edged in black, whitish throat, yellowish breast, gray flanks and belly, black and gray wings with rufous wing stripe, white undertail coverts, gray tail.

Size: L: 6.25"–7", WS: 9.75"–11"

Similar species: Eastern meadowlark is larger and has a bright yellow throat, breast, and underside. House sparrow is smaller, has no yellow areas, and its black breast patch is not in a V shape.

Season: Summer throughout most of the state; migrating over the Gulf coast

Habitat: Open farm fields, especially where grain is grown

Food source: Grain, seeds, insects

Nest: Near the ground among the plant stalks

Call: A clear series of notes followed by a hissing trill: *dick-dick-dick-cissss* or *dick-dick-cis-cis-cis*

Hot spots: Any open field is likely to attract dickcissels, but here are some very dependable sites: Balcones Canyonlands National Wildlife Refuge, Shin Oak Observation Deck, Bertram, 30.6600596 / -98.0494916; Hornsby Bend, Austin, 30.2181988 / -97.6458054; Mitchell Lake Audubon Center, San Antonio, 29.3105956 / -98.4996938; South Llano River State Park, Junction, 30.4391651 / -99.8128617; San Angelo State Park—South Unit, San Angelo, 31.4669145 / -100.5013617.

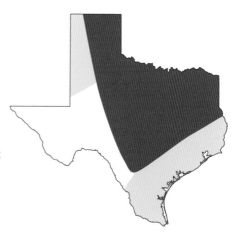

SPARROWS AND THEIR ALLIES

Towhees

SPOTTED TOWHEE
Pipilo maculatus

Watch for leaves rustling on the ground to find a spotted towhee as it searches for seeds and insects.

Field marks: Male has an all-black head, back, and throat; white underside, dark rufous flanks, brown wings with white spots, and a long, black tail, often held up at a 45-degree angle from the body. Female is very similar, but the head and breast are brown.

Size: L: 6.5"–8.5", WS: 11"

Similar species: Eastern towhee, whose territory barely overlaps with spotted towhee in central Texas, looks very much the same as the spotted towhee, but lacks the white spots across the shoulders of the wings.

Season: Winter through most of the state, year-round in part of westernmost Texas

Habitat: Open grasslands with high grass, forest edges, hedgerows, thickets, canyons with plenty of underbrush

Food source: Insects found under leaves on the ground, acorns, berries, a wide range of seeds

Nest: On the ground, usually hidden by grasses or under a fallen tree branch

Call: Three clear notes in quick succession, followed by a 2-second rattling trill

Hot spots: Davis Mountains Preserve, Tobe Canyon, 30.6461274 / -104.1792727; Big Bend National Park, Chisos Mountains area trails, 29.2699985 / -103.3004522; South Llano River State Park, Junction, 30.4391651 / -99.8128617; Hornsby Bend, Austin, 30.2181988 / -97.6458054; Lewisville Lake Environmental Learning Area, Lewisville, 33.0662579 / -96.9750008.

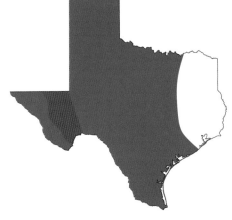

CANYON TOWHEE

Melozone fusca

Homeowners in west Texas know this bird from its visits to platform feeders, where they are one of the only birds that will eat milo seeds.

Field marks: Tawny brown overall with a rufous undertail area, and a long brown tail.

Size: L: 8"–10", WS: 11"–11.5"

Similar species: California and Abert's towhees and clay-colored thrush all look similar to canyon towhee, but their ranges do not overlap in Texas.

Season: Year-round

Habitat: Desert areas with grasses, rocks, low trees and shrubs; also in human neighborhoods, especially where there are feeders

Food source: Seeds and berries

Nest: On a tree branch close to the trunk, anywhere from 3 to 12 feet up

Call: A rapid *chill, chill, chill, chekit*, sometimes with only two *chill* before the final note and sometimes with four

Hot spots: TX 118 at Musquiz Creek, Fort Davis, 30.53569 / -103.80343; Big Bend National Park, Dugout Wells, 29.2712002 / -103.1352997; Twin Buttes Reservoir, San Angelo, 31.3774555 / -100.5366611; South Llano River State Park, Junction, 30.4391651 / -99.8128617; Milton Reimers Ranch Park, Cypress Creek Ranch, 30.3641504 / -98.1237811.

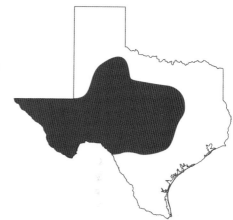

DOMINIC SHERONY

GREEN-TAILED TOWHEE
Pipilo chlorurus

A winter resident of west Texas, this secretive sparrow migrates through the panhandle to its breeding grounds just outside the state.

Field marks: Gray overall with a bright, rusty crown, a white throat, and an almost chartreuse wash over its wings and tail.

Size: L: 7"–7.5", WS: 9.5"–10"

Similar species: Olive sparrow is smaller, has a brown cap and a brown line through the eye, and its back and shoulders are a darker, duller green. Rufous-crowned sparrow has no green areas, and is mottled gray and brown across the wings and back.

Season: Winter in west Texas; spring and fall migration in the western panhandle

Habitat: In open shrubland, desert grassland, sparse forest, or areas with new growth after a fire; although their breeding habitat is at high altitudes, they spend the winter at lower elevations.

Food source: Seeds and insects found on the ground. Watch for a bird hopping forward and immediately backward as it redistributes woodland detritus under its feet.

Nest: Deep in a shrub or low tree, close to the ground (not in Texas)

Call: A combination of chirps, syrupy notes, and trills in succession; also a call note like a squeeze toy, similar to a catbird

Hot spots: Fort Peña Colorado Park, Marathon, 30.152997 / -103.2874735; Hueco Tanks State Park & Historic Site, El Paso, 31.9214283 / -106.0467612; Davis Mountains State Park, Fort Davis, 30.60079 / -103.92579; Christmas Mountains Oasis, Alpine, 29.4917768 / -103.4670389; Big Bend National Park, Chisos Mountains area trails, 29.2699985 / -103.3004522.

Sparrows

FIELD SPARROW
Spizella pusilla

Listen for a song that accelerates like a bouncing Ping-Pong ball to find this bird in an open field or meadow.

Field marks: Rufous and gray crown, gray head, rufous line behind eye, white eye ring, pink bill, buff breast, gray underside with light rufous flanks, rufous and brown wings with black primaries and two thin white wing bars, long gray tail.

Size: L: 5.75", WS: 8"

Similar species:. Chipping sparrow has a white eyebrow and a dark bill.

Season: Year-round in east Texas; winter in central, south, and parts of the west

Habitat: Disused pastures and farm fields, grasslands

Food source: Insects, seeds

Nest: On the ground or very low in a shrub

Call: An extended, accelerating song on one note: *twee, twee, twee, tweetitititititititi*; also a thin, high, sharp chip note

Hot spots: Commons Ford Ranch Metro Park, Austin, 30.3373826 / -97.8930759; Guadalupe River State Park, Spring Branch, 29.8736946 / -98.4859303; Kickapoo Cavern State Park, Kinney County, 29.61154 / -100.4533; Palo Duro Canyon State Park, Lake Tanglewood, 34.9651086 / -101.671257; San Angelo State Park—South Unit, San Angelo, 31.4669145 / -100.5013617.

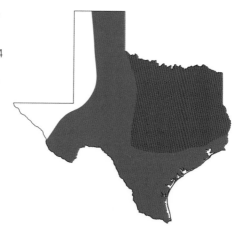

LARK SPARROW
Chondestes grammacus

This boldly patterned sparrow is easy to spot in the state's ample open country.

Field marks: Rufous cap with white center stripe, wide gray-white eyebrow, black eye line, rufous cheek, white lower eye ring, white malar stripe with black edge, gray throat, clear whitish breast with dark center spot, grayish-white underside, buff flanks, gray wings and tail with white outer tail feathers.

Size: L: 5.75"–6.5", WS: 10.5"–11"

Similar species: Clay-colored sparrow has a similar but browner facial pattern, buff underparts, and no black dot on the breast.

Season: Year-round through most of the state, winter in southernmost Texas, and summer in the panhandle.

Habitat: Scrubby areas and dunes along shorelines, open grasslands

Food source: Insects, seeds

Nest: On the ground or very low in a shrub or sapling; midwestern and western United States

Call: A long series of whistles and trills, not unlike a song sparrow; also a very high, thin *tsp* chip note

Hot spots: Any open area may host its own lark sparrows, but these spots are particularly productive: Palo Duro Canyon State Park, Lake Tanglewood, 34.9651086 / -101.671257; Salineño Wildlife Preserve, Roma, 26.5148584 / -99.116206; Cook's Slough Nature Center, Uvalde, 29.1873567 / -99.7886572; Big Bend National Park, Rio Grande Village, 29.1809226 / -102.9557133; Ascarate Park/ Lake, El Paso, 31.7532135 / -106.4023923.

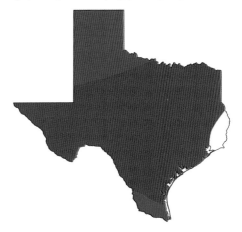

BLACK-THROATED SPARROW
Amphispiza bilineata

It's easy to spot this dapper sparrow in desert habitat, with its black throat nicely embellished with a white stripe on either side.

Field marks: Gray head with a bold white stripe above the eye, black throat with a white stripe on either side of it; soft brown body, wings, and tail; white underside.

Size: L: 4.5"–5.5", WS: 7.5"–8"

Similar species: Black-chinned sparrow has an all-gray head and body, with no white on the face and a bright pink bill. Other similar sparrows, including five-striped sparrow, do not have territory in Texas.

Season: Year-round

Habitat: Open desert and canyons with low shrubs

Food source: Insects, seeds

Nest: In low shrubs, close to but not on the ground

Call: A three-syllable chirp, followed by a buzz, then a repeated chirrup, ending with a musical trill. Variations in this song may use just one phrase of this complex construction.

Hot spots: Big Bend National Park, Dugout Wells, 29.2712002 / -103.1352997; Balmorhea Lake, Balmorhea, 30.9583956 / -103.7123108; Seminole Canyon State Park, Comstock, 29.6935703 / -101.3185787; Inks Lake State Park, Buchanan Dam, 30.7329965 / -98.3682132; Fort Lancaster Overlook, Sheffield rest area, 30.6780349 / -101.6727483.

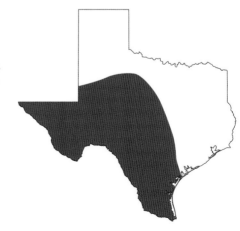

CHIPPING SPARROW
Spizella passerina

Common from backyards to woodland edges, this little sparrow's rusty cap and white eyebrow make it easy to spot as it forages on a lawn.

Field marks: Rufous cap, white eyebrow, black eye line, gray face, white malar stripe, grayish bill; gray throat, breast, and underside; gray nape, brown wings with two white wing bars, long gray tail. *Fall plumage:* Rufous cap fades to brown with buff eyebrow, pink bill.

Size: L: 5.5", WS: 8.5"–9"

Similar species: Field sparrow has a bright pink bill year-round, a white eye ring, and a duller brown crown.

Season: Summer across Texas, spring and fall in the panhandle, and winter in the Lower Rio Grande Valley

Habitat: Woodland edges, parks, gardens, mowed lawns in neighborhoods and commercial areas

Food source: Insects, seeds

Nest: Among a mass of vines, in a brush pile, or low in a shrub

Call: A long, one-note trill; also a high chip note, repeated incessantly

Hot spots: Chipping sparrows gather in small flocks under trees in landscaped gardens, in backyards with feeders, and in parks with arboretums or grassy paths. One of the best places to find them is on the ground on a rail trail, where they forage for seeds and tiny insects in full view of passers-by. They are far more numerous in residential neighborhoods than in wilderness areas.

SAVANNAH SPARROW
Passerculus sandwichensis

Common throughout grassland and marsh habitats in winter, this may be the first bird you see perching on a fence post or gritting on the edge of a road when you arrive at its habitat.

Field marks: Brown crown stripe, light brown head with dark brown eye line, yellow lores, white throat outlined in dark brown; buff breast, flanks, and underside streaked with brown; whitish undertail coverts, light brown back and wings streaked with darker brown, brown tail.

Size: L: 5.5"–6.25", WS: 6.75"–8"

Similar species: Song sparrow has a large dot in the center of its chest and no yellow on its face. First-year white-throated sparrow has a buffy head with two wide black stripes across the crown, no yellow on its face, and is generally a rounder bird.

Season: Winter

Habitat: Grasslands, marshes, open fields and meadows, farms, beach dunes

Food source: Seeds, insects, spiders

Nest: On the ground among tall grasses

Call: Two quick notes followed by a long trill, ending with a lower note: *chip-cheet-laeeeeeee-cheep*; also a thin, high chip note

Hot spots: Every marsh or open field you visit in winter will have savannah sparrows. Watch along roadsides or on fences and fence posts for the very vocal, very streaky sparrows with the yellow spot at the base of the bill.

WHITE-THROATED SPARROW

Zonotrichia albicollis

If you don't see this bird at your backyard feeder, look for it on the woodland floor turning over leaves in search of seeds and bugs.

Field marks: Black and white–striped cap, yellow lores, gray face and bill, white throat edged in black, gray breast and underside, brown wings with two thin white wing bars, brown tail. Young lack the bright white cap and throat.

Size: L: 6.75"–7.75", WS: 9"–10"

Similar species: White-crowned sparrow has a gray throat, a pink bill, and no yellow on its face.

Season: Winter

Habitat: Mixed woods with open understory, parks, gardens, backyards

Food source: Maple and oak leaf buds, seeds, insects

Nest: On or just above the ground, in a wooded area or in brush along a roadside or power line right-of-way

Call: Thready, musical song often transcribed as *old-sam-peabody-peabody-peabody*; also a sharp *chik* note

Hot spots: Throughout the winter, Texas residents enjoy white-throated sparrows under their sunflower seed feeders. If you don't feed birds at your home, any wooded area near you has overwintering white-throats, so check your closest city and state parks for these birds on the ground wherever seeds may have dropped from oak or maple trees.

WHITE-CROWNED SPARROW
Zonotrichia leucophrys

Habitat helps distinguish this sparrow from its white-throated cousin: The white-crowned prefers the edges of woods, fields, and marshes, where scrubby brush dominates.

Field marks: Black and white–striped crown, gray face, pink bill; gray throat, breast, and underparts; black and white back, brown and black wings with two thin white wing bars, brownish-gray rump, gray tail.

Size: L: 6.5"–7.5", WS: 9.5"–10"

Similar species: White-throated sparrow has a white throat and yellow lores and is usually found in different habitat.

Season: Winter

Habitat: Brushy grassland edges, dense scrub fields

Food source: Insects, seeds, grass, fruit, leaf buds

Nest: Near the ground or up to 30 feet up in a shrub, scrubby bush, or tree

Call: A descending series of clear notes with a buzzy ending: *Wee-weedle-doo-zee-zee-trzzzzz*

Hot spots: Even more numerous than white-throated sparrows, white-crowned sparrows are likely to appear under feeders in residential areas, especially if your yard is on the edge of a wooded area or a field. Watch the edges of these areas throughout the winter to find birds feeding on the ground, tossing leaves out of their way in search of seeds and insects, and "gritting"—gathering gravel they use in their digestive process—along roadsides.

SONG SPARROW

Melospiza melodia

There are many variations in the song sparrow's appearance across the United States. The dark brown sparrows found in most of Texas are of the Eastern race, while birds in west Texas may be paler and more reddish.

Field marks: Dark brown crown with a gray stripe up the middle, which sometimes stands up like a crest; gray eyebrow and cheek, brown eye line and malar stripe, white throat and chest, dark brown streaks on chest and flanks, culminating in a dark breast spot; gray back with brown stripes, brown and rufous wings and tail.

Size: L: 6.25", WS: 8.25"

Similar species: Savannah sparrow has a yellow stripe over the eye, and its bill and tail are shorter.

Season: Winter

Habitat: Woodland edges, brushy fields, stands of thick shrubs, open wetlands, marshes, beach dunes, parks, gardens, backyard feeders

Food source: Seeds, berries, grasses, some insects

Nest: On the ground, usually surrounded by taller grass or weeds

Call: A varied series of rising and falling warbles, usually ending in a trill; also a high-pitched *seet*, sometimes followed by a single, much lower *hup* note

Hot spots: Virtually every open field, forest edge, and neighborhood in Texas has resident song sparrows. Detectable first by song, they often pop up to stand at the top of a small shrub or on a blade of tall grass and sing, throwing their heads back and pumping out the notes using their entire bodies for emphasis. These sparrows are easy to spot and cooperative in giving birders good looks.

HARRIS'S SPARROW
Zonotrichia querula

Large for a sparrow and striking in appearance, Harris's sparrow winters in the state's central plains.

Field marks: Nonbreeding adult is most often seen in Texas: tan head and back with a black, white-speckled cap that extends down to the throat, encircling the pink bill; bright white breast and underside, with some brown streaking on the flanks and undertail coverts; tan and brown wings with two white wing bars; brown tail. Breeding bird has a grayer head and back.

Size: L: 6.5"–8", WS: 10.5"–11"

Similar species: House sparrow is darker overall with a gray cap, dark brown face, and grayish underside.

Season: Winter

Habitat: Farm fields, pastures, sod farms, areas of low vegetation near a water source, hedgerows, backyards with feeders

Food source: Seeds, berries, plants, and some insects when available

Nest: In northern Canada, on the ground but sheltered by a tree or shrub

Call: One long note, followed by a shorter one on the same pitch: *WHEEE, wee*, repeated often with short pauses between songs

Hot spots: Most winter flocks congregate north of Austin, with concentrations around the Dallas–Fort Worth metroplex. Small flocks of ten to thirty birds are often seen on roadsides in areas of open fields. These spots are very dependable for this sparrow throughout the winter: Trinity River Audubon Center, Dallas, 32.703804 / -96.705555; Lake Waco Wetlands, Waco, 31.607359 / -97.3040521; Hornsby Bend, Austin, 30.2181988 / -97.6458054; Cedar Hill State Park, Dallas, 32.6227136 / -96.9800091; Heard Natural Science Museum and Wildlife Sanctuary, McKinney, 33.1584503 / -96.6153376.

OLIVE SPARROW
Arremonops rufivirgatus

This south Texas specialty frequents feeders in the Lower Rio Grande Valley, making it easier to see than you might expect, especially in refuges and parks that maintain platform seed feeders.

Field marks: Large sparrow with a gray head striped in brown, pink bill; olive green back, wings, and tail; mottled gray underside. Often holds its tail upright when foraging on the ground or plundering a platform feeder.

Size: L: 5.5"–6", WS: 8"

Similar species: Green-tailed towhee is larger and more chartreuse than olive, with a white throat and a rusty crest. Rufous-crowned sparrow is not green at all. Canyon towhee is grayish brown overall with a rusty patch under the tail.

Season: Year-round

Habitat: Fields and woods with low, dense vegetation

Food source: Seeds, insects

Nest: In a low shrub or under a fallen branch, on or near the ground

Call: A series of simple chips, accelerating over 2 or 3 seconds: *chit, chit, chit, chit-chit-chit-chit-chi-chi-chi-chi-chi*; also a high, insect-like, often-repeated single chip

Hot spots: Hugh Ramsey Park, Harlingen, 26.1857402 / -97.6641657; Bentsen–Rio Grande Valley State Park/World Birding Center, Mission, 26.1849709 / -98.3793885; National Butterfly Center, Mission, 26.1796025 / -98.3664483; Resaca de la Palma State Park/World Birding Center, Brownsville, 25.9965839 / -97.5690513; Estero Llano Grande State Park World Birding Center, Llano Grande, 26.1268335 / -97.9578167.

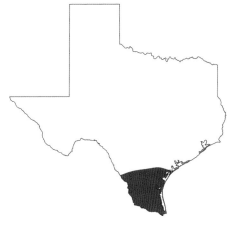

Junco

DARK-EYED JUNCO
Junco hyemalis

If you travel across Texas, you may encounter this bird in at least three of its six different plumages: slate-colored (above left), pink-sided (lower right), and red-backed (above right). The red-backed variety is the only one that breeds in Texas, and only in a small area of the Guadalupe Mountains.

Field marks: *Slate-colored:* Male is solid slate gray above, with pink bill, white belly, gray rear, white undertail coverts, gray tail with white outer feathers. Female has slate gray head, breast, and back; gray wings with some brown feathers, white belly, gray rear, white undertail coverts, gray tail with white outer feathers. Red-backed: All gray with a rusty patch on its back. *Pink-sided:* Gray head, dull pinkish body, grayish-brown wings.

Size: L: 5.75"–6.25", WS: 9.25"–10"

Similar species: Tufted titmouse has a gray crest, nape, back, and wings; a white throat, breast, and belly; rosy flanks. Spotted towhee is larger and has a black head, white underside, and bright rust-orange flanks.

Season: Winter

Habitat: Woodland edges, neighborhoods, parks, gardens, fields with adjacent woodlands, roadsides

Food source: Seeds, insects, fruit, berries

Nest: On the ground or just above it, in a shrub or brush pile, or under a log

Call: High, full-bodied, 3-second trill, sometimes broken halfway through

Hot spots: Juncos are numerous throughout the winter, especially feeding on the ground under seed feeders, on roadsides, and in parks and gardens. With so many different plumages, it may take some time to realize that you are looking at juncos, so using a photo identification app like Merlin (Cornell Lab of Ornithology) can help you determine whether your bird is indeed a junco.

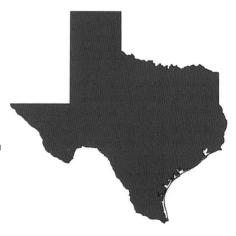

MEADOWLARKS, BLACKBIRDS, AND ORIOLES

Meadowlarks

EASTERN MEADOWLARK
Sturnella magna

A large, brightly colored songbird with a high, clear voice, this bird's song fills local meadows and farm fields.

Field marks: Breeding adult has black and white–striped head, light brown cheek, white malar stripe, gray bill, bright yellow throat, wide black V on breast, yellow breast and underside, buff and black streaks on flanks; scaly brown and buff pattern on wings, back, and tail; white outer tail feathers. In nonbreeding plumage, black on the crown and black breast band fade to gray.

Size: L: 9.5"–11", WS: 14"–17"

Similar species: Western meadowlark (seen only in west Texas) is identical, and can only be differentiated in the field by song. Female bobolink has a similar but more muted head pattern, and a buff breast with faint black streaks and no black V. Dickcissel male has a gray head with a single white eye line, yellow malars, and a white throat with a black V patch, but it has rufous shoulders and a brown and black–streaked back and wings.

Season: Year-round

Habitat: Farm fields, open meadows, grasslands

Food source: Insects, berries, seeds

Nest: On the ground and hidden among tall grasses and crops

Call: A whistled *seeyu, SEE-oh-yu*, sometimes with a trill on the last note, sometimes ending with a downward slide; also a chattering call that ends in another *see-yu*

Hot spots: Every large, grassy field or stretch of cultivated farmland in east and central Texas has its share of eastern meadowlarks. Listen for the distinctive, melancholy song and watch for one to pop up on top of a corn stalk or a fence post, where it will pose for pictures and sing for some time.

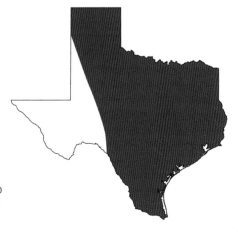

WESTERN MEADOWLARK
Sturnella neglecta

Nearly identical to the eastern meadowlark—the territories of these birds overlap in eastern and central Texas—the western is more easily differentiated by song.

Field marks: Light brown head with black stripes on crown and through the eye, yellow throat and breast extending to the belly, black V on chest; whitish underside with dark brown streaks, mottled light and dark brown back and wings, short tail with white outer tail feathers.

Size: L: 6"–10", WS: 16"

Similar species: Chihuahuan meadowlark, recently promoted to a full species by the AOS, has a lighter face with less yellow on it. Eastern meadowlark is virtually identical with darker, more defined facial lines and a little more white on its tail. All meadowlarks are best sorted out by song.

Season: Winter in east and central Texas, year-round in west Texas

Habitat: Farm fields, open meadows, grasslands

Food source: Insects, berries, seeds

Nest: On the ground and hidden among tall grasses and crops

Call: A distinctive, multisyllabic whistle: *ooh-WEE-hoo, weedelee-oo*, remarkably easy to separate from an eastern meadowlark's song; also a number of call notes, including a low *purlll*, a rattling call on one pitch, and a simple, slim *cheep*

Hot spots: Every open field with tall grasses has its own population of meadowlarks, so the trick is to determine which are eastern and which are western (and if you're in westernmost Texas from Big Bend to El Paso, whether you are hearing and seeing a Chihuahuan meadowlark). Song is your best friend for this process.

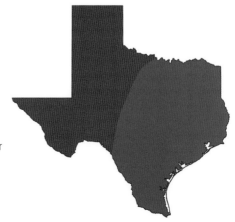

Cowbirds

BROWN-HEADED COWBIRD
Molothrus ater

Cowbirds are notorious in the birding world for laying their eggs in the nests of other birds, abandoning their babies for others to raise.

Field marks: Male has brown head, black body with a slightly turquoise sheen. Female is uniformly drab gray-brown, with slightly darker wings.

Size: L: 7.5", WS: 12"

Similar species: Rusty blackbird is uniformly blue-black with a yellow eye. Common grackle has an iridescent blue head, a blackish body, and a very long tail.

Season: Year-round

Habitat: Edges of wooded areas, farm fields, neighborhoods, parks

Food source: Insects, seeds

Nest: Lays one egg per nest of another bird species. In one season, a single cowbird may lay as many as thirty-six eggs in other birds' nests.

Call: A liquid-sounding burble, ending in a very high squeal: *blug-lug-EET*

Hot spots: Find cowbirds in just about any green space, especially those with open fields adjacent to forest edges. These birds usually move and feed in flocks, so if you discover one cowbird, you are likely to see many more.

BRONZED COWBIRD
Molothrus aeneus

A shorter, heavier cowbird than the much more common brown-headed variety, this one makes its year-round residence in the Lower Rio Grande Valley and heads only slightly north to breed.

Field marks: Red eye, black head with thick ruff on back of neck, bronze sheen in reflective light; black body and tail, iridescent dark blue wings. Female is similar but not as iridescent. Juveniles are gray-brown with streaky breast and underside.

Size: L: 8.5"–9", WS: 14"–15"

Similar species: Brown-headed cowbird is slimmer and has a distinctly brown head and a dark blue body.

Season: Year-round in southeast Texas, summer from Houston to Big Bend and the Davis Mountains

Habitat: Open areas including grasslands, farmlands, golf courses, airports

Food source: Seeds, some insects

Nest: These birds lay their eggs in other birds' nests and leave their young for the host birds to raise as their own.

Call: A series of whistles, gurgles, and very high-pitched wheezes

Hot spots: Resaca de la Palma State Park/World Birding Center, Brownsville, 25.9965839 / -97.5690513; San Benito Wetlands, Harlingen, 26.1739485 / -97.6235167; Estero Llano Grande State Park World Birding Center, Llano Grande, 26.1268335 / -97.9578167; Bentsen–Rio Grande Valley State Park/World Birding Center, Mission, 26.1849709 / -98.3793885; Big Bend National Park, Cottonwood Campground, 29.1366997 / -103.5220032.

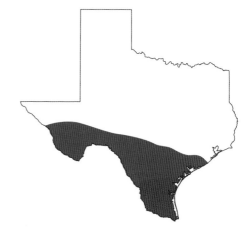

Blackbirds

RED-WINGED BLACKBIRD
Agelaius phoeniceus

No open field is complete without a colony of these highly visible, always active blackbirds.

Field marks: Male is solid black from head to tail with a red and yellow patch at the shoulder. Female is like a large sparrow, with a brown cap, lighter brown eyebrow and malar stripe, brown cheek, buff underside streaked with dark brown, brown wings with two white wing bars, brown tail.

Size: L: 8.75"–9.5", WS: 13"–14.5"

Similar species: Rusty blackbird, common grackle, European starling, and brown-headed cowbird have no wing patch. Female rose-breasted grosbeak has a more vivid facial pattern than female red-winged blackbird, and has more finely streaked underparts and a yellow patch under each wing.

Season: Year-round

Habitat: Open fields, farmlands, meadows, wetlands of all varieties, beach dunes, woodland edges, neighborhoods

Food source: Insects, seeds, fruit, marine invertebrates, crop grains; also come to backyard feeders

Nest: Firmly attached to reeds or other canes in grassy marshes or other wetlands

Call: A familiar three-note *onk-or-REE*; also a piercing, descending whistle and a deeper descending trill

Hot spots: Any plot of land with tall grasses contains red-winged blackbirds, whether it's in an agricultural area, a wildlife refuge, in a creek near a shopping mall, along a drainage ditch on a roadside, or alongside a schoolyard. Red-wings perch on top of cattails and phragmites, hop through low shrubs and the lowest branches of trees on woodland edges, and show up at backyard feeders when natural food sources become scarce.

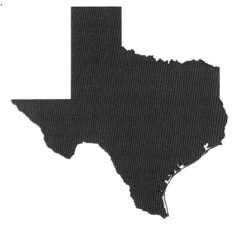

YELLOW-HEADED BLACKBIRD
Xanthocephalus xanthocephalus

The black bird with the bright yellow head is easy to spot in wetlands and open fields, especially when blackbirds gather in flocks.

Field marks: Males are all black with bright yellow head and chest, black around the eye to the bill, white patches on black wings. Females are brown with yellow and brown markings on face, a yellow throat.

Size: L: 8.5"–10", WS: 16.5"–17"

Similar species: Bobolink has a yellow patch on the back of its black head, and much more white on the wings. Red-winged blackbird is smaller and has an all-black head, as well as a red and yellow patch on each shoulder.

Season: Winter in west Texas, summer in the northern panhandle, and spring and fall migration throughout the east and central regions

Habitat: Open spaces including prairies, wetlands, meadows, some parks

Food source: Insects when available; seeds of many kinds in winter, including those offered by backyard feeders

Nest: Deep among the reeds or other vegetation in a wetland or field, always very near water

Call: Three or four rising and falling *plip* notes, followed by a raspy *squaaaa*. The flight song recombines these sounds into a continuous burble, with more emphasis on the longest one.

Hot spots: Balmorhea Lake, Balmorhea, 30.9583956 / -103.7123108; Canyon Lake 6, Lubbock, 33.5676571 / -101.8033202; Leonabelle Turnbull Birding Center, Port Aransas, 27.8275297 / -97.0789558; Sandia Wetlands, Balmorhea, 30.98631 / -103.70718; Twin Buttes Reservoir, San Angelo, 31.3774555 / -100.5366611.

BREWER'S BLACKBIRD
Euphagus cyanocephalus

All black with a yellow eye, this blackbird stands out from similar birds in Texas.

Field marks: Solid, glossy black from head to tail, with a yellow eye and a short bill; long tail. Female is dull grayish brown with a black eye.

Size: L: 9", WS 15"–16"

Similar species: Rusty blackbird is similar in size and shape, but is not shiny. Red-winged blackbird has red and yellow shoulder stripes.

Season: Winter

Habitat: Marshes and grassy areas near small bodies of water

Food source: Seeds; insects in summer

Nest: In colonies in shrubs or low trees, usually near water

Call: A sharp, rising *pit-TWEEEE*, followed by a single *cht*

Hot spots: It's very common to find Brewer's blackbird associating with large flocks of other birds like great-tailed grackle, common grackle, and red-winged blackbird. Watch for the smaller, sleeker bird with the yellow eye when you see flocks perched on utility wires along open shrubland.

Grackles

COMMON GRACKLE
Quiscalus quiscula

This grackle's long, rudder-shaped tail makes it easy to differentiate from the straight tails of cowbirds and blackbirds.

Field marks: Blue-black, iridescent head and breast, yellow eye, large black bill, uniformly brown-black body, long tail with flat, triangular end. Juvenile (pictured right) is browner and lacks the iridescence.

Size: L: 12.5"–13.5", WS: 17"–18.5"

Similar species: Red-winged blackbird is smaller, has a red and yellow patch on its wings, and has a shorter tail. European starling is much smaller and has a short tail. Great-tailed grackle is quite a bit larger and has a much longer and larger tail.

Season: Year-round through east and central Texas, with a summer population in the western panhandle

Habitat: City streets, parks, and neighborhoods; meadows, farm fields, beaches, dunes, shrubby areas

Food source: Insects, seeds, fish, fruit, eggs and nestlings in other birds' nests

Nest: Up to 12 feet off the ground in a tree or tall shrub

Call: An unmusical *chaa-ak, chaa-REE*, like the creak of metal against metal

Hot spots: All it takes to find a common grackle is a walk down any city or suburban street, a stroll through a beach parking lot or along a shopping center's edges, or a scan of the trees near an open field. Grackles often crowd other birds off backyard feeders (especially the platform variety), and they have been known to peck the head of a house sparrow until the smaller bird relinquishes a prime feeder perch.

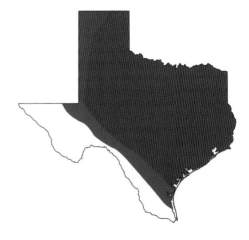

GREAT-TAILED GRACKLE
Quiscalus mexicanus

Here's the big black bird with the wide tail you see on every utility wire in the state.

Field marks: Large, all-black bird with an iridescent sheen, a yellow eye, and a long, wide, rudderlike tail. Females are all brown and smaller, with a shorter tail.

Size: L: 15"–18", WS: 19"–23"

Similar species: Common grackle is much smaller with a shorter tail. American crow is bulkier with a heavier bill and a shorter, fanlike tail. Brewer's blackbird is much smaller with finer features and a comparatively short tail.

Season: Year-round

Habitat: Urban, suburban, and rural areas where people live, as well as in agricultural areas with crops

Food source: Seeds and grains, fruit, small animals, insects and invertebrates, human leavings

Nest: Very high in a tree

Call: A series of long whistles, croaks, clicks, more whistles, squeals like a rusty hinge, and more. When they come together in flocks, these very loud birds can raise a cacophony that rivals any construction site.

Hot spots: These grackles are everywhere in Texas, to the point that some nature centers no longer feed birds from feeders all day to keep the grackles from bullying other birds and eating all the food themselves. The grackles often amass in the middle of cities shortly before sunset to roost overnight. Most metro areas have a corner or a shopping center that the grackles have claimed for their own, often congregating in the tens of thousands to crowd along utility wires. Check eBird to see where this is happening near you—even if you consider great-tailed grackles a nuisance, this is a phenomenon any birder would like to see.

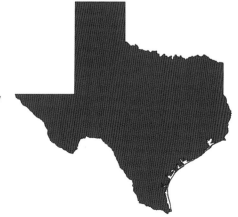

Phainopepla

PHAINOPEPLA
Phainopepla nitens

All black and gleaming in the sun, this bird's name means "shining robe" in Greek.

Field marks: Male is all black with a high, feathery crest, a red eye, a slim bill, and a long tail. Female is the same shape and size and has the red eye, but is all a tawny gray-brown with some white along the edges of the wing feathers.

Size: L: 7"–8.5", WS: 10.5"–11.5"

Similar species: Cedar waxwing is brown and sleek with a black mask and a lighter underside tinged with yellow. Black phoebe has a white belly.

Season: Summer in far western Texas only

Habitat: Deserts with low trees, especially where the trees contain mistletoe, a parasitic plant

Food source: Mistletoe berries, as well as small fruits from other trees

Nest: Often inside a mistletoe plant in a tree, usually more than 6 feet up

Call: A varied series of *whupps, squees*, and spirals; also a single, clear *wha-DEET*

Hot spots: Christmas Mountains Oasis, Alpine, 29.4917768 / -103.4670389; Big Bend National Park, Dugout Wells, 29.2712002 / -103.1352997; Big Bend National Park, Chisos Mountains area trails, 29.2699985 / -103.3004522; Davis Mountains State Park, Fort Davis, 30.60079 / -103.92579; TX 118 at Musquiz Creek, Fort Davis, 30.53569 / -103.80343.

Orioles

BALTIMORE ORIOLE
Icterus galbula

One of the most hoped-for backyard birds, this stunning orange and black creature comes readily to jelly feeders.

Field marks: Male has black head, throat, and back; orange breast and underside, black wings with orange patches at shoulder and one white wing bar, orange lower back and rump, black tail with orange outer feathers. Female has yellow-orange head and body with patchy black pattern on head, white throat, black wings with white wing bars, paler yellow flanks, yellow-orange rump and tail.

Size: L: 8.75", WS: 11.5"

Similar species: Spotted towhee has a black head and white breast and underside, with dark orange flanks. Orchard oriole has a darker, burnt-orange body. Bullock's oriole has an orange face, a slim black line through the eye, and large white wing patches.

Season: Spring and fall migration through east and central Texas

Habitat: Wooded areas, parks, gardens, suburban backyards with mature trees

Food source: Caterpillars, moths, other insects, fruit, flower nectar; also hummingbird nectar, oranges, grape jelly from backyard feeders

Nest: In a tree in a woven basket nest, usually more than 20 feet from the ground

Call: A syrupy, musical series of clearly defined, whistled notes: *hee-doo-HEE-dee-doo-dee-hoo* and variations of this; also a simple *peep* note, followed by a descending whistle (like a pennywhistle)

Hot spots: Just about any park with large trees may attract Baltimore orioles, but if you're striking out, try one of these near-certain spots in spring or fall. White Rock Lake & Old Fish Hatchery, Dallas, 32.8156276 / -96.7264652; Tyler State Park, Tyler, 32.4799358 / -95.2991867; Lick Creek Park, College Station, 30.562224 / -96.213541; Rose Hill Cemetery, Corpus Christi, 27.7908875 / -97.4213639; Laguna Atascosa National Wildlife Refuge, Brownsville, 26.2338009 / -97.3643036.

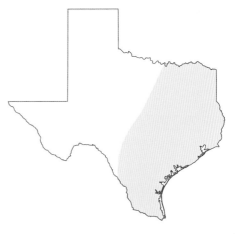

ORCHARD ORIOLE
Icterus spurius

Smaller and darker than its Baltimore cousin, this less-common oriole shares much of the same habitat.

Field marks: Male has black head, throat, upper back, wings, and tail; black eye, sharp black bill, dark orange breast and underside, dark orange patch on upper wing, one white wing bar, orange lower back and rump. Female has yellow head and body with darker wash on head, black eye, gray bill, dark gray wings with two white wing bars, yellow-green tail, white patches on underwings. First-summer male is similar to female, but with a black eye ring and throat.

Size: L: 7.25"–7.75", WS: 9.25"–10.5"

Similar species: Baltimore oriole is a brighter orange. American robin has a brown head, back, wings, and tail; a white eye ring, and white undertail coverts.

Season: Summer

Habitat: Woodlands, orchards, arboretums, neighborhoods with mature trees, parks

Food source: Insects, fruit, flower nectar, feeders with oranges and grape jelly, hummingbird nectar

Nest: In a tree or bush, usually well above the ground

Call: A musical series of whistles, faster and more numerous than a Baltimore oriole: *wee-WHOO-purwee-HOO-teewee-ta-dee-pur-dee,* and so on.

Hot spots: Lake Travis, Bob Wentz Windy Point Park, Austin, 30.4128174 / -97.9008651; San Antonio Botanical Garden, San Antonio, 29.4601113 / -98.4572897; South Padre Island Birding and Nature Center, 26.1374628 / -97.1739367; Clapp Park, Lubbock, 33.5550145 / -101.8639944; South Llano River State Park, Junction, 30.4391651 / -99.8128617.

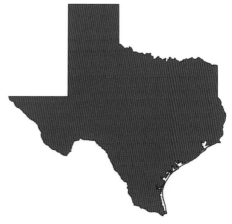

BULLOCK'S ORIOLE
Icterus bullockii

One of several bright orange orioles in Texas, this one lives and breeds in the western half of the state.

Field marks: Bright orange head and body with a black cap, a black line through the eye, and a black throat; black wings with wide white patches, orange and black tail. Females are a lighter shade of orange with a gray back, whitish underside, and brown wings with white wing bars.

Size: L: 6.5"–7.5", WS: 12"

Similar species: Baltimore oriole is a deeper orange with an all-black head. Hooded oriole has an all-orange head with a black face, including the eye. Altamira oriole has no black cap, and its black face surrounds the eye.

Season: Summer

Habitat: Deciduous woodlands, state and city parks, riparian areas

Food source: Insects, small invertebrates, nectar, fruit; also grape jelly from feeders

Nest: A long, woven, socklike nest hanging high in a tree

Call: A buzzy sound followed by several clear, syrupy notes, sometimes ending with clicks or buzzes

Hot spots: Mitchell Lake Audubon Center, San Antonio, 29.3105956 / -98.4996938; Falcon State Park, Roma, 26.5836148 / -99.1452921; Fort Peña Colorado Park, Marathon, 30.152997 / -103.2874735; Twin Buttes Reservoir, San Angelo, 31.3774555 / -100.5366611; Buffalo Lake National Wildlife Refuge, Umbarger, 34.9101471 / -102.1138.

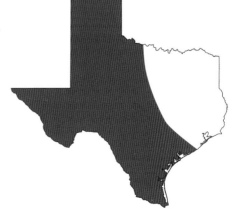

SCOTT'S ORIOLE
Icterus parisorum

Brilliant yellow and jet black, this oriole prefers desert habitats filled with the yucca plants it uses for food, nesting locations, and nest-building materials.

Field marks: Male has an all-black head, upper back, and breast; bright yellow body with black wings and a white wing bar; black and yellow tail. Female is olive overall with gray wings and a white wing bar.

Size: L: 9", WS: 12.5"

Similar species: Hooded oriole is orange with a black face and throat. Audubon's oriole is a more muted yellow with a greenish wash, and its tail is solid black.

Season: Summer

Habitat: Desert scrubland with lots of yucca plants

Food source: Insects, plant nectar, fruit

Nest: In a yucca, usually about 6 feet off the ground

Call: A short series of clear, tumbling notes: *deet, deet, deedle-deedle-deedle-WEET*; also soft *whit, whit, whit* call notes

Hot spots: Fort Lancaster Overlook, Sheffield rest area, 30.6780349 / -101.6727483; Big Bend National Park, Chisos Mountains area trails, 29.2699985 / -103.3004522; Davis Mountains State Park, Fort Davis, 30.60079 / -103.92579; Guadalupe Mountains National Park, Pine Springs, 31.9074905 / -104.8013279; South Llano River State Park, Junction, 30.4391651 / -99.8128617.

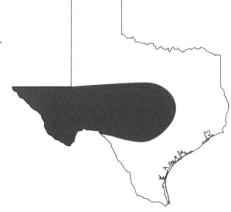

ALTAMIRA ORIOLE
Icterus gularis

It can be tricky to tell this bird apart from a hooded oriole, but Altamira's size and more delicate facial markings help with the identification.

Field marks: Orange head and body with a black band from eye to bill and a black throat; black shoulders and wings with a white wing bar.

Size: L: 8.5"–9.5", WS: 14"

Similar species: Hooded oriole is smaller and has a more extensively black face, as well as a smaller bill.

Season: Year-round

Habitat: Areas with woods and water features in the Lower Rio Grande Valley

Food source: Insects, nectar, fruit; also come to grape jelly feeders and plunder nectar feeders meant for hummingbirds

Nest: A long, socklike nest high in a tree, often near water

Call: A definite whistle, with a long string of rising and falling notes, sometimes broken up by a staccato buzz

Hot spots: Laguna Atascosa National Wildlife Refuge, Brownsville, 26.2338009 / -97.3643036; National Butterfly Center, Mission, 26.1796025 / -98.3664483; Estero Llano Grande State Park World Birding Center, Llano Grande, 26.1268335 / -97.9578167; Hugh Ramsey Park, Harlingen, 26.1857402 / -97.6641657; Bentsen–Rio Grande Valley State Park/World Birding Center, Mission, 26.1849709 / -98.3793885.

AUDUBON'S ORIOLE

Icterus graduacauda

A prized sighting for Texans and visiting birders, this oriole puts in its annual appearances in a concentrated area along the Lower Rio Grande Valley.

Field marks: Creamy yellow body with an all-black head and breast, black wings feathers outlined in white, all-black tail.

Size: L: 7.5"–9.5", WS: 12.5"

Similar species: Scott's oriole is a more lemony yellow, with a yellow and black tail. As a rule, the two orioles do not share habitat in Texas, as their preferences vary widely from each other.

Season: Year-round

Habitat: Woods alongside a creek or stream, canyons with vegetation, backyards with feeders

Food source: Insects, fruit, spiders

Nest: In trees, up at least 5 feet

Call: A languid whistle, lower in pitch than most orioles; also a raspy call note

Hot spots: Laguna Atascosa National Wildlife Refuge, Brownsville, 26.2338009 / -97.3643036; Resaca de la Palma State Park/World Birding Center, Brownsville, 25.9965839 / -97.5690513; Estero Llano Grande State Park World Birding Center, Llano Grande, 26.1268335 / -97.9578167; National Butterfly Center, Mission, 26.1796025 / -98.3664483; Bentsen–Rio Grande Valley State Park/World Birding Center, Mission, 26.1849709 / -98.3793885.

FINCHES

HOUSE FINCH
Haemorhous mexicanus

This small, long-tailed finch came from the western United States and found its way east through New York City pet stores in the 1940s. Today it is widespread in Texas, where it is a native species; in neighboring Louisiana, it's consider exotic.

Field marks: Male has red forehead, face, throat, breast, and rump; pale gray nape, white underside with gray streaks and a pink wash, black wings with thin white wing bars, long dark tail. Female has drab gray-brown head, throat, and back; light gray breast and underside with darker gray streaks, dark wings with two slim white wing bars, gray tail.

Size: L: 6", WS: 9.5"–10"

Similar species: Purple finch is more uniformly pink overall.

Season: Year-round

Habitat: Neighborhoods, cities, parks, gardens, arboretums, backyards with feeders

Food source: Seeds, fruit

Nest: In a tree cavity, deep in a shrub, or in a crack or hole in a building

Call: Continuous, often lengthy series of warbles, whistles, trills, and chatter

Hot spots: Every neighborhood has at least a small flock of house finches, especially if some of the residents keep their seed feeders stocked. House finches are particularly easy to see from late summer through winter, when they bring their fledglings to feeders and birdbaths. They often flock together in a single large shrub a short distance from a ready food source.

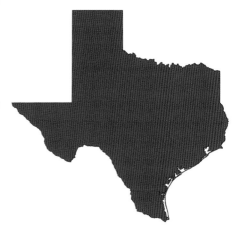

PINE SISKIN
Spinus pinus

Pine siskins can be plentiful in open coniferous woods, but they also spend much of their winters visiting feeders in suburban and rural areas.

Field marks: Male has brown head and back, thin gray bill, white breast with dark brown streaks, black wings with bright yellow stripes, short yellow tail with black tip. Female has a browner breast and underside and has white wing bars instead of yellow stripes.

Size: L: 4.5"–5", WS: 8.5"–9"

Similar species: Female house and purple finches are grayer overall and have no yellow. Female purple finch has buffy flanks.

Season: Winter

Habitat: Forests and woodlands, parks, neighborhoods, farm fields with wooded edges

Food source: Seeds, insects, spiders, road salt; seeds at feeders during the winter months

Nest: On the branch of a conifer well above the ground

Call: A long, continuous warble with occasional buzzy notes

Hot spots: White Rock Lake, Dallas, 32.8337313 / -96.7121315; Mitchell Lake Audubon Center, San Antonio, 29.3105956 / -98.4996938; Hornsby Bend, Austin, 30.2181988 / -97.6458054; Jesse H. Jones County Park, Houston, 30.024 / -95.295; Jenna Welch Nature Center I-20 Pond, Midland, 31.9630947 / -102.1210903.

AMERICAN GOLDFINCH
Spinus tristis

The only all-yellow bird with black wings in the United States, this goldfinch is a regular visitor to backyards, gardens, and parks in winter.

Field marks: Male has black forehead; yellow head, back, upper wings, throat, breast, and underside; pink bill, black wings with one white wing bar, white rump, black tail. Female has olive-gray head, yellow eye ring, yellow throat, dull yellow breast and flanks with indistinct olive-gray streaks, olive-gray back, black wings with one white and one buff wing bar, white patch under the wing, white undertail and rump, black tail. *Fall plumage:* Male has gray head, back, and underside; yellow patch around eye, gray bill, yellow throat, yellow shoulders, black wings with one whitish wing bar, black tail. Female is uniformly drab brownish gray with black wings, one brownish wing bar, white undertail, black tail with whitish edges.

Size: L: 5", WS: 9"

Similar species: Yellow warbler is yellow overall with red streaks on its breast and flanks. Lesser goldfinch has a full black cap, as well as olive-green cheek, nape, and back.

Season: Winter

Habitat: Open grassland, farm fields, marshes, thickets, woodland edges, neighborhoods, parks, gardens

Food source: Seeds, particularly from flower heads; nyjer and sunflower seed at feeders

Nest: In a shrub or young tree, not far from the ground

Call: A simple, lilting *twee-twee-twee-twee-twee*; also a rising *per-WEE* alarm call and a descending *DEE-dee-dee-dee* in flight

Hot spots: Goldfinches are one of the most common winter birds in Texas, found in virtually every grassy area. They are frequent visitors to feeders, especially if you offer nyjer seed.

LESSER GOLDFINCH
Spinus psaltria

Not quite as bright as their more northerly cousin, these goldfinches crowd feeders and birdbaths throughout much of the state.

Field marks: Black cap that comes down to the eye, olive head, yellow face, small bill; olive-green nape and back, black and olive wings with white patches, all-yellow underside, dark tail. Female is brown all over with a yellowish patch on the chin, muted yellow flanks.

Size: L: 3.5"–4.5", WS:6"–8"

Similar species: American goldfinch is a brighter yellow overall, with striking black cap and black wings.

Season: Winter on the Gulf coast, year-round through west Texas, summer on the panhandle

Habitat: Fields, woods, scrubland, agricultural areas, riparian areas

Food source: Seeds, plant buds, some fruit

Nest: In a leafy tree, often near a water source

Call: A long, continuous, quite musical string of warbles and trills; also a high-pitched, twittering call

Hot spots: If you live in central, western, or southern Texas and you have a yard that can accommodate a seed feeder or two, you can have lesser goldfinches attending your feeders all day, often with a large flock of their friends. There's little need to travel to see these gregarious birds—but if you don't have a place for a feeder, your nearest local park is sure to have its own resident goldfinches.

Old World Finch

HOUSE SPARROW
Passer domesticus

No household is complete without a dozen or so of these in the backyard. This introduced species from England can be found anywhere that humans frequent, from front porches to city centers.

Field marks: Male has gray cap, wide brown stripe from eye to back, gray cheek; black eye, bill, throat and breast; white collar, gray belly and flanks, brown back, brown and black wings, white patch on wing, gray tail. Female is drab grayish tan overall with small yellow bill, thin white eye line, brown and gray wings with thin white wing bar, brown tail.

Size: L: 6.25", WS: 9.5"

Similar species: No other Texas bird has the facial pattern of a male house sparrow.

Season: Year-round

Habitat: Cities, towns, parks, neighborhoods, backyards with bird feeders

Food source: Seeds, fruit, crumbs from human discards, some insects

Nest: In a tree cavity, a hole in a building, a bowl created by a man-made sign, or a man-made nest box. House sparrows are known to evict bluebirds from nest boxes and take them over for their own broods.

Call: A simple, fairly dry *cheep* from a male and a chattier series of *cheeps* from a female are familiar sounds in most neighborhoods.

Hot spots: This ubiquitous sparrow is found in every backyard, park, garden, beach, city street, outdoor restaurant, and even inside big-box stores and malls, where they plunder the crumbs humans leave behind in food courts. No hot spot is required to find a house sparrow; chances are you can see one outside your window as you read this.

APPENDIX A: A REALISTIC CHECKLIST OF THE BIRDS OF TEXAS

The following checklist is compiled from official bird checklists of Texas. The original checklists each included rare species that are not seen regularly in Texas, as well as accidentals—birds very far from their native habitat, brought here by storms or other forces of nature—and species that are extirpated from the region or believed to be extinct. We have omitted these accidental and extirpated birds to help you set realistic expectations for the birds you are most likely to see on an average day in the proper habitat, season, and time of day. Should some surprising birds make an appearance, there's room at the end to write in these unusual sightings. (* = Exotic or Introduced species.)

Loons
☐ Common loon

Grebes
☐ Eared grebe
☐ Pied-billed grebe
☐ Least grebe

Pelicans
☐ American white pelican
☐ Brown pelican

Cormorants and Anhinga
☐ Double-crested cormorant
☐ Neotropic cormorant
☐ Anhinga

Herons and Egrets
☐ Great blue heron
☐ Great egret
☐ Snowy egret
☐ Tricolored heron
☐ Little blue heron
☐ Cattle egret
☐ Reddish egret
☐ Green heron
☐ Black-crowned night-heron
☐ Yellow-crowned night-heron

Ibises and Spoonbill
☐ White ibis
☐ White-faced ibis
☐ Roseate spoonbill

Waterfowl
☐ Greater white-fronted goose
☐ Snow goose
☐ Canada goose
☐ Black-bellied whistling duck
☐ Wood duck
☐ Mallard
☐ Gadwall
☐ Northern pintail
☐ American wigeon
☐ Northern shoveler
☐ Blue-winged teal
☐ Cinnamon teal
☐ Green-winged teal
☐ Mottled duck
☐ Canvasback
☐ Redhead
☐ Ring-necked duck
☐ Lesser scaup
☐ Bufflehead
☐ Hooded merganser
☐ Ruddy duck

Duck-like Birds
☐ Common gallinule
☐ Purple gallinule
☐ American coot

Vultures
☐ Black vulture
☐ Turkey vulture

Hawks, Kites, and Eagles
☐ Osprey
☐ Swallow-tailed kite
☐ Mississippi kite
☐ White-tailed kite
☐ Bald eagle
☐ Northern harrier
☐ Cooper's hawk
☐ Red-shouldered hawk
☐ White-tailed hawk
☐ Common black hawk
☐ Harris's hawk
☐ Swainson's hawk
☐ Zone-tailed hawk
☐ Red-tailed hawk
☐ Crested caracara
☐ Merlin
☐ American kestrel
☐ Peregrine falcon
☐ Aplomado falcon

Quail and Turkey
- ☐ Northern bobwhite
- ☐ Plain chachalaca
- ☐ Scaled quail
- ☐ Wild turkey

Rails
- ☐ King rail
- ☐ Clapper rail

Cranes
- ☐ Sandhill crane
- ☐ Whooping crane

Stilt and Avocet
- ☐ Black-necked stilt
- ☐ American avocet

Plovers
- ☐ Black-bellied plover
- ☐ Piping plover
- ☐ Semipalmated plover
- ☐ Wilson's plover
- ☐ Snowy plover
- ☐ Killdeer

Oystercatcher
- ☐ American oystercatcher

Sandpipers
- ☐ Lesser yellowlegs
- ☐ Greater yellowlegs
- ☐ Solitary sandpiper
- ☐ Willet
- ☐ Spotted sandpiper
- ☐ Upland sandpiper
- ☐ Long-billed curlew
- ☐ Marbled godwit
- ☐ Ruddy turnstone
- ☐ Red knot
- ☐ Sanderling
- ☐ Semipalmated sandpiper
- ☐ Western sandpiper
- ☐ Least sandpiper
- ☐ White-rumped sandpiper
- ☐ Pectoral sandpiper
- ☐ Dunlin
- ☐ Stilt sandpiper
- ☐ Buff-breasted sandpiper

- ☐ Long-billed dowitcher
- ☐ American woodcock
- ☐ Wilson's snipe

Gulls and Terns
- ☐ Laughing gull
- ☐ Ring-billed gull
- ☐ Herring gull
- ☐ Caspian tern
- ☐ Royal tern
- ☐ Sandwich tern
- ☐ Forster's tern
- ☐ Black skimmer

Doves and Pigeons
- ☐ Rock pigeon*
- ☐ Eurasian collared-dove*
- ☐ White-winged dove
- ☐ Mourning dove
- ☐ Common ground dove
- ☐ Inca dove
- ☐ White-tipped dove

Parrot and Parakeet
- ☐ Red-crowned parrot*
- ☐ Monk parakeet*

Cuckoos
- ☐ Yellow-billed cuckoo
- ☐ Groove-billed ani
- ☐ Greater roadrunner

Owls
- ☐ Barn owl
- ☐ Eastern screech-owl
- ☐ Western screech-owl
- ☐ Great horned owl
- ☐ Burrowing owl
- ☐ Barred owl

Nightjars
- ☐ Lesser nighthawk
- ☐ Common nighthawk
- ☐ Common pauraque
- ☐ Common poorwill

Swift
- ☐ Chimney swift

Hummingbirds
- ☐ Ruby-throated hummingbird
- ☐ Black-chinned hummingbird
- ☐ Buff-bellied hummingbird
- ☐ Rufous hummingbird

Kingfishers
- ☐ Belted kingfisher
- ☐ Green kingfisher
- ☐ Ringed kingfisher

Woodpeckers
- ☐ Red-headed woodpecker
- ☐ Red-bellied woodpecker
- ☐ Yellow-bellied sapsucker
- ☐ Downy woodpecker
- ☐ Hairy woodpecker
- ☐ Red-cockaded woodpecker
- ☐ Ladder-backed woodpecker
- ☐ Golden-fronted woodpecker
- ☐ Acorn woodpecker
- ☐ Northern flicker
- ☐ Pileated woodpecker

Flycatchers
- ☐ Eastern wood-pewee
- ☐ Eastern phoebe
- ☐ Black phoebe
- ☐ Say's phoebe
- ☐ Vermilion flycatcher
- ☐ Ash-throated flycatcher
- ☐ Brown-crested flycatcher
- ☐ Great-crested flycatcher
- ☐ Eastern kingbird
- ☐ Couch's kingbird
- ☐ Western kingbird
- ☐ Scissor-tailed flycatcher
- ☐ Great kiskadee

Shrike
- ☐ Loggerhead shrike

Vireos
- ☐ White-eyed vireo
- ☐ Plumbeous vireo
- ☐ Red-eyed vireo
- ☐ Black-capped vireo
- ☐ Warbling vireo

Jays, Crows, and Ravens
- ❏ Blue jay
- ❏ Woodhouse's scrub-jay
- ❏ Green jay
- ❏ American crow
- ❏ Common raven
- ❏ Chihuahuan raven

Swallows
- ❏ Purple martin
- ❏ Tree swallow
- ❏ Cliff swallow
- ❏ Cave swallow
- ❏ Barn swallow

Titmice, Chickadees, and Allies
- ❏ Tufted titmouse
- ❏ Black-crested titmouse
- ❏ Carolina chickadee
- ❏ Horned lark
- ❏ Verdin
- ❏ Bushtit

Nuthatches
- ❏ Red-breasted nuthatch
- ❏ White-breasted nuthatch

Wrens
- ❏ Carolina wren
- ❏ House wren
- ❏ Bewick's wren
- ❏ Marsh wren
- ❏ Sedge wren
- ❏ Rock wren
- ❏ Canyon wren
- ❏ Cactus wren

Bulbul
- ❏ Red-vented bulbul*

Kinglets and Gnatcatchers
- ❏ Golden-crowned kinglet
- ❏ Ruby-crowned kinglet
- ❏ Blue-gray gnatcatcher
- ❏ Black-tailed gnatcatcher

Thrushes
- ❏ Eastern bluebird
- ❏ Western bluebird
- ❏ Mountain bluebird
- ❏ Hermit thrush
- ❏ Wood thrush
- ❏ American robin
- ❏ Clay-colored thrush

Mimic Thrushes
- ❏ Gray catbird
- ❏ Northern mockingbird
- ❏ Brown thrasher
- ❏ Curve-billed thrasher

Starling
- ❏ European starling*

Waxwing
- ❏ Cedar waxwing

Warblers
Many warblers pass through Texas during migration. These remain to breed.
- ❏ Orange-crowned warbler
- ❏ Nashville warbler
- ❏ Northern parula
- ❏ Yellow warbler
- ❏ Golden-cheeked warbler
- ❏ Colima warbler
- ❏ Yellow-rumped warbler
- ❏ Pine warbler
- ❏ Black-and-white warbler
- ❏ Common yellowthroat
- ❏ Wilson's warbler

Tanagers
- ❏ Scarlet tanager
- ❏ Summer tanager

Sparrows
- ❏ Chipping sparrow
- ❏ Field sparrow
- ❏ Lark sparrow
- ❏ Savannah sparrow
- ❏ Black-throated sparrow
- ❏ Harris's sparrow
- ❏ Olive sparrow

- ❏ Song sparrow
- ❏ White-throated sparrow
- ❏ White-crowned sparrow
- ❏ Spotted towhee
- ❏ Canyon towhee
- ❏ Green-tailed towhee

Blackbirds and Orioles
- ❏ Red-winged blackbird
- ❏ Eastern meadowlark
- ❏ Western meadowlark
- ❏ Chihuahuan meadowlark
- ❏ Yellow-headed blackbird
- ❏ Brewer's blackbird
- ❏ Common grackle
- ❏ Great-tailed grackle
- ❏ Phainopepla
- ❏ Bronzed cowbird
- ❏ Brown-headed cowbird
- ❏ Baltimore oriole
- ❏ Orchard oriole
- ❏ Bullock's oriole
- ❏ Scott's oriole
- ❏ Altamira oriole
- ❏ Audubon's oriole

Finches and Allies
- ❏ House finch
- ❏ Pine siskin
- ❏ American goldfinch
- ❏ Lesser goldfinch
- ❏ Northern cardinal
- ❏ Pyrrhuloxia
- ❏ Black-headed grosbeak
- ❏ Blue grosbeak
- ❏ Indigo bunting
- ❏ Lark bunting
- ❏ Painted bunting
- ❏ Dickcissel
- ❏ Dark-eyed junco
- ❏ House sparrow*

Accidentals
- ❏
- ❏
- ❏
- ❏

APPENDIX B: RESOURCES

"All About Birds." Cornell Laboratory of Ornithology. allaboutbirds.org.

Arnold, Keith A., and Gregory Kennedy. *Birds of Texas*. Tukwila, WA: Lone Pine Publishing Int'l., 2007.

"Birds of North America." Cornell Laboratory of Ornithology, birdsna.org/Species-Account/bna/home.

Bryan, Kelly, et al. *A Checklist of Texas Birds*, seventh edition. Texas Parks and Wildlife, 2006.

Common, James. "Birders Behaving Badly." James Common, September 21, 2017. https://commonbynature.co.uk/2017/09/21/birders-behaving-badly/.

Dunn, Jon L., and Jonathan Alderfer. *Field Guide to the Birds of North America,* seventh edition. Washington, DC: National Geographic Society, September 12, 2017.

eBird (globally crowdsourced content). Cornell Laboratory of Ornithology, ebird.org.

Lockwood, Mark W. *Basic Texas Birds: A Field Guide*. Austin: University of Texas Press, 2007.

Peterson, Roger Tory. *A Field Guide to the Birds: A Complete New Guide to All the Birds of Eastern and Central North America*, sixth edition. Boston: Houghton Mifflin Harcourt, 2010.

Sibley, David Allen. *The Sibley Guide to Birds*. First edition. New York: Alfred A. Knopf, October 3, 2000.

Tekiela, Stan. *Birds of Texas Field Guide*, second edition. Cambridge, MA: Adventure Publications, 2020.

Williamson, Sheri L. *Hummingbirds of North America*. Peterson Field Guides. New York: Houghton Mifflin Co., 2001.

INDEX BY HOT SPOT

INDEX BY SPECIES

ABOUT THE AUTHOR AND PHOTOGRAPHER

Avid birders for many decades, bestselling author/photographer team **Randi** and **Nic Minetor** have produced more than forty books for FalconGuides and its parent company, Globe Pequot, including *Birding New England, Birding Florida, Best Easy Birding Guide: Acadia National Park, Best Easy Birding Guide: Cape Cod, The New England Bird Lover's Garden*, and *Backyard Birding and Butterfly Gardening*. Their work includes guides to a number of national parks and historic cities, as well as *Hiking Waterfalls in New York State, Hiking the Lower Hudson River Valley*, and *Hiking Through History New York*. Nic's photography also appears in eight foldout Quick Reference Guides to the birds, trees, and wildflowers of New York City and New York State, and the trees and wildflowers of the Mid-Atlantic region. Randi is the author of seven books that tell the true stories of people who have died in national and state parks: *Death in Rocky Mountain National Park, Death on Mount Washington, Death on Katahdin, Death in Acadia National Park, Death in Glacier National Park, Death in Zion National Park*, and *Death in the Everglades*. Randi also writes for *Birding* magazine and *North American Birds*, and her work has appeared in *The Kingbird* and *Bird Watcher's Digest*.

When not in the field, Nic is the resident lighting designer for Eastman Opera Theatre and the Memorial Art Gallery at the University of Rochester, and for theatrical productions at Rochester Institute of Technology and the National Technical Institute for the Deaf. Randi writes for other book publishers and for a number of trade magazines, and she serves as a ghostwriter for executives and entrepreneurs in a wide range of fields. She is also the president of the Rochester Birding Association.